Tove Jansson

Tove Jansson

WORK AND LOVE

TUULA KARJALAINEN

Translated by David McDuff

PARTICULAR BOOKS
an imprint of
PENGUIN BOOKS

PARTICULAR BOOKS

Published by the Penguin Group
Penguin Books Ltd, 80 Strand, London WC2R 0RL, England
Penguin Group (USA) Inc., 375 Hudson Street, New York, New York 10014, USA
Penguin Group (Canada), 90 Eglinton Avenue East, Suite 700, Toronto,
Ontario, Canada M4P 2Y3 (a division of Pearson Penguin Canada Inc.)
Penguin Ireland, 25 St Stephen's Green, Dublin 2, Ireland
(a division of Penguin Books Ltd)
Penguin Group (Australia), 707 Collins Street, Melbourne, Victoria 3008,
Australia (a division of Pearson Australia Group Pty Ltd)
Penguin Books India Pvt Ltd, 11 Community Centre, Panchsheel Park,
New Delhi – 110 017, India
Penguin Group (NZ), 67 Apollo Drive, Rosedale, North Shore 0632,
New Zealand (a division of Pearson New Zealand Ltd)
Penguin Books (South Africa) (Pty) Ltd, Block D, Rosebank Office Park,
181 Jan Smuts Avenue, Parktown North, Gauteng 2193, South Africa

Penguin Books Ltd, Registered Offices: 80 Strand, London WC2R 0RL, England

www.penguin.com

First published in Finnish as *Tove Jansson: Tee Työtä ja Rakasta* by Tammi 2013
First published in Great Britain by Particular Books 2014

1

Copyright © Tuula Karjalainen, 2013
Translation copyright © David McDuff, 2014

The moral right of the author and the translator has been asserted

Particular Books gratefully acknowledges the financial assistance of FILI
(Finnish Literature Exchange) for this translation.

Typeset by Richard Marston
Printed in China

A CIP catalogue record for this book is available from the British Library

978-1-846-14848-4

www.greenpenguin.co.uk

Penguin Books is committed to a sustainable
future for our business, our readers and our
planet. This book is made from paper certified
by the Forest Stewardship Council.

Contents

To the Reader

The child moved for the first time. Just a small kick, but one clearly felt through the abdominal wall, and it sent a message – I am me. Tove Jansson's mother, Signe Hammarsten-Jansson, was out walking in Paris, and had just arrived at rue de la Gaîté – Street of Joy. Was it a portent? Did it mean the child would be happy? At any rate, she would bring an enormous amount of joy to the world.

Times were hard. The threat of war hovered over Europe like the oppressive, stagnant air that precedes a thunderstorm. Despite, or perhaps just because of this, life in the art world was intense. Early twentieth-century Paris saw the birth of modern art – Cubism, Surrealism and Fauvism – and the city was home to writers, composers and artists whose names would soon become guiding stars. These included Pablo Picasso, Georges Braque, Salvador Dalí and many others. Among them were Viktor Jansson from Finland and Signe Hammarsten-Jansson from Sweden, who had only been married a few months – and their as yet unborn daughter. The First World War had already broken out when Tove Jansson was born in Helsinki on 9 August 1914.

In writing a biography you inevitably enter another person's reality and begin to live in a kind of parallel universe. Stepping into Tove Jansson's life has been a rich and wonderful experience, though I had constantly to be aware that I might not necessarily be welcome. Tove has been the subject of biographies, studies and dissertations written from many different points of view. She permitted it during her lifetime, despite not always being very interested. She usually said that if one was going to write about an author it would be better to wait until he or she was dead, if at all. Yet it is also clear that she prepared for future researchers, as she preserved most of her extensive memoirs, correspondence and notebooks.

I met Tove once, in 1995. By then she was already eighty-one. I was preparing an exhibition about the artist Sam Vanni, who had died a few years earlier, and I was interested in the years that Tove and Sam had shared in the 1930s and 40s. For me, too, Vanni was a very dear and close friend whose work had formed the basis of my doctoral dissertation a few years earlier. I feared that Tove would have neither the time nor the strength for a meeting, but she wanted to see me. We sat in her turret studio in Ullanlinna and talked about art, life and Sam Vanni. Tove told me about their youth, about Maya Vanni and their visit to Italy, and about Sam's teaching methods, and their friendship. I received answers to my questions, and for the exhibition catalogue Tove also promised to give us a story from her notebook that Sam – then still Samuel Besprosvanni – had told her. Suddenly Tove suggested that we take a little whisky. And so we drank whisky and smoked cigarettes, as people did in those decades. And the interviewee became the interviewer. Now I was able to tell her all about Sam, his wife and his sons, of whom Tove did not seem to know much at all. We realized that many other people who were important in Tove's life had also touched mine. Of these, Tapio Tapiovaara was someone I knew quite well, and I had also met Tuulikki Pietilä and Vivica Bandler many times.

The next time I was in Tove's studio was when I was writing my book and studying her archive. For me, the most important items were her letters and notebooks. For months I sat alone in the Ullanlinna studio reading letters, as I couldn't copy them or remove them from the apartment. The studio still looked almost the same as it had done in Tove's lifetime. Her self-portrait *Lynx Boa* (1942) gazed directly at me from the easel. On tables and windowsills were seashells and bark boats, and on the wall a gigantic library stretched from the floor high up to the ceiling, together with paintings stacked closely together. On the wall of the toilet there were pictures of disasters, sinking ships and stormy seas that Tove had cut out from various periodicals. It was all as it had been when she was alive. Her presence could be clearly felt.

There were a great many letters, which Tove had written over some thirty years. The most important were those she had sent to her friend Eva Konikoff in the United States: a large stack of them, written on thin tissue paper in small handwriting that filled each page, some blacked out or even mutilated by wartime military censors. Eva's letters were not there. In a strange way the letters particularly brought to life the 1940s, the war and subsequent recovery. They gave a sense of what the war felt like to a woman who at that very time should have been enjoying her youth, making a career and building the framework of her life. And how it felt when the war was over. In addition to Eva's letters I was also given access to Tove's notebooks and her correspondence with other people, especially her letters to Vivica Bandler and Atos Wirtanen, which have been important for my book. Many of her short stories are based on material from these letters and notebooks, often very directly.

Once I was deep inside Tove Jansson's world, I wanted to connect her work as closely to her life as possible, to the wider society and to her inner circle. This determined my method and the focus of my book. Of particular importance was the war and its final years. So difficult did she find the war that in later years she could not even bear to think about it. Yet those years were not wasted, even though Tove herself sometimes felt and said that they were. It was during them that she created and decided many of the most important elements in her life and career. In the midst of the war, and as a result of it, she created her first Moomin stories, matured as a painter, created a fine series of self-portraits, and produced her uniquely courageous war drawings.

The book's title, *Tove Jansson: Work and Love*, is based on her *ex libris* motto (*Laborare et Amare*). Work and love were the things that mattered most to her throughout her life – and in that order. Tove's life and art were closely interlinked. She wrote and painted her own life and found her inspiration very near to her – in her friends, her islands and her travels and personal experiences. Her life's work is enormous. It should really be discussed in the plural, because she had several careers – as an author of fairytales, as an illustrator, painter, writer, stage designer, dramaturge, poet, political caricaturist and cartoonist.

Her output is so vast that anyone writing about it is almost overwhelmed by its volume. I felt like Aunt Gerda in Tove's book *The Listener* (1971) – the old lady who decides to make a chart of her friends and relatives to show the various relations between them. The children and their parents are connected by red lines, while she marks the love affairs in pink. If they deviate in any way from the norm, or are forbidden, she marks them with double lines. But the passage of time renders the task impossible: the relationships between people keep changing, the chart has to be corrected constantly and no piece of paper can ever be big enough to encompass it all.

Aunt Gerda's work is never finished. Nothing ever stops and, what's more, time changes the past. Sometimes it feels as though the past is particularly susceptible to change. There are countless perspectives on man and art, and yet life has no plot. There are only scattered, overlapping parallel events that highlight or conceal one another. The closer one looks, the more complex the picture becomes. This is especially true in relation to Tove. She did several different things at the same time. She painted for almost the whole of her life, she created the Moomin books for more than thirty-five years, and she illustrated various publications and wrote adult fiction for decades.

The breadth and diversity of Tove's career have also affected the structure of my book. Its basis is both chronological and thematic, and is a compromise between the two. A mere chronology would lead only to a jumble of trivial facts, and the times in which she lived and the ideas and phenomena that accompanied them are also an essential part of the themes of her art and her life.

Much has been written about Tove. Erik Kruskopf wrote a detailed study of her work as an artist some twenty years ago. The Swedish critic Boel Westin has written a great deal about the Moomins, and published an extensive biography of Tove (translated and published in English in 2014). Juhani Tolvanen has written much over the years about Tove's comic strips. And this is to mention but a few of the names. In particular, the Moomins have been the subject of countless books, even dissertations, of which Sirke Happonen's wide-ranging work is probably the most recent. The undercurrent of homosexuality in Tove's books has also interested a number of researchers.

I wanted not only to focus on Tove's art, but also to show her in the context of her time, its values and cultural history. The importance of her inner circle is given particular emphasis here. Tove's life was fascinating. She challenged conventional ways of thinking and moral rules in a country where old prejudices, especially on the subject of sexual behaviour, maintained a strict hold. She was a revolutionary, but never a preacher or a demagogue. She influenced the values and attitudes of her time, but was no flag-bearer – instead, she was a quiet person who remained uncompromising in her own life choices. The status, independence, creativity and esteem of women vis-à-vis men were absolute values for her. She did not submit to the average female role, either in her career or in the way she lived. When she was still a little girl she wrote that 'freedom is the best thing'. It remained of utmost importance throughout her life.

Per il mio carissima Trinca. Self-portrait, oil, 1939

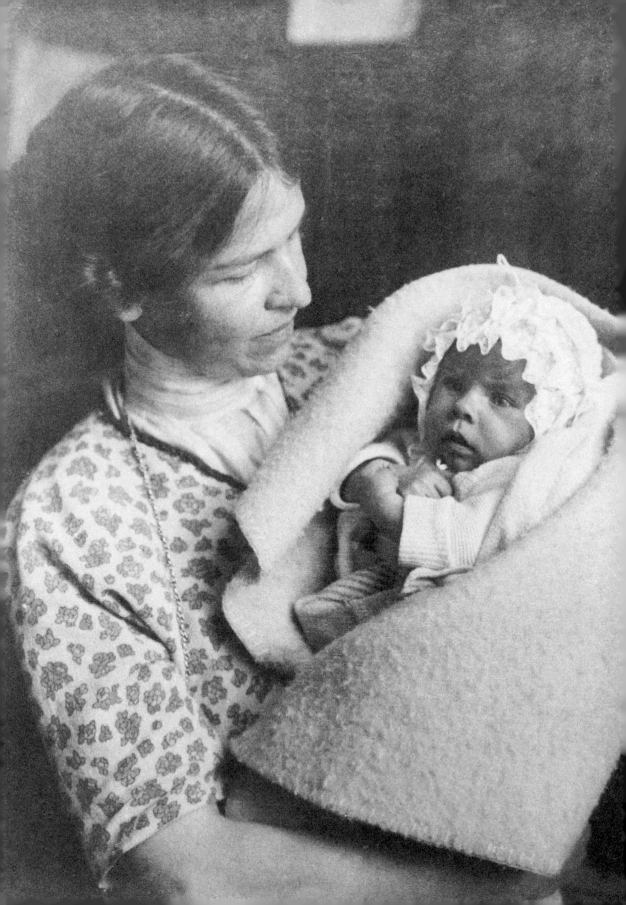

I
Father's Art, Mother's Pictures

THE WAR-DAMAGED FATHER

Tove's first and most important artistic role model was her father. He viewed art as a great and serious endeavour, and Tove appears to have learned this from him at an early age. The relationship between father and daughter was contradictory: filled with great love, it also contained deep hatred. Viktor Jansson wanted Tove, the first-born child of two artists, to be an artist too. And Tove did become one. However, she also became much more – in ways that to her father were alien, incomprehensible and repugnant – and yet she became an artist of whom he remained enormously proud.

Tove's father, Viktor Jansson (1886–1958), came from a Finland-Swedish merchant family. His own father died when he was still young, but his widowed mother continued to run a haberdashery business and the young Viktor frequently had to help her, together with his brother. Although the business was not particularly profitable and life not always free from financial strain, Viktor received several opportunities to visit Paris in order to study sculpture there.

Viktor Jansson's career as a sculptor had started promisingly, but he never became one of the truly great artists of his day. For a man of ambition who sought to get ahead, this probably rankled. During this period, the Finnish sculpture scene was largely permeated by the cult of Wäinö Aaltonen, and all the others remained in his shadow. In a small country, there was only room for one artist to be declared a god – or a genius – at any one time.

In those days it was not easy to be an artist and a paterfamilias. Following the value system of the time, in order to preserve his honour a husband had to be able to provide for his family. Viktor Jansson doubtless found it hard to accept the family's reliance on his wife's income, let alone now and then having to receive financial assistance from his wife's well-off relatives in Sweden.

Tove as a newborn infant in her mother's arms, 1914

The family's financial position was often uncertain, which was not unusual for artists. A sculptor's income depended on so many factors – coincidence, luck and the estimation of a volatile art world. The family lived modestly, sometimes in near poverty. Art and its creation came first, but the rewards were vanishingly small. Vivica Bandler has recalled Tove's relationship with money: Tove said she had been brought up 'to feel sorry for all the people who weren't artists'. This attitude softened the misery that inevitably accompanied being hard up.

War memorials and statues of White Guard heroes were a source of employment for Viktor Jansson, as they were for many other Finnish sculptors in the 1920s and again after the Second World War. 'Faffan', the name by which he was generally known, made four monuments commemorating the War of Independence, the two most important of which are in Lahti and Tampere. The bronze men in them are naked, young and handsome, and look as though from Ancient Greece. In the Tampere Statue of Freedom (unveiled in 1921), the soldier has raised his sword straight up towards the sky as if about to attack. Placed on top of a column, the male figure towers above all things earthly and mundane. The total effect is heroic, while the composition is undoubtedly phallic. The soldiers combine beauty, aggression and defiance, qualities that the period and its ideology considered important, and that therefore required artistic representation.

For Viktor Jansson, sculpting heroic monuments had more to do with economic necessity than with any genuine desire. His regular work consisted mostly of soft, erotic female figures and delicate portrayals of children. In her book *The Sculptor's Daughter*, Tove wrote that her father did not like women. He thought they were too noisy, wore large hats at the cinema, were anti-social and would not obey orders in wartime. Only when they were made into sculptures did they become real women. The only living women he actually approved of were his wife and daughter.

The family members and their closest friends were used to being the models and muses of artists. Viktor's wife, Signe, or Ham (1882–1970), posed as a model for his sculptures, as did the young Tove. For the piece *A Girl's Head* (*Flickhuvud*, 1920), her father carved her face from marble. The soft light of the pale marble glows in the sculpture's delicate features and peaceful expression. Viktor Jansson also created a number of fountain sculptures, and Tove posed as the model for one of the mermaids in the outdoor *Play* (*Lek II*) sculpture near the Kappeli Restaurant on Helsinki's Esplanade. She had already grown into a young woman when her father depicted her in his sculpture *Convolvulus*, and the girl in this piece is indeed as supple and erotic as a climbing vine, as the title suggests. In 1931 the sculpture was installed in Kaisaniemi Park, where it remains. At the ladies' croquis evening at the Lallukka Artists' Home in 1937, Tove described her experience of being a nude model: 'I adopted the pose of Papa's *Convolvulus*. A step forward, one raises one's arms a little. A very small, lingering step, the tips of one's toes turned slightly inwards, a parrying, fumbling movement with one's hands – it's supposed to depict awakening, or youth. Papa said.'

Though Tove's relationship with her father was burdened by many conflicts and sometimes coloured by plain hatred, the bond between them never completely broke. They had such different and strong views on society and politics that they could not understand each other's values. Tove's mother had explained to the children that during the Civil War something had snapped in their father and created irreparable cracks in his soul. Through the war, the once sunny-tempered, playful and amusing Viktor changed into an austere and embittered man, inflexible in his opinions. He smiled only on the rarest of occasions and in other ways found it extremely hard to express his feelings. Tove's father remained on the periphery, so the nuclear family was formed from mother and children. Yet Tove admired her father tremendously, and in her art she depended on his views.

Faffan was a typical patriot of his time. Like many war heroes, he remained emotionally fixated on the war, reliving past battles over and over again with his comrades. The men drowned their gloomy thoughts in wild revelry. They gathered in restaurants, leaving their wives at home, so that they could drink and talk freely about lofty matters, art and life, without being bothered by women, children and everyday concerns. The evenings were spent soaked in liquor, even though the prohibition laws of the time meant that alcohol was hard to come by.

Viktor Jansson's best friend was a fellow student, the painter Alvar Cawén, another hero of the Finnish Civil War. As young men at the turn of the century they had shared a studio in Paris, and also one in Helsinki. Their friendship endured throughout their lives, and they caroused and worked together. Their wives also became friends. The families organized parties together, and during the Prohibition they brewed illicit liquor. The painter Marcus Collin was a friend of both Faffan and Cawén and from 1933 onwards the Jansson and Collin families lived at Lallukka. As neighbours in the same building, they formed a friendship that was lasting and trouble-free.

During Prohibition there were speakeasies in Helsinki, but to visit them

Self-portrait at age fourteen,
charcoal drawing

was risky as they could be raided without warning. For this reason the junketing also took place at home. The Janssons often held after-parties that sometimes lasted through to the following day. Frequent among the guests were Tyko Sallinen, Jalmari Ruokokoski and other acclaimed artists of the time. As a young child, Tove would watch the men's parties, or *hippor*, as they were called in Swedish, from her hiding place. Thus from a very early age she got a feel for the art world and the artists of her time, as well as for war and male aggression. She later wrote about these experiences in a short story in which the nature of male friendship is aptly summed up: 'All men party (*hippar*) and are chums who will never leave one another in the lurch. A chum may say dreadful things, but the next day it's forgotten. A chum doesn't forgive, he just forgets and a woman forgives everything but never forgets. That's how it is. That's why women aren't allowed to party. Being forgiven is very unpleasant.'

In the story Tove remembers her childhood and her mother who, at Christmas, would carefully dust her father's miniature sculptures. No one else was ever allowed to touch them. Yet in the home there were objects even more sacred – hand grenades from the Civil War. These items were revered symbols of the war for her father. It was totally forbidden to dust them – no one had permission to do that, ever. The men's war memories and their wild behaviour during the *hippor* were the subject of a short story in which Tove recalls the warlike celebrations through the eyes of a little girl: '. . . I love Papa's parties. They sometimes go on night after night. I wake up, go back to sleep and am rocked in the smoke and the music [. . .]. After the music come the memories of war. Then I wait for a bit under the covers, but I always get up again when they attack the wicker chair. Then Papa fetches his bayonet that hangs above the bags of plaster in the studio and everyone jumps to their feet and shouts and then Papa attacks the wicker chair. During the daytime it has a rag rug over it so no one can see what it looks like.'

Like many other Whites[1] in the Civil War, Viktor Jansson saw left-wing politics and Communism in particular as a major threat to his country. Germanophilia was on in Finland, especially during the Winter War and Continuation War. Jansson had faith in Germany and saw it as a liberator and a friend. He took a hostile attitude towards Jews, and it was particularly her father's anti-Semitism that deeply wounded Tove. She was quite categorical on the matter, '*Feuer und Flamme*', as she herself put it. Several of her best friends, like Sam Vanni (until 1941 Samuel Besprosvanni) and Eva Konikoff, were Jewish. Viktor Jansson found it hard to accept when in her drawings for the magazine *Garm* his daughter took a strong stand against Germany and Hitler. In her letters she often complained about her father's shameless intolerance and 'hair-raising' political views.

Viktor found it hard to accept his daughter's male friends. They were often either Jews or Communists, or at any rate prominent men with left-wing ideas. Tapio Tapiovaara, the artist with whom Tove continued an affair for several years during the war, belonged to the group known as *Kiila* ('the Wedge') and had adopted its strongly left-wing view of the world. Even more prominent was Atos Wirtanen, the leftist politician, intellectual and critic who remained Tove's steady companion for many years. As a personality, Wirtanen had a reputation for inflexibility and unwillingness to compromise, and according to Tove was generally known as 'Parliament's enfant terrible'.

Tove's free and public liaison with the well-known and highly prominent Atos Wirtanen sparked widespread moral indignation and intolerance. Her father was also not at all happy, and the situation was made even worse by Wirtanen's leftism and social prominence. The marriage-like affair clashed with the customs of the time – in the Janssons' social class such affairs were severely condemned: sexual experiments had to be carried out in secret, they were not discussed, and women were assumed to be virgins until marriage. In a society that demanded sexual abstinence, it was very hard for an unmarried couple living together as husband and wife to claim any respect or credibility. Sexual relations were in no sense a private matter. Tove's father found it impossible to overcome the attitudes with which he had grown up and in which he deeply believed. And yet, in spite of this, many of these undesirable male companions were allowed to visit the Janssons' home.

1. The Whites were one of the two parties in the Finnish Civil War of 1917–18, the other being the Reds, or socialists. The Whites were supported by the White Guards, Jäger troops and the political right. They also received military support from Germany.

Tove was very family-centred. She did not move away from home until the age of twenty-seven, and her ties to her family remained strong throughout her life. The Janssons lived in Helsinki, first in Katajannokka, and then in Töölö. During her childhood and youth Tove lived at 4 Luotsikatu Street in Katajannokka, where the budding young artist's imagination was likely to have been influenced by the neighbourhood's decorative art nouveau architecture. Even as a small child she looked through the apartment's oval window at the houses and roof turrets opposite. Their pointed shape and proportions recall the Moominhouse, and especially the contours of the bathing hut. The same shape recurs in Snufkin's hat.

There was art in progress all over the home, and from an early age Tove became used to living among the bags of plaster-of-Paris, half-finished clay sculptures on trestles and numerous plaster figures awaiting bronze casting in her father's studio. And she also grew accustomed to her mother sitting at a corner of the table and designing postage stamps, cover art and book illustrations. There was always some new creation on the go.

During the summer, often from early spring until late in the autumn, the Janssons were archipelago-dwellers. The Pellinki archipelago near Porvoo, some fifty kilometres from Helsinki, was an important place for them. One had to cross to the islands by public ferry, and travel the rest of the way by small boat. Among the middle classes of the time it was customary for families to move to the country for the summer at the end of the school year, and the Janssons were no exception. Tove's mother, Ham, had a steady job, and so she only visited the island for holidays and at weekends. While her mother was away a housekeeper looked after the family. The Janssons lived in several different villas in the Pellinki archipelago, but they were all close to each other. They rented their first villa from the Gustafsson family: the Gustafssons' son Albert ('Abbe') was the same age as Tove, and they became lifelong friends. Later, for many years the family spent the summer on the island of Bredskär, where Tove and her brother Lars built a cabin. In the 1960s Tove moved to Klovharu, perhaps the island she loved best. A love of the sea and of islands united all the family members. The summers at Pellinki were their best times – they were 'more at home' there than in the city, as Tove's brother Per Olov has recalled.

In 1933 the family moved from Katajannokka to the recently completed Lallukka Artists' Home. Artists with different specialities lived together there,

At home. Tove's father and mother, Faffan and Ham, after plaster casting

and there was an active social scene among close neighbours. Alone or with her fellow students Tove rented modest workrooms, but for a long time her home was at Lallukka. It was there that she was officially registered, and had her own bed and personal effects. But life at Lallukka was cramped, especially since Tove had grown up and begun to paint, and because the three Jansson family artists worked there in a space intended for one. Tove badly needed a workroom of her own, but maintaining a studio was expensive for a young artist – often too expensive. Many incipient careers, such as hers, were nipped in the bud due to a lack of work space.

Tove rented the first workroom she could really have to herself in a building next door to Helsinki's Kristuskirkko church in 1936. In the following year she

Tove and Ham in the Lallukka Artists' Home, 1944

found a better one on Vänrikki Stoolin Katu. In 1939 she acquired new premises at 18 Urheilukatu. The place was in a rather poor state, and Tove recalls trying subsequently to get a studio of her own at Lallukka. This remained a dream, as to her annoyance the house manager started mentioning Faffan's unpaid rents. So Tove stayed in Töölö, close to Lallukka. During the Winter War she had a studio on Töölönkatu, where life was made difficult by a landlady who kept a watchful moral eye on the young woman's comings and goings and among other things disapproved of painting with nude models. Fortunately Tove got back her old studio on Vänrikki Stoolin Katu in April 1940.

Various kinds of living spaces, including interiors such as apartments and hotel rooms, were important subjects for Tove. She painted the rooms where she stayed overnight when travelling and the studios where she worked. The studio on Vänrikki Stoolin Katu is the location and subject of *Evening Interior* (*Kvällsinteriör*, 1943). In it one can sense the atmosphere that the young Tove experienced when she moved away from home, an atmosphere that combined a fear of loneliness with all manner of practical problems, starting with cooking. She wrote to Eva Konikoff, telling her optimistically that everything was being taken care of. The Janssons had a maid called Impi who seemed to manage all the everyday chores brilliantly, and so the daughter of the house did not need to bother about them.

Life for the family girl was not easy, though: because of their opposing views of the world, father and daughter often had extremely strained relations, to the point where Tove, in her own words, sometimes felt so ill that she had to go to the bathroom and vomit. For the sake of family peace Tove had to keep quiet, which meant she suppressed her rage. Her concealed emotions eventually exploded, and the anger that had been hidden for years burst out. 'Faffan and I said that we hated each other.' The Janssons' family friend and doctor Rafael Gordin seriously recommended that Tove should move away from home and become independent. Tove herself wrote that she would not be able to endure one more hour at home. If she stayed there she would suffer some kind of mental breakdown and would neither be able to be happy nor develop into a good painter. A deep bitterness, even mercilessness, was particularly reflected in Tove's assessment of her father's relationship with her mother Ham: 'I see how Faffan, the most shiftless and most short-sighted of us all, tyrannizes the whole house, I see that Ham is unhappy because she has always said yes, smoothed things over, given in, given up her life and not got anything back except children, whom the men's war will kill or make into bitter, negative people . . .'

The move, though only to a temporary studio, meant a new life – liberation, independence and new living arrangements. It also meant inconvenience and removal crates, but above all it meant taking responsibility for herself. Tove reflected on how the mere decision to move affected her entire existence: 'Since I decided to leave the family everything has changed [. . .] even my tastes. Played the Adagio from Beethoven's Violin Concerto which I used to love the most – and didn't like it at all. And for the first time enjoyed Bach [. . .] The field is open for anything, I've done the spring cleaning.'

With the move, the great crisis with her father was, if not over, then at least under control. Tove suffered from guilt, for she knew that her mother missed her. But after the move her relationship with her father improved, and the two learned to be more understanding towards each other. Tove never cut off her links with home, and even during the worst times she had dinner at Lallukka and joined the family at the summer cabin in Pellinki during the months of spring, summer and autumn. Yet even years later she sometimes found it quite hard to be with her father, and said: 'I go to Lallukka every Sunday, but no more often than that, as I really don't like being with Papa.' The relationship between Viktor and his youngest son, Lars, or Lasse, was also difficult at times, and became alarmingly fraught during the Continuation War, when Lasse openly rebelled against his father. Tove wrote to Eva that she would have liked to say to her father: 'Be careful you don't drive the last one of us away!'

LIFE WITH MOTHER UNDER A BELL JAR

Tove's mother, Signe (Ham) Hammarsten-Jansson, was the centre of her life and her greatest love, so great that no one else would ever match it. In many ways they had grown together. While her father was out in the Helsinki night,

Tove drawing in her mother's arms, *c.* 1915

making merry with his friends, little Tove and her mother grew accustomed to being alone with each other, and became somehow welded together early on. Ham's influence on her daughter's future and on her career was crucial. She was her daughter's first and most demanding teacher. Tove quite literally learned to draw in her mother's arms. It is said that Tove could draw when she was only one or two years old, even before she was able to walk.

Ham worked hard, and at home the little girl watched her drawing, hour after hour. It convinced her that Indian ink, pen and paper and the act of drawing itself were a fixed and natural part of a woman's life. This early intimacy with the making of pictures, together with her mother's guidance, facilitated Tove's artistic precocity: for with this background she became a trained illustrator at a very young age, easily acquiring an excellent mastery of pen and pencil drawing. She was only fourteen when her drawings were first published, and the following year she made several illustrations for various newspapers.

Mother and daughter lived in a symbiotic relationship. Tove said that she spent her childhood with her mother as though they were living together under a bell jar – just the two of them in a private world of their own, from which the rest were excluded. The strength and depth of the relationship are to some extent reflected in the story 'Snow' from *The Sculptor's Daughter*, in which Tove describes a little girl and a mother alone in a house that is buried under white snow. The daughter is filled with calm and happiness: she imagines that no one can get in or out and expresses her joy by shouting to her mother, 'I-love-you, I-love-you', laughing and throwing cushions at her, and not wanting the house to be dug out of the snow. Together in isolation they are safe from the world like bears in a den. All that is bad is outside: 'What was most fantastic was the sense of disaster as the snow just kept rising and rising – over the windows – it was as if we were living in a green aquarium [. . .] And at the same time the feeling of absolute security – seclusion – and one felt that now no one could go out, and no one could come in. Mother and I are in our winter den – we're like bears who have filled their tummies with spruce twigs and the world has ceased to exist, it's dead, it's not there anymore.' Tove said that the incident was real, though she was thirty when it happened, during a week she spent drawing with her mother when the house was snowed in.

Signe Hammarsten-Jansson was the daughter of a Swedish pastor and court chaplain. She had studied art at Konstfack[2] in Stockholm. Viktor and Signe,

2. Konstfack: the University College of Arts, Crafts and Design.

or Ham as everyone called her, met in Paris, where they were both continuing their art studies. They fell in love, held their wedding in Sweden and spent the early part of their marriage in Paris, where Tove was conceived.

Ham maintained extremely close relations with her parents and siblings. As a child, Tove spent her summers with her uncles and grandparents on the island of Blidö in the Stockholm archipelago. The landscape of Blidö has often been considered the original prototype of Moominvalley. It is equally lush and gentle, with its large trees and sea beaches. While Tove studied in Sweden, she lived with her maternal uncle. The Swedish side of the family was large and relatively wealthy, and judging by Tove's writings the personal relationships were warm and easy-going. In the story 'My Friend Karin', Tove portrayed her cousin Karin, her religious experiences and the life of her grandparents: 'Once Mother and I travelled to Sweden and stayed with Grandpa and Granny in their big rectory that is situated in a valley by the sea. The house is full of uncles and aunts and their children.'

The years of the Civil War, its aftermath and the early 1930s were rather gloomy in Finland. Like other families, the Janssons experienced material shortages. During the Winter and Continuation Wars, and also during the economic depression that followed them, they needed help from the Swedish side of the family and Swedish relatives helped them in many ways – by sending food, artists' paints and building materials. By marrying a sculptor and moving far away from her family to Finland, Ham had given up a great deal. In poor and war-beleaguered Finland she is likely to have missed the land of her birth and her family. In her new homeland, she was in the process of coming to terms with the final years of Finland's existence as an autonomous region of Tsarist Russia, the First World War and the Civil War, when she fled with her daughter back to Sweden. A couple of decades later came the Winter War, the Continuation War, the Lapland War and the economic depression. For a young woman who had been used to quite different conditions, Finland was not an easy country to move to and live in, but Ham seems to have endured the trials of her new homeland with bravery: 'Mama never talked about homesickness, but as often as possible I was taken out of school and sent to Sweden to meet her brothers and find out how life was for them and tell how life was for us . . .'

In *The Sculptor's Daughter*, Tove wrote about her mother's homesickness and longing for Sweden. Many of the household utensils and items she had brought from Sweden were reminders of the land of her birth, and she tried, often unsuccessfully, to protect them. 'At home we never hold parties in the studio, only in the drawing-room. That's where [. . .] all of Grandpa and Granny's curly-grain wood furniture is. It reminds Mama of the land where everything is as it ought to be. At first she was very afraid it would be damaged, and got angry about cigarette burns and glasses leaving rings, but now she knows that it's just the patina.'

Viktor Jansson was Finland-Swedish, and most of his friends were Swedish-speakers. Thus his young wife could manage perfectly well with her native language, and everyone spoke Swedish in the home. Moreover, in the early part of the twentieth century, Swedish was used far more widely in Helsinki than it is today. So Ham had no particularly compelling reason to learn another language, and so she never learned Finnish properly. But her lack of fluency in the language increased her isolation and restricted her circle of friends. Her family and close friends therefore became all the more important.

Upon marriage, Ham gave up the career of an independent artist that she had dreamt of while studying art as a postgraduate in Paris. In those days it was thought particularly suitable for women to specialize in textile art, and Ham tried her hand at it, taking part with Ragni Cawén in events like the exhibition organized in Copenhagen by the Friends of Finnish Handicraft (*Suomen käsityön ystävät*) in 1919. But art and the ambition associated with it were no longer the focus of her life: instead, like so many women at that time, Signe Jansson lived primarily for her family. When she looked at the lives and careers of couples who were both artists, they did not present an attractive example to her. Within such families, the husband took most of the time and space for the making of art. Often for the wife there was none at all. She had to be flexible in her expectations and desires, as well as looking after the children and coping with the daily routine of running the household. After that, there was no room left for anything else.

If a woman chose to pursue her art, and especially if she was more successful than her husband, there was not much chance of the marriage working. At Lallukka, Ham found it easy to follow the lives of artists' families at close quarters, and it is possible that the living examples she witnessed convinced her of this. The wives of Faffan's best friends, Alwar Cawén, Marcus Collin and Ragnar Ekelund, had trained as artists but after embarking enthusiastically on their careers had remained in their husbands' shadows. Women were judged by a different standard. Female artists were often discussed in relation to their husbands, and their work was also reviewed by comparing the two. It was convenient for critics to say that a woman had been influenced by her husband, and that the husband had all too obviously been the example she followed. Women's art was not viewed independently and not really taken seriously. Such a reception was unlikely to encourage women in their careers, and it did not encourage Ham either.

The wives of artists bore financial responsibility for the family, and were often in paid employment. In the family the husband's career took priority, and the wife had to do all she could to help and support him, so that he could focus on making art. The life of a woman married to an artist did not look easy. Many women, like Ragni Cawén, felt that one artist in a family was enough, or, as Ham Jansson said, 'one sculptor in the family is enough'. Husband and children went before all else, as Ham discovered. And yet her own work was still essential, and she could not even think of living without it. In order to be able to create, she needed her family's well-being and her own personal happiness among her nearest and dearest.

Ham was an efficient personal assistant to her husband, thanks to the professional qualifications she had obtained. A wife's contribution to her spouse's career could be considerable, while at the same time being anonymous and invisible, as was common in those times. Under her own name Ham focused on illustrating, and built a distinguished career. But it was not 'Art' – true art, that 'noble fire of the spirit'. The era was marked by an immense disparity in the value placed on applied art and fine art, and the difference persisted for almost the whole of the twentieth century. Applied art was seen almost as tinkering – hand-craft at best.

Ham brought in the family's steady income. From 1924 onwards she had a drafting job at the note-printers for the Bank of Finland, and also worked hard at numerous illustrating jobs for various periodicals and book publishers. She is regarded as the first professional Finnish postage stamp designer, virtually the mother of the genre in Finland. She produced enormous quantities of book covers and illustrated several newspapers. Her work for the satirical magazine *Garm* was significant, and her involvement with it lasted throughout its existence, from 1923 to 1953. The most memorable works among her vast output of illustrations for it were probably the caricatures depicting personalities from the cultural and political life of the time. Her work on the liberal *Garm* was also significant in that it passed directly from mother to daughter. Ham played a prominent role in the magazine during the 1920s and 1930s, while from the late 1930s onwards Tove was the artist who did most to create the magazine's visual style. To her, as to her mother, *Garm* offered a modest but regular income. And they had to make a living, even though they also made their name as artists with independent works.

Her mother's life with her father made Tove assess women's role in marriage, and their work. She saw at very close quarters the low esteem in which women and their work were held. Faffan was not the easiest of life partners: the family doctor Rafael Gordin had a habit of asking Ham how the 'fourth child of the family' was, referring to Faffan. Tove felt great sympathy for her mother when she saw how hard she had to work to keep the family's finances under control, and how she adapted to her husband's demands without complaining. Tove was troubled by her mother's life of subjection and wondered how she could make her happy. She imagined how they would go abroad together and leave everything behind, including Faffan. Tove thought of rescuing her mother and taking her somewhere far away to safety in a happier land and a happier life. She never seems to have wondered whether her mother would be willing to emigrate. At the same time she had dreams, sometimes plans that were far advanced, of moving abroad with her friends, sometimes with her brother, or her lover, to Africa or Polynesia. But in reality her love for her mother kept her in Finland: 'It's Ham who keeps me here, because I shall never find anyone whom I can love as much, and who loves me as she does.'

Everyone thought that Ham was a wonderful mother, and she was also a popular person. Judging by all the evidence, especially her daughter's letters, she was tolerant, wise, capable and all-accommodating. Tove's brother Per Olov has described how his mother, a former girl scouts leader, taught him how to orienteer by using the wind, tree trunks, mosses, clouds and anthills, and 'forgave all my stupid behaviour, radiating a calm, reassuring, Moominmamma-like warmth'. Tove's younger brother, Lasse, was also very attached to his mother – 'far too much so', as Tove wrote. As a young man during the war, while he lived at his uncle's house in Turku, Lasse sent his mother letters filled with love and affection. These epistles to her, full of deep love and longing, caused concern to the family and Ham asked a doctor she knew for help. According to Tove, he advised Ham to wean the boy away from her and to treat him coldly. He said she should even send him away to a labour camp, the thought of which terrified Lasse.

THE YOUNGER BROTHERS, PER OLOV AND LARS

There was a six-year gap between the births of Tove's brothers. Per Olov was first (1920), followed by Lars (1926–2000), the youngest in the family. According to Per Olov, the long intervals between them were due to the family's

The Jansson children, *c.* 1927

financial hardship. For six years Tove was an only child because her parents were not able to afford another baby. Tove's brothers were everything to her, and she was always deeply involved in their lives and their thoughts. During the war their fate weighed on her mind, and this uncertainty was a constant source of anguish to her. The three siblings worked together a lot. Per Olov took pictures of Tove's work and in 1980 they made the Moomin book *An Unwanted Guest* (*Skurken i Muminhuset*), with texts by Tove and photographs of the Moomin characters by Per Olov. Lars translated the Moomin comics into English and ultimately published them himself. The siblings remained close throughout their lives, and her brothers' wives and children were also an integral part of Tove's existence. All the siblings were talented and artistic: both brothers wrote books, and Per Olov was also a brilliant photographer.

As a young man during the war, Per Olov, also called 'Prolle' or 'Peo', ended up on the front line, to the family's great horror. He had been asthmatic as a child, which added greatly to Ham's concern about her elder son. Prolle could have pleaded infirmity on the grounds of his asthma and avoided the front, but he did not want to. Reading Tove's letters, one can sense her great love for her brother, and also her constant worry about his life at war. The same fear filled the whole family. Tove always wrote to her friends about how her brother was faring and about the happy celebration for all the members of the family when he came home on leave from the remote northern fronts. Communication with him was often broken when military operations meant the mail did not get through. Then life was full of fear and worry. At such times the most important place in the family home was the doormat, at which they would stare in the hope that the postman would finally bring a letter from Prolle at the front.

At an early age, Per Olov married Saga Jonsson, with whom he had exchanged letters during the war. They had a son, Peter, and a daughter, Inge, whose lives

Tove eagerly followed from the sidelines. Saga did not always understand Tove's uninhibited relationships, something that Tove complained about in her letters, and they remained a little distant from each other. Prolle took the best and most artistically accomplished photographs of his sister. Tove did not like having her picture taken, and it was not always easy to make her agree to it, but her brother did take many photographs, at her request, in connection with various projects.

After Ham, Lasse was the member of the family closest to Tove. In their gifts and personalities, brother and sister bore a strong similarity. They shared a sensitivity and a deep interest in life, people and the world, but also a tendency towards deep depression. According to Tove, they both had their own realms of darkness where at times they lost their way. Their particular worlds differed greatly, however, so it was not easy for one to gain access to the other's nightmares. Shortly after the war, Lasse tried to run away to South America with a friend in a sailing boat. Before they even reached Sweden their boat got into trouble and they nearly lost their lives. On their return home, Lasse said that for a long time he had been in despair, and that running away had been an attempt to escape from himself. He had been suffering from insomnia, and was depressed and suicidal. Fortunately he had not had the courage to act on his feelings. The event shocked the family, who had not suspected anything was wrong, and it weighed on them all for a long time. Tove tried to talk to her brother about it, but he rejected all his sister's overtures. Later they managed to re-establish contact and an open way of discussing things.

In 1949 Tove planned to emigrate with Lasse to the island kingdom of Tonga. Her brother's depression presumably fuelled the plan, and Tove made clear that it was Lasse's idea. But both of them wanted a change and freedom above all from Finnish society, which they found constricting. With conscious deliberation they collected money and other materials for the journey – and both could easily have taken their work with them. They wrote to the Governor of Tonga about their desire to emigrate there, and the Governor answered their letter. They were not welcome – the kingdom had such a great shortage of housing and materials that no new residents were wanted. However, Tove reflected, there were a lot of islands in Polynesia. The only thing that tied her to Finland was Ham, but the tie was so strong that the emigration plans came to nothing. Yet the dream, the idea of change, the planning for it as well as the recognition of its possibility, meant a great deal to the siblings. It was these attempts to flee

Tove's drawing of her school, 1920s

Cover illustration for Tove's magazine
The Christmas Sausage (*Julkorven*), 1920s

to Paradise – even though they remained no more than dreams – that helped them through periods that seemed gloomy and hopeless.

BECOMING AN ARTIST

Tove hated going to school and was rather a bad student. She never really writes about school, and there is nothing of the kind in Moominvalley, for example. When she occasionally mentions schools it is in a negative light, comparing them to prisons. Tove's own school years were difficult. The subject she hated most was mathematics, which she did not understand and from which, at Ham's request, she was excused. In the drawing class, the students had to make meticulous pictures of owls and the like, and Tove loathed it. But she drew constantly, among other things designing humorous magazines like the *Christmas Sausage* (*Julkorven*), copies of which she sold to her classmates. At the age of twelve she received a black mark for drawing a caricature of her teacher on the class blackboard. At school she obtained respect for her writings, but her drawings were the subject of laughter – and they were, indeed, often funny. It is probable that she was also bullied to some extent. At any rate, in a short story she recorded that in later life one of the bullies wrote to her, hoping for a meeting with the

A New Year card, signed 'T. Knark' by Tove
at age fourteen

Tove's first book, published under the
pseudonym 'Vera Haij', 1933

now famous artist under the pretext of sharing old school memories. The former classmate introduced herself: 'I'm Margit, the girl who punched you in the belly in the playground.' Tove said that she did not want to look back on her school years, and often repeated that school had been an unpleasant experience that she had mostly forgotten, including the reasons she had been so afraid of it. As an adult she suffered when giving interviews, as the questioning reminded her of the terrible years of school and lessons, as well as the endless questions of the teachers.

Life for the Janssons was financially challenging, as for so many Finnish families from the late 1920s until the middle of the following decade. It was a period of mass unemployment and recession. Ham had to work hard in order to secure a living for the family. Tove would have liked to stay at home and help her mother with her illustrations, but despite their worries and bad conscience her parents thought she must attend school.

With her parents' permission Tove was able to leave school and begin the study of art in Stockholm at the early age of sixteen. As she had dropped out of school, there were no other professions for her to fall back on. At an early age she was certain about what she wanted to do with her life and the qualifications she needed. So the years of her youth were not spent in superfluous studies.

In Stockholm Tove lived with her uncle Einar Hammarsten, Professor of Pharmacochemistry at the Karolinska Institute, and her art courses did not involve any major expense. The art school was the same one Ham had attended. Although homesickness and worry about her mother cast a shadow over her years in Stockholm, Tove's time with her uncle was a happy one, as she later stressed.

From 1931 to 1933 she studied at Stockholm's Konstfack, where she took an advanced course in arts and crafts, focusing on book illustration and advertising design. The first year of the course included a broad range of subjects, and was intended to introduce students to the different areas of the visual arts. The second year involved training of a more vocational kind. Tove took a critical view of the school and found the teaching of utility art that dominated the curriculum boring, but she consciously developed her technical skills in all the subjects. Her primary interest was in painting. She liked decorative painting, which she was also good at, and she received the highest grade in the subject and the teacher's recommendation that she should apply for a place at the Stockholm Academy of Fine Arts. A few years later these studies acquired unexpected importance when she produced a number of monumental decorative paintings and glass intarsia for kindergartens, restaurants and schools in various parts of Finland, as well as for the walls of the restaurant in Helsinki City Hall.

After completing the course, Tove did not want to stay in Stockholm but returned to Helsinki and began to study at the School of Fine Arts, or Athenaeum, as it was then called, as it was housed in the building of the Athenaeum Art Museum. It was the same school that Faffan had attended. Tove was not interested in sculpture, explaining that she did not have the spatial sense of form that it required. Painting was her passion and from 1933 to 1936 she studied it. Many things were happening in the art world at the time: small revolutions were under way, and there was an effort to change the prevailing values in the direction of internationalism and away from a rather narrow conception of art. This groundswell also affected the students at the Athenaeum. The students demonstrated their views by leaving the school, then returning to it and leaving again. Tove, too, had long breaks in her studies when together with her fellow students she protested against the instruction, which they all found boring. In 1935 Tove left the school and along with seven students from her painting class acquired a studio that they all shared. During this period Tove was a private student of Sam Vanni, and this formed a particularly important part of her artistic development. However, she later returned to the school and took the final exam.

Tove painting at the Athenaeum, sometime between 1933 and 1936, exact year unknown

The rector of the School of Fine Arts was Uuno Alanko, who in his art and opinions followed a reserved and somewhat inflexible classicism and lacked interest in modern international ideas. He did not inspire Tove. Perhaps he could not motivate a young woman who said that 'he set subjects from the *Kalevala*, always the *Kalevala*, which he viewed as the painter's Bible; it was all that one needed'. Alanko thought that in order to get into the right frame of mind one should go to the outdoor ethnographic museum on Seurasaari Island. *The Kalevala* and national motifs were very popular in 1930s Finland, but remote from the world of a young Finn-Swede who had returned from Stockholm after three years of study there.

In addition to Alanko, William Lönnberg was the other teacher at the art school whom Tove criticized severely, in particular for his strict post-Cubist use of shapes and forms. She recalled how Lönnberg would suddenly enter the room and rap out: 'Well, my young miss, you will never be a painter.' It may have been that he had a specific prejudice against his female pupils, but it was hard to tell. Among the artists, Lönnberg was a counterbalance to Finnish National Expressionism, while Tyko Sallinen and Jalmari Ruokokoski were its prominent representatives. Their art, based on impulsiveness and spontaneity, drew the young Tove's admiration, even though they had produced their most powerful paintings long before. These men had also been Faffan's fellow students, and Tove knew them from her father's parties.

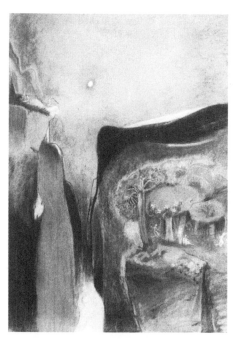

The Hermit, pastel, 1935

Tove may have made many criticisms of Lönnberg, but his teaching found fertile soil in her views on art. His most important principles of art production – controlled form and the use of colour as the fundamental element of painting – also came to be the distinguishing marks of Tove's art during the decades that followed. Lönnberg's principles were repeated in the private lessons she took with Sam Vanni, since Lönnberg was Vanni's great exemplar and master. Through Vanni, whom she loved and admired, Tove came to accept Lönnberg's views almost without noticing.

Mystical Landscape, oil, 1930s

Tove's student days, the mid-1930s, were a very active period in the Finnish art world. There was a desire to get away from the old atmosphere of the past, buried in layers of dust, and to open the doors and windows on European modernism. Maire Gullichsen was the era's great purveyor of change. She had wealth, skill and sufficient experience to set in motion a number of innovations in the field. In 1935 she founded Artek as a centre dedicated specifically to contemporary art. She also played an important part in developing the role of women in the art world. It is said that the exhibition of French art which Artek staged at Kunsthalle Helsinki in 1938, and which Gullichsen opened, was the first in the country to be opened by a woman. Like most of the modernists of the time, Gullichsen was Finland-Swedish.

Artek's aim was to merge art, science and technology in accordance with European models. The gallery functioned brilliantly, in spite of the intervening wars and the death of the gallery's other dynamo, Nils-Gustav Hahl, in 1941. Artek held dazzling international exhibitions, including work by Fernand Léger and Alexander Calder. In the 1950s Finnish modernists and artists who had taken up abstract art, like Sam Vanni and Birger Carlstedt, held exhibitions there which attracted a good deal of attention.

In 1939, in order to guarantee the future of major international exhibitions, the Nykytaide/Samtidskonst (Contemporary Art) Association was established on the model of the Swedish one set up in the previous year. The large exhibition of French art produced by Artek and held at Kunsthalle Helsinki in 1939 was a massive enterprise – too massive for a small organization like Artek. For the staging of such events a broader base was required, and the new association produced the country's most important international exhibitions.

As a counterweight to the school of the Finnish Art Society (Suomen Taideyhdistys), which many felt to be conservative and backward-looking, the Free Art School (Vapaa Taidekoulu) was established. Internationalism was its founding tenet, and so it tried to find progressive teachers from abroad. The school was free: there was no entrance exam and anyone could attend life-drawing classes. It was the brainchild of Maire Gullichsen, who had studied in France and familiarized herself with French art education. In addition to Hjalmar Hagelstam, who led the institution, the other teachers at the Free Art School were William Lönnberg and later Sam Vanni and Sigrid Schauman. Tove went there in the evenings to draw, and when she had completed the course at the Athenaeum she officially enrolled as a student. She was lucky to have as one of her teachers Hagelstam himself, who inspired and encouraged all his pupils. Initially, the school was housed in Hagelstam's turret studio on the corner of Ullanlinnankatu and Kasarminkatu. These were the same premises that Tove acquired after the war. By then, however, many things had changed, and 'Hageli', the studio's director, had been killed in action.

The works that Tove painted before the war are particularly fascinating and indicate an artist who is quite different from the one she was to become. Several of the works are large in size, some even more than two and a half metres wide, but among them there are also small watercolours and pastels. Common to them all is a mystical and fairytale-like atmosphere, strangely exciting colours and frequent strong contrasts of light and darkness.

The titles of the works emphasize a striving for the imaginary, as in the painting *Mystical Landscape* (*Mystiskt landskap*, 1930s), where brightly lit fields of colour cut across a landscape filled with dark blue tones. In the painting *Fairytale* (*Saga*, 1934), though the palette is uniformly brownish, the subject is fairytale-like. A prince rides in the forest, a girl in a red dress plays with a goat, flowers grow straight into the sky, and everything is make-believe. The central element is a kind of otherworldliness, as in *Foreign City* (*Främmande stad*, 1935), which depicts an urban stone environment.

The paintings reflect the foundations in monumental art that were instilled in Tove during her years in Stockholm, for they remain controlled despite their large size. But they also display an interest in storytelling: above all, in a story that transports viewers beyond the moods of the everyday, sometimes to the

House, watercolour, 1930s

realms of fairytale and sometimes to an inner world. In her youth Tove was very engaged with the Surrealism of her time, yet for one reason or another she abandoned it in her paintings. And yet we can see visual echoes of this period in her later monumental works, her fairytale works and paintings based on paradisal themes.

In the 1930s, young Finnish art students did not really travel much, even in Europe, and this was one of the reasons why modern art remained fairly unknown in Finland. Thanks to her mother's family background, Tove had visited Sweden and studied there, where the range of art on offer was broader and more international than at home. The exhibitions she saw included 'Paris 1932', which featured many post-Cubist and Surrealist works, with so many of the latter that the exhibition was dubbed 'The Surrealist Expo'. Tove wrote about the exhibition in *Svenska Pressen*, complaining that this kind of art left her cold, and she could not understand it.

Tove received an opportunity to travel outside the Nordic countries in 1934, when she went to stay with her mother's sister in Germany, and then continued on her own to Paris. The Impressionist paintings in the museums had a great impact on her, especially the purity and richness of their colours. German art, on the other hand, interested her much less. The young woman noted the forces of German nationalism and the rising tide of Nazism; she drew Nazi flags and

Foreign City, oil, 1935

parades, perhaps with a sense of how these forces would come to change her life and that of all Europe. Tove travelled alone around Germany. At that time it was most unusual for a young woman to travel unchaperoned. Considered morally unacceptable, it was certainly daring behaviour.

Four years later, in 1938, Tove set off for Europe again – this time to France, including Paris and Brittany. Again she travelled alone. This time she had a bit of money. A scholarship and earnings from her illustrations meant she was able to stay in France for several months, from May to mid-September. In Paris she stayed among Finnish artists, at the same hotel as Birger Carlstedt and Yngve Bäck, both experienced visitors to the French capital. Hjalmar Hagelstam and the young Irina Bäcksbacka were also there. Tove was sensitive to conflicts: she suffered as a result of the group's internal bickering and intrigues and sought her own peace and quiet. Initially, like many other Finns, she enrolled at the Académie de la Grande Chaumière. Then she changed to taking classes at L'École d'Adrien Holy. She was accepted at the prestigious École des Beaux Arts, where she began her studies. Tove had already trained at two institutions and obtained two degrees, so she could be selective about the teaching she received. She found the prestigious school conservative, and decided to return to Holy. There she worked hard at her painting, and some of the works she produced there have been preserved.

Asleep among the Tree Roots, gouache and Indian ink, 1930s

Perhaps the happiest point of her stay in Paris was when Faffan visited. He had also obtained a scholarship to travel to France, and now father and daughter strolled through the streets of Paris just as her parents had once done. Their relationship was warm and free of discord, the emotional bonds between them strengthened, and they understood each other better. This period was the best time they had together during Tove's adulthood, and the happy memory of it went a long way.

After Paris, the time that Tove spent in Brittany was the most productive for her in terms of her career. She created many paintings there, mostly of the seashore. In many of the works depicting seaweed-burners we see the region's wonderful beaches, the sea, the lighthouses and among them the burners themselves. These paintings are more or less authentic portrayals of normal life in the period before the Second World War. During her stay, Tove also painted *Blue*

Hyacinth (Blå hyacint). A window stands open on a typical Breton landscape, and in the window, forming the centrepiece of the work, is a blue hyacinth. The Brittany paintings were exhibited in several of Tove's shows during the years that followed.

Just before the outbreak of the Winter War, Tove also managed to travel to Italy, the dream of many Finnish artists. The journey began in April 1939. First she took the ferry to Tallinn, then travelled on to Berlin and finally to Italy. Europe was holding its breath, everything sagged under the inevitability of war, and not many months later the conflict broke out. The heavy shadow of the Blackshirts and the Fascists, which no one could avoid, spread over Italy's ancient, noble art and culture. Tove was hungry for new adventures and travelled from one place to another at speed. She saw and experienced many things, but there was not much time for painting. She got to know Venice, Rome, Florence, Sicily and Capri, with the high point of the trip being the Vesuvius volcano. It was living its own mighty life of fire and ashes, though it did not erupt until 1944. The volcano is the basis of Tove's second Moomin book, *Comet in Moominland*, where she describes a fire-belching world in a way only a person acquainted with something similar would be able to. For a long time Tove was sad that she had to stay with the group she was travelling with and could not leave it behind. She dreamed of spending a night alone on the side of the volcano and conversing with it in peace and quiet. It appears that pressure to conform made her return to the hotel on the bus with the others for tea and an evening snack.

Her mother had taught her many things, and hard work was the one that took precedence. Ham had always been very conscientious, and although her output was extensive its quality never suffered. The same, in full measure, was true of the daughter. Tove took an active part in the events of the art world and frequently exhibited her work. The paintings she showed in her early years received positive notices, particularly in the Finland Swedish press; she was often considered to be not only young and promising, but also bold and innovative. Sigrid Schauman, a close

Blue Hyacinth, oil, 1939

friend of Faffan and Ham, who had known Tove since she was a little girl, wrote very encouragingly about Tove's first shows. At the early age of eighteen, Tove's drawings were included in Salon Strindberg's 'The Humorists' exhibition with those of her mother. Some four years later, in 1936, she took part in the exhibition held by the Finnish Designers Association (Suomen Piirtäjäliitto) at Kunsthalle Helsinki, while in the following year her work featured in the spring show of Helsinki Artists (Helsingin Taitelijat), and a few months later in the exhibition at Kunsthalle presented by the Academy of Fine Arts. To the state art prize competition she sent paintings that included her *Self-Portrait with Wicker Chair* (*Självporträtt med korgstol*) of 1937. Though she did not win the prize, the work was the only one to be published in *Svenska Pressen*. In the paper Schauman wrote a positive review of this self-assured and humorous portrait of a girl. And Tove really does look confident. She has portrayed herself from below, and her gaze is fixed, almost sullen. Beside her is a wicker chair, the same one that Faffan had attacked with a bayonet during his parties. Just before the Winter War she showed work in numerous major and minor exhibitions. The Finnish Art Society bought one of her paintings in its spring exhibition, and she received the Society's Ducat Prize for young artists, as well as a travel scholarship. Now she had recognition and an award. The future looked bright: Tove was young and promising, but the world was changing. War had just broken out.

FRIENDS

Tove had many Finland-Swedish friends whom she had known since childhood. In her youth she moved in a circle of art students, and her friends were both Finnish- and Swedish-speaking. Her fellow students at the Athenaeum remained close to her, especially Tapio Tapiovaara. During her student years she met the slightly older Sven Grönvall ('Svenkka') and Gunvor Grönvik. Wolle Weiner (1913–63) belonged to the circle of Tove's closest friends: he was a stage designer, but also worked from time to time as a critic, and he wrote about Tove's works. A large number of her other friends, such as Essi and Ben Renvall, Ina Colliander and many others, were artists. Her lovers' friends were also important to her. Through them she gained access to new cultural circles. Through Tapio Tapiovaara and Atos Wirtanen she met the most important left-wing and liberal-minded writers, artists and politicians of her time. They included Jarno Pennanen and Arvo Turtiainen, as well as the author Eva Wichmann, who became a close and

Sketch for the book *The Dangerous Journey*, gouache and Indian ink, 1970s

valued friend. Through Vivica Bandler she became acquainted with the theatre world and its directors, actors and musicians, among them Birgitta Ulfsson and Erna Tauro, who set several of Tove's poems, like the well-loved 'Autumn Song', to music.

In one of her short stories, Tove recalls her last day at the Athenaeum, her last day with her fellow students. It was still peace time. The expectation of war hung like a black cloud in the sky, though one did not always have to believe in it, or at least not have it in one's thoughts all the time. 'It was May, a cold, bright day, the clouds flew over the sky like large sails in a storm. But in the drawing class at the Athenaeum it was hot, and there sat Alanko, giving us all his farewell speech. [. . .] sang sentimental songs [. . .] our Communist Tapsa shouted to me that he had made an abominably pretty picture with no propaganda and couldn't we swap our works of art for a mark or two now and then? [. . .] We decided to go to Fennia, as a few of us had some money. [. . .] There were eight boys, Eva Cederström and me. [. . .] Tapsa and I went whirling round in such a crazy Viennese waltz that no one else had room to dance, and then he bought me a rose.'

A young woman often has a knack for being happy in spite of everything.

She was admired, she could dance, and she loved to dance. The city was waking up and the spring was beautiful. There were no barriers to happiness, it was all pure joy, she felt: 'I ran up on the rocks, birds were already starting to chirp here and there and a faint red dawn was waking in the east. I was so happy that it hurt and I stretched my arms straight up and let my feet dance as they wanted to. [. . .] I walked very slowly through the city with my coat on my arm. A slight wind had started to blow, a cool morning breeze. The town was absolutely deserted. I thought it amusing, what they say about how hard it is to be happy.'

After her art studies, her fellow students continued to mean a great deal to her. The most important was Tapio Tapiovaara ('Tapsa'), but her friendships with many of the others also lasted a long time. The handsome Unto Virtanen sat as a model for several of Tove's paintings, such as the frescos in Helsinki City Hall. In 1943 Tove painted a portrait of Runar Engblom, giving it the succinct title of *The Furniture Architect* (*Möbelarkitekten*). It shows a man with a dog that is closely watching what is happening. The man sits in the background, looking slightly shy. He is holding a pair of dividers. In what is otherwise a rather matter-of-fact painting, a mysterious, almost surrealistic atmosphere is created by a white rose that lies on the floor between the man's feet.

Tove's dearest and closest friend was Eva Konikoff, also known as 'Koni', or 'Konikova', as Tove called her. She was a photographer and belonged to the same Finland-Swedish circle of friends as Tove. Like many other émigrés at the time, Eva felt insecure in a country on the brink of war because of her Russian-Jewish background. As a child she had already fled St Petersburg in tragic circumstances, and now she was again forced to leave, this time for the United States.

SAMUEL BESPROSVANNI – LOVER, TEACHER,
ROLE MODEL AND FRIEND

Samuel Besprosvanni (later Sam Vanni, 1908–92) played many important roles in Tove's life, as her lover, teacher, adviser, critic and friend. His future wife, Maya London, was also Tove's friend. So close to Tove were the Vannis that she planned to found an artists' colony in Morocco with them. She accompanied them on painting trips in Europe. When in the late 1950s the Vannis divorced, Maya moved to Jerusalem. But Tove and Maya's friendship only grew deeper as time went by, and they wrote to each other often.

Tove met Samuel Besprosvanni in 1935 at Kunsthalle Helsinki, where she was making decorations for a charity event. Unaware of the relationship that had begun between the two young people, Faffan suggested that Vanni should start to teach Tove. Vanni was the great love of Tove's youth, her artistic role model and primary influence. He was six years older than her, which was quite a lot when one was twenty-one. Because of his tuberculosis he had spent time at a number of sanatoriums abroad, where he became acquainted with international art. In those days travel was still rare, and few international art exhibitions were held in Finland. In matters of life experience, as an artist and expert on art, Vanni had the advantage over Tove. He was also a man of the world, an intellectual with an interest in the theory of art and a charismatic conversationalist. To cap it all, he was startlingly handsome and a brilliant artist. The relationship could be seen as a classic one

A drawing by Sam Vanni which Tove copied for her publisher, charcoal, 1935

between teacher and student. During a process in which professional and emotional life merged, Vanni gained even more influence on an embryonic artist, who as yet lacked experience. Sam had strong views on art, and for a long time he remained Tove's artistic authority. His influence was often inspiring and positive, but occasionally he damaged her fragile self-esteem, and his criticisms would echo in her mind for years afterwards.

Vanni's influence on Tove's work is sometimes all too striking. They had the same artistic heroes and ideals: the Impressionists, especially Henri Matisse, and an ardent love of colour. They painted similar subjects – classic window views, self-portraits, still lifes and landscapes. Vanni was a legendary teacher and loved teaching. His authority and influence on several generations were so considerable that people talked about 'the shadow of the great Vanni'. When Tove met him he was only at the beginning of his career, but his magical aura was already well established.

Tove recalled the conversations she had with Vanni in his studio when she went there to do figure drawing. He was a fascinating person, and in order to understand him one really had to concentrate on listening and raise oneself to his level. In 1935, when Tove took an active interest in his work, she was inspired by his large canvases and felt an urgent longing for bright colours. From time to time she realized that she no longer had the strength for her 'own poor daubings', so involved had she become with the work of her admired teacher.

It appears that Vanni had noticed her reverence, for she wrote that he had serious misgivings about their relationship. He was afraid that she would lose herself and blend completely into his world, something he found a deplorable prospect, as in such cases one person became a mere reflection of the other. A person, Tove wrote, who only 'thinks his thoughts and sees with his eyes. Someone who lives in him. Do you promise that you won't lose yourself in me? Yes, of course I do, I said, obediently.' It was a promise she sometimes found hard to keep.

From Tove's notes it is possible to gain an idea of Vanni's inspiring methods of instruction: 'Samuli was cheerful and chatty, he put an empty canvas on his easel and said: "We're going to paint a still life, so you can see how it's done. [...] You must pay close attention, and before you paint you must ask God for forgiveness. The first brush-stroke is deadly dangerous, it determines everything [...] You must use your brain and not just paint according to a theory..."'

Just as many artists' wives, many lovers, children and friends were made to sit as models for Vanni, so too did Tove. He painted several portraits of her. One of the first is strong and heavy, a sculptural portrait dominated by dark earth colours that fail to do justice to the model's sensitivity and cheerfulness.

Tove's portrait of Sam Vanni,
charcoal, 1939

In the picture we see a much older woman gazing ahead of her with a purposeful look. There is something gloomy and mournfully brown about it all. It does not look like the painting of a man in love with his model. However, Vanni's portrait of Tove in 1940 does have that loving quality. It is suffused by a weightless light. The deep glowing red of the floor is reflected in the young woman's cheeks and powerful arms, making her skin glow with vigour and health. Her dress is blue, shading into purple, its fabric glistening silk or velvet with beautiful folds. In the background a mist of light blue impressionistic tones surrounds her like the halo of a Madonna. In spite of her beauty, she looks active and self-assured – gazing straight

Portrait of Tove by Sam Vanni,
oil, 1940

towards the painter and the viewer. She has a sketchpad on her knee, a pen in her hand, and on the table beside her there are jars of brushes, as if to underline the fact that she is a creative artist. She looks as though she is drawing Vanni while he paints her.

It may have been then, as she sat there with her sketchpad and pen, that Tove began the portrait of the man she loved – a work that many would later recognize in photographs of her studio, where it always occupied a prominent position This charcoal drawing of Sam Vanni was completed in 1939, on the very eve of the Winter War. Vanni stares ahead to his right, immersed in thought and looking slightly dreamy. His posture is that of Auguste Rodin's sculpture *The Thinker*. The work is large for a charcoal drawing, the rhythm of the lines attractive and nimble yet powerfully building the male figure.

Religious differences may have exerted some influence on the way their relationship developed. Although Tove came from a pastor's family on her mother's side, religion does not seem to have featured greatly in her way of thinking, and it seems unlikely that she would have looked down on someone because of their religious faith. In one of her stories she describes what reads like a very realistic episode in a restaurant, and something very similar to it also appears in a notebook entry probably written soon after the event. The cigarette smoke has given her a headache, and the loud music makes it difficult to hear what Samuel is saying as he 'delivered his usual monologue on his rather obscure and ambiguous philosophy'. The restaurant meeting captures a moment of the relationship between the teacher and his admiring student, but it also clearly shows that by this time Tove had developed an amused and critical attitude towards him.

Signs of the end of the affair, perhaps even of its aftermath, could be detected:

His voice is so quiet, but it is unlike all other voices, one believes instantly and blindly what it says. [. . .] It was like this, you see: at the beginning I was attracted to you sexually, but then it changed, I simply felt at home and calm and warm with you.

35

That was something I had never found in a woman before. Then I began to love you. [. . .] But now, Samuel continued, now I don't feel any desire at all. Instead, I have come close to you spiritually. And now I would like to keep your friendship as a kind of supreme super-friendship, do you understand? [. . .] What happened in spring was a warning – that we must sublimate, and instead form a spiritual fellowship. [. . .] Well, you remember that time you took it so badly because it wasn't working. Don't you see, that was God's intention, it was to show me for the last time that it was not what he planned. We have been warned many times.

Besprosvanni (Rus. Беспрозванный, literally 'nameless') was the surname given by the Russian military to Sam Vanni's grandfather whom they had kidnapped as a boy. Vanni's grandfather later escaped to Finland but kept his newly given name. During the Second World War, Vanni changed his name, as it met with a great deal of prejudice – anti-Semitism on the one hand (Samuil) and on the other Russophobia. Like many others, he wanted a name that was free from hatred, and changed it to the more Finnish-sounding 'Sam Vanni'. The name change made Tove furious. She wrote about it to Eva Konikoff perhaps without reflecting that it was precisely for this reason that Eva had emigrated to the United States – away from the narrow, frightening and racially intolerant atmosphere of wartime Finland. In Tove's opinion, Samuel had eliminated his roots and, by doing so, had also disposed of the dear, bohemian 'vagabond' she knew so well.

Tove's anger increased when she learned that Vanni's father had bought him a fashionable studio and villa in Westend – a 'château' or 'palace', as she scornfully described it. The new house was large and grand and full of stylish objects that Tove listed in their entirety, from standard lamps to different kinds of wallpaper. She also seemed vexed by the young couple's new elegance. Maya and Sam now talked about books and theatre, and to her they both seemed too exclusive. This change irritated her – the irritation was mixed with a certain amount of jealousy, but above all with sorrow and yearning for what had been lost. She wrote that Sam 'was so elegant that I burst out laughing. Maya is even posher. [. . .] You would not recognize our mucky old eccentric Samuel Besprosvanni in the Sam Vanni he's become!'

Tove was still eagerly looking forward to the next works Sam would show in public. And sure enough, at the end of the year he had a couple of paintings in an exhibition at Kunsthalle Helsinki. In Tove's opinion they were somehow 'dingy', and she did not like them very much. Her active interest in Vanni's art and its reception was marked by an admiration that alternated with harsh criticism. Sam's manner of painting had become heavy, Tove thought – the works lacked the quality she considered to be most important: radiance. Without radiance none of the paintings were worth anything at all. Vanni had also noticed its absence, for he told her: 'I'll put the radiance in later, some time.'

Portrait of Maya Vanni by Tove, oil, 1938

In spite of it all they maintained good relations. Vanni was still Tove's mentor and instructor in making art, her ever faithful helper and adviser. In Tove, Sam also had a friend and confidante; he turned to her when the roof of the new villa leaked, the pipes acted up, snow had to be shovelled and there was not enough money for heating. It was also to her that he went when the relationship with his wife was going badly. While preparing an exhibition during a period of intense creativity he was often wholly preoccupied. His wife would take her revenge by going away to Sweden at the very time when he needed her company and support. Like other artists' wives, she could not expect him to support her work and she could not retreat to it for long, ignoring him and the housework. An artist's wife was supposed to be ready with help, sympathy and companionship whenever her husband needed it. No wonder that such wives felt envy for their husbands, sometimes even amounting to hatred, for the husbands always had peace and quiet for their work. Vanni told Tove of his terror on seeing his wife's eyes grow dark with hatred when she saw his latest paintings.

In 1938 Tove painted Maya's portrait. In this unusual picture the background dominates, filled with large, firework-like flower patterns. The woman sits in front of them expressionless, almost apathetic. Surprisingly and somehow without motivation her blouse is open, revealing the breasts of a beautiful young woman. Her skin glows, soft and flawless. But why are her breasts revealed when otherwise she is fully clad and portrayed in daylight? Pornographic collections often contain pictures of semi-clothed women, their partial nudity being used to increase sexual excitement. This picture contains nothing of that kind. Its strange, contradictory quality prompts questions, making the viewer feel like a voyeur.

II

Youth and War

WAR LETTERS

The war existed not only on the front line, but everywhere: its sound was the tinkle of shattering glass, the thunder of bombs, the rifle salutes at the graves of heroes. It dictated everyday lives – housing, nutrition, health and relationships. The war brought with it death, loss and great sorrow. People's feelings during the war were extreme. There was a great deal of deep and irreconcilable hatred, officially permitted and encouraged by many as being patriotic. As the conflict dragged on, bitterness grew. Love and sex also found particularly fertile soil. People were said to be dancing on graves with a hysterical energy born out of a fear of death. People wanted to forget and they drowned their sorrows in liquor. With sobriety came silence; fear only being shown when they were drunk. Each day was a constant struggle for survival in different ways.

The heavy weight of living paralysed people, consuming and emaciating them.

The war drove friends apart. Eva Konikoff left for the United States: as a Russian Jew she had originally fled to Finland from St Petersburg, and she found the atmosphere between the Winter War and the Continuation War particularly oppressive. The threat of a new war was constant. Tove did not seem fully to comprehend her friend's fear, just as she did not understand Sam Vanni's reasons for changing his Russian-Jewish name. In Tove's letter of 1941 one can hear a doubt about Eva's anxiety: 'And by the way, think carefully about why you buzzed off, are you really sure why you did? I think you're just using the approaching war as an excuse, you want to go away again, it's your continual wish to move on – and of course to fret endlessly about all that you're giving up and want to leave behind. Isn't that so?'

Tove wrote many letters to Eva, around a hundred over a period of thirty years. The young women shared their dreams and fears, reflecting on life, work and love. During the war, letters took a long time to reach their destination, and some disappeared along the way. Postal censorship was strict, traces of which could be seen by the blacked-out areas of the letter or those portions cut right out. As the arrival of a reply was never certain and not expected, the letters seem more like diary entries than a dialogue between two women. Indeed, Tove explained to Eva that in her letters she wanted above all to unravel her own thoughts. The letters are like direct greetings from a bygone era, with its values, its problems and the horrors of war. They describe Tove's everyday existence, her constant worry about food supplies and, above all, her concern for the survival of her lover, her brothers and her friends in the fighting. But because of censorship, the war was the one subject she could not write about directly.

As might be expected, the letters highlight the things that mattered to young women of their age and experience. They reflect the story of Tove's passage to adulthood, the young artist's hopes, disappointments and aspirations. To her friend, Tove confessed her abstract fears – will I ever be able to love, will I ever love enough, and will I ever be able to give people something through my art? Will I ever be happy? Above all, Tove wondered what was most important in life and art. Like any young person, she was preoccupied with love and the choice of a future life partner. Happiness alternated with despair, rapture with depression. Aside from the war, Tove lived on this emotional roller-coaster.

Often her mind was governed by a depression that threatened to kill her desire

Eva Konikoff, c. 1939

to create, and not even art could bring her solace or a spiritual home: 'Eva, the things that really mattered have become superfluous! They have made a completely different world, no, we have let it become a different world where we don't have a place any longer. Yes, painting has always been hard, but now there is no point in it, and that is due to the war.' The feelings prompted by the war reflected a deep sense of hopelessness and, at times, a desire to leave it all behind. The Continuation War had been in progress for six months when she declared: 'War everywhere, the whole world at war. [...] Sometimes it feels as though some of the earth's accumulated anguish were weighing on me like a lump, threatening to explode.

Never has sympathy been so blended with bitterness, love with hatred, the will to live – in decency and dignity – with the desire just to crawl away and let go.'

Tove was deeply affected by sorrow. The Collins and Cawéns, close friends of the Janssons, lost their sons on the front, and the Nelimarkkas' son, an artist, was also killed at war. The well-liked teacher and friend Hjalmar Hagelstam lost his life in 1941, as did Tapio Tapiovaara's brother Nyrki, and many other friends. All of this formed a backdrop to the constant anxiety, especially when a longed-for letter from a brother or a lover failed to arrive. Then they expected the worst, and kept quiet: 'At home it's like a silent well, we are each shut up in our thoughts.'

During the war the importance of all that was good and peaceful became more pronounced. In 1941 Tove wrote about the lovely Christmas they had just had, a counterweight to the bleakness of life and the nagging fear, and she wished that in wartime there could be not just one but several Christmases. When it came to the truly frightening events of the war, she described them curtly, saying, for example, '[they're] furious now, the Russians'. More space was devoted to the description of bottled preserves. Tove's letters repeated her constant concern about the supply of food. During the summer and autumn they picked all sorts of things for the winter. The whole family picked berries, mushrooms and a variety of herbs and leaves, as well as fruit and vegetables from the vegetable garden. Flour was bought, and fish preserved. Impi, who managed the Jansson family's household, gathered clover and raspberry leaves. Tove wrote: 'We've become veritable herbivores – if we ever get a bit of meat to eat, we feel as weird and wild as Tarzan afterwards.'

To counteract the sorrow and the greyness, there were social gatherings at which everyone partied frenetically as if the last day were at hand. Despite the war, people wanted to dance, and Tove loved dancing. All they had to do was draw the blackout curtains, put some music on, and dance. For a part of the war this was forbidden, but then people danced in secret, drank and talked too much. And every conversation ended with the sentence: 'but just wait till the war is over!' If one managed to feel happy, one felt guilty. The war-weariness frequently turned into pure mayhem, as at a May Day party at Ben and Essi Renwall's apartment, where everyone drank uninhibitedly and danced like mad, arguing and laughing. Tove found the party scene desperate, as the mix of war anxiety and alcohol made people's emotions spiral out of control. In Tove's studio they also gathered for after-parties that bore some resemblance to Faffan's *hippor* when she was a child.

The After-Party (also known by the title *The Morning After*), oil, 1941

This party, or one like it, is depicted in Tove's painting *The After-Party* (*Nachspiel*) from 1941, also known as *The Morning After* (*Dagen efter*). It shows a bride and groom dancing in Tove's studio. The wedding bouquet has been carelessly thrown on the floor, and on the table there are liquor bottles and glasses. A couple sitting at the table are kissing, and a solitary man looks on at this theatrical scene. The characters are faceless, and the room contains props that are typical of Tove: a cello, sheets of paper and bentwood chairs. The party in her painting is not a cheerful one, and on the canvas she has written 'The Morning After'. In a letter she said that while it was pleasant to meet people, 'I would rather turn to the wall and not see a human face. I would rather not live at all, as long as there is a war.'

Even minor everyday events were coloured by war. Tove wrote that she spent entire days painting on the terrace of the Uspenski Cathedral, working hard from morning to night. She found it difficult to paint outside, and sometimes had panic attacks. The factory chimneys and buildings in the surrounding district made it interesting and inspiring. It was also a quiet place, the only people around being black-clad worshippers on their way to the Orthodox service. There she could paint in peace. 'A little old Russian lady came cautiously up to me to take a look, and burst out in a spontaneous flood of words in her own language. As soon as I looked at her, her smile died away and she retreated, apologizing. *Khorosho?* I said – and the smile returned. [...] ... But I can't hate.'

The young female painter did not arouse much admiration in the streets of Helsinki. In 1941 Tove wrote that while she was painting down at the harbour, 'a few rascals came up to me and told me that young ladies should go home to her children, as war was going to break out at any moment'. Women were supposed to bear children and produce new life, new soldiers to replace the men who had fallen – it could be expressed as bluntly as this. The country needed children, and it favoured large families. These were demands that Tove was unwilling to meet. She never tried to avoid the obligation to work that the war imposed, however. She did voluntary agricultural labour of various kinds, made snowsuits and bread bags for the soldiers at the Athenaeum, and engaged in other charity work. As the values she espoused were strongly pacifistic, she did not want to join the Lotta Svärd women's paramilitary organization. She was resolute in her opposition to war – an attitude not at all common in a nation now steeped in military propaganda and enthusiastic in its self-defence. Over and over again she pondered the war's rationale and justification, and wrote: 'Sometimes I am gripped by fathomless despair at all the young people who are being killed at the front. Do not they all – Finns, Russians, Germans – have the same right to live and do something with their lives?'... Can one have hope, make new life, in this hell that goes on repeating itself?'

When on leave from the fighting, her friends were tired, hungry, desperate and afraid to return to the hell of war. Mentally and physically frayed, they were shattered by the conflict and the conditions. They needed all the care they could get: food, clean clothes and rest. But above all else those young men wanted a woman's embrace, and 'the calm of the body'. From a human perspective it was understandable, but for women it meant difficult personal decisions and a morality that deviated from the norm.

Sometimes it was terrible to perceive, let alone understand, how much the conditions of war had affected the young men and changed them. Tove wrote that an old friend, Matti, had once come to her 'railway station' as she jokingly called her studio because of all the visitors it had. She was shocked by the encounter. Before the war the young man had been a shy and sensitive dreamer with an interest in poetry, philosophy and art. Now he had changed completely.

He adored the war, relished the prospect of victory, and was full of the ecstasy of conquest. Power was all that mattered, Nazism the correct orientation and the destruction of small states justified. That world no longer had room for individualism, books or poems. He had set his hopes on the war, enjoyed it, and expressed these views loudly to Tove in her studio. In the very studio – she wrote – where she kept her still-life paintings, where she sewed lace on her nightgown, listened to Beethoven and sent poems to the front.

PICTURES OF LAUGHTER AND HORROR

For Tove, the sale of her paintings was a good source of additional funds, but she derived a regular income from her work as an illustrator, of which she produced an increasing amount after completing her studies. In addition to the Christmas and New Year cards she made for the Art Card Centre (Taidekorttikeskus) in 1941–2, she also produced Easter cards and cards with bird and animal themes, earning a decent amount from them. Above all, she created illustrations for many periodicals, numerous Christmas almanacs, newspapers and children's magazines, and drew caricatures, book covers and artwork for various publishers and journals. Publications such as *Garm*, *Lucifer*, *Svenska Pressen*, *Astra* weekly, *Hepokatti* and many others in Finland and Sweden employed her. She was a highly regarded graphic artist, and in 1946 *Garm* advertised itself by stating that Tove Jansson, 'indisputably Finland's foremost cartoonist', was its 'house illustrator' (*hovtecknare*).

And Tove was indeed productive. Illustrations paid very badly, and in order to make the work at all worthwhile she had to create a large number of them. No wonder she sometimes sighed and said she was only 'an Indian ink machine'. She often complained that she did not receive as many artist's grants as she thought she deserved. She suspected that people thought her rich because of her illustration work.

Tove could shroud almost anything in sharp humour, at once intellectual and familiar, through which she viewed the horrors of the war. In Sweden in 1941 she was voted the most humorous

One of Tove's many postcards with animal motifs, gouache, early 1940s

cartoonist in the Nordic region. She wrote to Eva about this with some perplexity, saying that it appeared the humour remained in her fingers, though everything around her was so infinitely dreadful.

The political drawings, particularly those published in *Garm*, form a special and significant part of Tove's output. They are incredibly courageous, reflecting the painful moods of the time. They show exceptional boldness, perhaps even an indifference to her personal future. If Finland were to be occupied or conquered, it would either be by the Soviet Union or Hitler's Germany. The victor would then purge the country of the forces that had put up the most opposition; thus many people had to maintain a low public profile. It was safest to publish pic-

BARA ALLMÄNHETEN GER SIG TILL TÅLS LITE SÅ FÅR DEN NOG STRÖMMING!
GOTT NYTT ÅR !

Patience is needed in the herring queue.
Cover sketch for *Garm*, New Year 1941–2

tures and texts that defamed Finland's enemies anonymously. Neither Hitler's concentration camps nor Stalin's Siberia were a particularly tempting prospect.

Tove's drawings for *Garm* condemned the war and wars in general. They reveal her deep hatred of it, and her pacifism. In a country at war, the idealization of war, or at least the people's unbroken will to defend their country, was official policy. The military censor gave priority to victorious battles, the bravery of Finland's soldiers, their will to fight, and the monstrous nature of the enemy. The misery at home, the major defeats in battle and the large numbers of dead and wounded were subjects the authorities were anxious to hush up. As such, Tove's pictures were not to the liking of all Finns.

With her own particular humour, Tove also described the deprivation and hunger that accompanied war. In a 1942 New Year's greeting illustration she drew a lonely old man fishing through a hole in the ice while the people in a queue hundreds of metres long wait to buy the fish he might possibly catch. The winter of 1941–2 was one of the worst periods of famine during the war years.

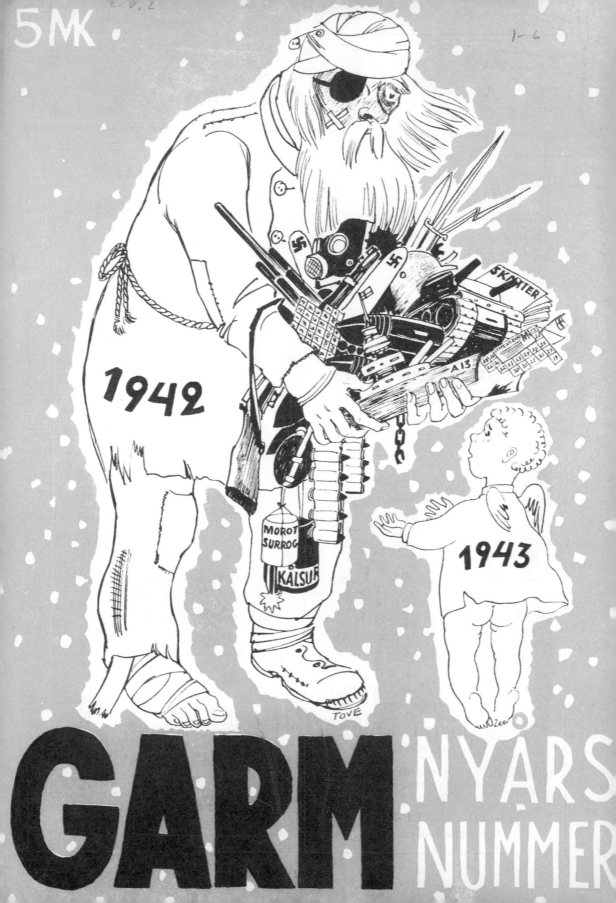

'Good Lord, do they lay eggs now, too?' *Garm*, 1938

People were not allowed to discuss unpleasant realities in public but the famine was shared by all, and despite the military propaganda everyone felt it in their belly. The greeting for 1943 is thought-provoking: it shows the wounded, ragged, one-eyed Old Year handing presents to the young New Year. He has nothing to give except food coupons, guns, a gas mask, bullets and war toys.

Tove was daring; she defied official policies of the time, never trying to cover her back through silence or anonymity. Ever since the turn of the century – even earlier in cultural terms – Germanophilia had traditionally been quite widespread in Finland, and in 1940 the country had entered an alliance with Germany. After that, the political cartoons in anti-Nazi publications like *Svenska Pressen* and *Garm* tended to cause deep offence among Finns. In matters of politics the Finland-Swedish press took a bolder stand than the Finnish-language one, sometimes to its own detriment. *Svenska Pressen* was forced to cease publication because of its open resistance to Germany. However, the paper continued to appear under a new name – *Nya Pressen*. *Garm* was also frequently threatened with closure.

Though her heightened sensibility meant that Tove suffered deeply during

The Old Year presents his gifts to the New Year.
Cover for the New Year issue of *Garm*, 1942–3

47

The saleswoman in a toyshop tells a girl that the new dolls
no longer say 'Mama' but 'Heil Hitler', *Garm*, 1935

the war, we can see some delight in her drawings that savagely mock Hitler and Stalin. At *Garm* she had a free hand, which she made the most of, and later said that she thoroughly enjoyed illustrating the magazine: '[. . .] what I liked most of all was being able to be beastly to Hitler and Stalin'.

Even before the war, the positive attitude towards Hitler taken by many Finns was revealed in the background of a cartoon that shows a little girl in a toyshop. The girl is looking for a doll that can say 'Mama', but the saleswoman tells her they only have dolls that say 'Heil Hitler'. The cartoon appeared in *Garm* in 1935.

Tove mocked Nazism and Hitler in such a way as to reveal a pathetic and ridiculous clown behind the monster who threatened Europe. In her satire, the image of Hitler was still recognizable, and it contained both humour and terror. In October 1938 Tove drew a caricature of Hitler as a whining, greedy toddler. Baby Hitler screams for 'more cake', even though on all sides he is being offered pieces of cake that bear the names of various countries, and a large gateau baked in the shape of a globe. The cartoon alludes to the Munich Agreement of a few weeks earlier when the great powers ceded to Hitler the strategically important Czech Sudetenland, which in turn gave him more or less free access to the whole of Czechoslovakia.

Garm's editor-in-chief said that he and the magazine came very close to being charged with 'insulting the head of a friendly state'. There is similar mockery in a drawing where Hitler sits on a throne between a pair of bombs while his subjects sit around him with dynamite, powder and nitroglycerin, waiting for the order to light a match. Hitler is plucking the petals from a daisy: 'yes, no, yes, no'. Perhaps one of the more blackly comic depictions of Hitler shows him in nine different guises, as he plunders Lapland. Everything must be taken, and what cannot be carried is burned – exactly what happened in Lapland.

A double portrait of Stalin was to have been the cover illustration for *Garm* in November 1940, but it was censored. Stalin is depicted here as a fearless and fear-inducing warrior about to draw his enormous sword. Garm, the symbolic dog, quivers in the background. A moment later, in the accompanying picture, Stalin's posture has begun to wilt, and the sword revealed in the scabbard is small and pathetic. The dog is now yapping at the poor dictator. By means of small changes in the pictures Tove rendered Stalin's familiar, intimidating and powerful figure harmless – so harmless that not even *Garm* dared to publish the picture as it was, for no one wanted to cause too much offence to Stalin and the Soviet Union during the peace negotiations that were then in progress. Stalin's recognizable features therefore had to be changed into those of an ordinary Russian soldier.

The *Garm* magazine cover for Christmas 1941 shows a Santa Claus who has jumped up with his sack of presents to the safety of a cloud. Poor Santa looks sadly down at the earth. Beneath the clouds, bombers are strafing a burning terrain and even the angels are flying away in terror. The picture is at once amusing, seasonal and harshly realistic. In 1943 Tove approaches the horrors of war in quite a different way: drawn with delicate lines, a little boy is shown at the foot of a Christmas tree. He is firing a toy gun and has just pierced the heart of an angel who is hanging from one of the branches. The bullet is still on its way into the flame of a gently burning candle. In September of the same year *Garm* published a distressing cover illustration in which, at the intersection of two searchlights in a sky reddened with gunfire and explosions above a blackened earth, a frightened angel gazes in wonder at the horrors of the world. When the end of the war arrived, the magazine celebrated with a cover showing a white dove, the symbol of peace, flying above a charred and ruined landscape. Life

Hitler frets, *Garm*, 1938

'No, yes, no . . .' Hitler asks a daisy for advice
and his subjects stand ready with matches,
Garm, 1938

was hard, but there was hope if one could manage to believe in it. In September 1944, *Garm*'s cover depicted the uncertainty and fear felt by many, in the form of a large, bright red question mark against black, twisted barbed wire.

Although her political drawings were work, and painful work at that, the illustrations that Tove made for *Garm* were a vital outlet for her feelings of aggression, and her own fears. Through them the readers also found a way to cope with their anxiety. Tove's immediate circle was very politically active, and this in turn gave her the courage to challenge public opinion and be resistant to caution born of fear.

COLOURS IN A WICKED WORLD

The war affected everything that mattered to Tove, and everything she did. Yet the war is not particularly visible in her painting, nor does it feature directly in the work of many other Finnish artists. She did, however, produce some paintings of bomb shelters, which show groups of frightened, faceless people fleeing the air raids. These works movingly recreate the oppressive atmosphere

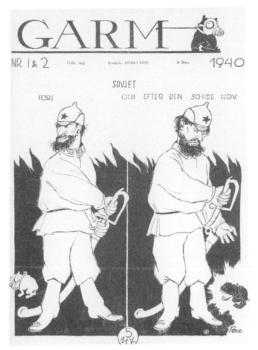

Unpublished and uncensored cover sketch for *Garm* portraying Stalin.
On the right is the censored cover that was actually published, *Garm*, 1940

of a dimly lit space. Tove has vividly captured the everyday reality of war as only someone who had been in air raid shelters and experienced the anxiety of wartime could.

To counteract the fear, greyness and gloom of the war, Tove liked to paint beautiful and cheerful flower arrangements. Was it simply a flight from painful reality, or a moment's recourse to colour and beauty? Probably both. Tove loved any kind of radiance, a word she repeated many times in her letters over the years. Flower painting provided her with a good opportunity to capture it. She painted flowers on their own, as an element in still-life works, in clusters or as parts of portraits, but always with enthusiasm and application. There was a commercial demand for paintings of flowers, and Tove met it. In 1941 the salon of the Helsinki Artists group held an exclusively flower-themed exhibition, in which Tove took part with the Brittany painting *Blue Hyacinth*, mentioned earlier. Sigrid Schauman wrote enthusiastically about this work, seeing the flower as a symbol of dreams rather than as a mere flower, and drawing attention to the delicate colour scheme. The blue hyacinth is surrounded by bright bluish light streaming in through an open window. For Tove, flowers reflected her emotions. At a time when her love life was going badly, she wrote to Eva that she had begun to paint a white orchid, wax-like but beautiful.

All her life Tove was fascinated by the human face and it formed a large part of her output, sometimes as part of the whole body, but often as a close-up of facial features. Self-portraits are central to her work. Through them we see the emotions that each phase of her life brought with it and we can trace her artistic development. In 1940 Tove painted a self-portrait called *Girl Smoking* (*Rökande flicka*). The work focuses on her face and one of her hands, and she portrays herself as defiant and challenging. At the time of its completion, the Winter War was over and the waiting for the Continuation War had begun. There was peace, however, and for a short time at least the greatest fears receded. As the title suggests, the woman is enjoying a cigarette, its grey smoke blending with the blue background. Tove was a heavy smoker – it was the custom of the time, especially in artistic circles. With its pink, yellow and blue nuances, the portrait is a cheerful one. It was bought by a tobacco merchant who used it as an advertisement for his business. Although Tove found this slightly disconcerting, the money was welcome.

At around the same time, Tove sketched a portrait of Eva, which she finished in 1941, after her friend had already left for America. At its first public showing it was well received, something that Tove reported to Eva with delight, telling her that she had deliberately given it such a high price that no one would buy it – she wanted to keep it for herself. Much later she gave it to Eva as a present, sending it to her in America. In the painting, Eva sits on a bentwood chair. Someone has thrown sheets of paper, perhaps music, on the chequered floor, and in the corner is a cello. In the background is a door and a heavy, pleated baroque-style curtain. The woman is dressed only in her underwear and is barefoot, suggesting she has either just got up or is on the way to bed. Eva's parents were shocked by their daughter's semi-nudity, a reaction that Tove appears to have found amusing. The woman in the portrait has strong features that resemble those of Eva Konikoff as they appear in the photographs that have survived. She is leaning her forearms on her thighs, looking thoughtfully to one side. Attention is focused on her appearance: she is stylish, but this is no sweet and pretty female portrait. Nothing about the woman makes an appeal to the viewer or is intended to please. She is self-sufficient, and indifferent to the gaze of others.

In Finland, the wartime period was not at all bad where artists' incomes were concerned. The value of money was uncertain, as there was really nothing to buy – a universal shortage of everything reigned, with a constant fear of inflation

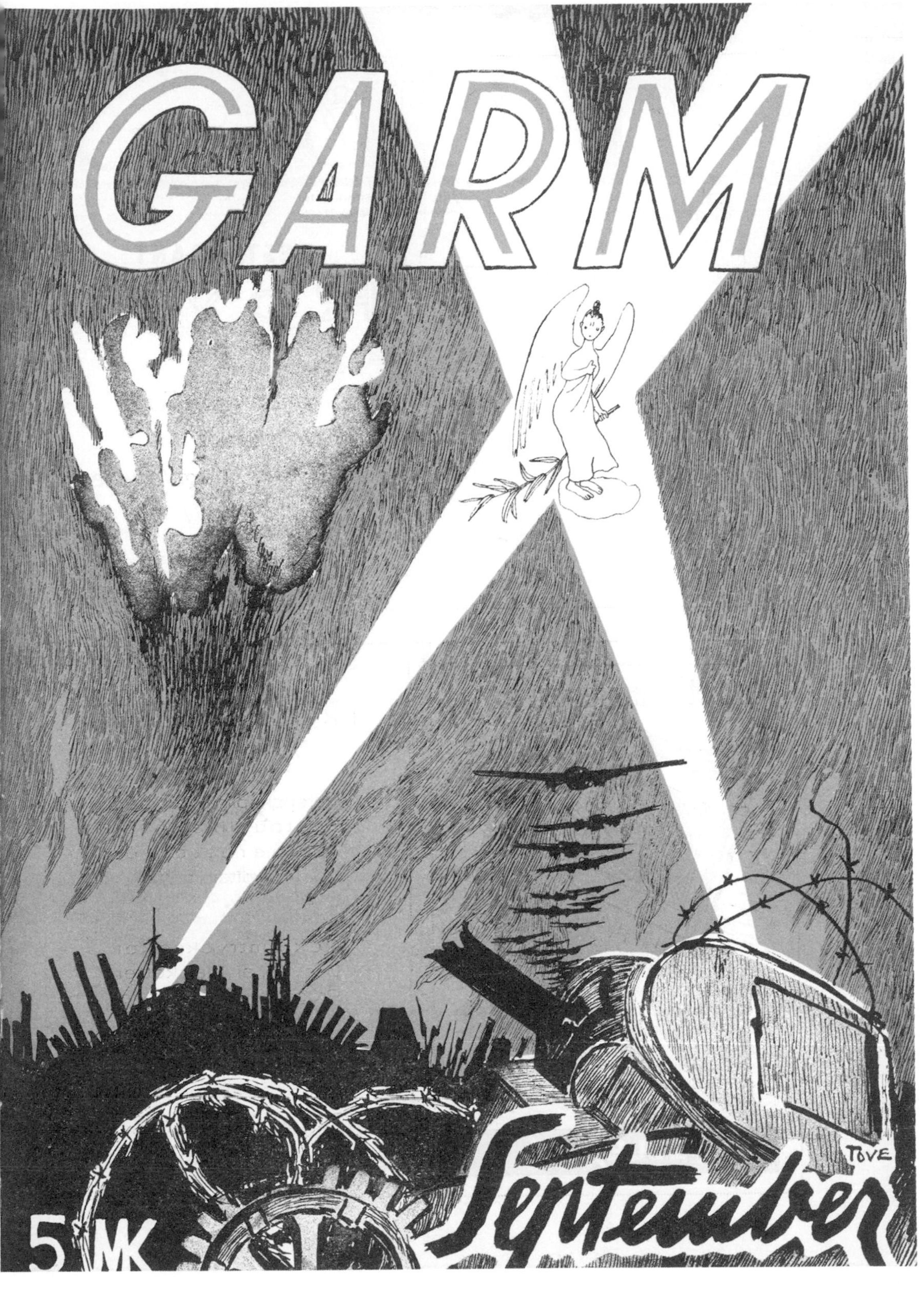
GARM
TOVE
5 MK
September

Self-portrait, *Girl Smoking*, oil, 1940

and a sinking currency. The fear was not unfounded and became most acute shortly after the war, with the so-called 'banknote cutting'. This understandably led people to want to invest their money in property as soon as possible in order to protect and possibly increase its value. Art was one investment option. For *Garm*, Tove drew a witty cartoon of art buyers flocking to the studio of a hardworking artist. Trade is brisk, it is all going well, and the artist continues to paint and paint while children bring more and more paints and brushes. Perhaps Tove herself did not fare quite as well, though she did sell her works, and wrote to Eva each time she succeeded in doing so. Her accounts show that in 1941 she sold nineteen works, in 1942 twenty, in 1943 twenty-nine, in 1944 thirteen and in 1945 as many as thirty-nine. The arrival of peace saw a marked decline in the number of art purchases. During the two wars and the subsequent economic depression, Tove also exchanged paintings for essential items whose practical value exceeded their monetary value. She needed capital not only to live on, but also to pay the rent on the studio and maintain it – and ultimately to buy it. Selling paintings was not always a simple matter, and during the final period of the war in 1945 she complained about buyers' unreasonable demands. One person bought a work, but after some time brought it back and asked to have it exchanged for a larger one. The subject of the new painting was to be a silver vase of violets.

A LOVE DEFINED BY WAR – TAPIO TAPIOVAARA

Tove Jansson and Tapio Tapiovaara (1908–82) studied at the Athenaeum together, and in the early years of the war they became lovers. Their affair was stormy, with war as its backdrop. But by the end of the war their love had burned out. They continued to be friends, and the friendship was important to them both. Tapiovaara, or Tapsa, as he was always called, had a personality quite different from Sam Vanni's. But both men seemed to share an enthusiasm for attempting to 'preach' to the young Tove and thereby to influence her ideas and values. However, the guidance they offered took very different directions.

The war defined the framework of Tapio Tapiovaara and Tove's relationship, and also the manner in which it ended. Tove seems to have put up with a great deal from Tapsa solely because she believed that his life would be a short one. Although she does not say so directly, she thought he would be killed at the front. To her, he was a kind of living corpse: still alive, but soon to be dead.

For this belief she had perfectly realistic grounds: many men of this generation fell in the war, and many of those who were sent off to fight at the same time as Tapsa did lose their lives, as Tove wrote.

In their relationship Tove became the one who nurtured, understood and forgave. She was determined to make sure that not one hour, not even a moment of Tapsa's leave would be boring, let alone unhappy, and she felt obliged not to make him upset. What he did became less important to her than loving and being kind to him. By thinking in this way she buried her own desires and needs.

Of Tove's friends, Tapsa was one of the first who really belonged to Finland's Finnish-language culture, and his social circle was very different from hers. From an early age he had been a staunch left-winger, 'our Communist', as Tove called him during their student years. Tapsa's brother Nyrki was an admired film director, a promising star in his field. He was also one of the most prominent activists in the Kiila group. He figured among its leading artists, and on the political left as a whole: some of his graphic art and large mosaics were the result of commissions he received in the Soviet Union and they formed a notable presence in the polarized society of his time. He opened Tove's eyes to

Tapio Tapiovaara, c. 1939

left-wing ideas, something for which she had been prepared neither by her home (especially her father's view of the world), nor by the tolerant liberalism prevalent in Swedish-speaking cultural spheres. But although she moved in a social circle of people who were interested in party politics, Tove did not share their interest. Her best friend Eva also eagerly took part in such debates, and when Eva moved to the United States, Tove said that Tapsa missed their 'sacred political discussions', as she playfully called them.

Sam Vanni and Tapio Tapiovaara belonged to the same circle of young artists. Quietly, Tove moved from the one to the other. She wrote to Eva about her worry that Samuli and she were drifting apart, but at the same time said that Tapsa had come closer to her. Only gradually had she begun to realize how strong and independent he was, and how much he meant to her. Each day, or at least on days when there was no fighting, he wrote wonderful letters to her from the front, so wonderful that she reflected:

If the war does not take Tapsa, I want to keep him. There has grown within me a new longing for something permanent and stable, something warm that I can trust – I'm tired of episodes and violent infatuations. Tapsa and I know where we are with each other, there is so much more there than sex [. . .] He has taught me not to be afraid of life. If he comes back it must be I (all of us here at home) who am brave and cheerful and try to make him forget 'what no human being should have to see'.

Yet Tove's longing was pensive: she worried that the man who returned to her might be thoroughly changed. The war broke many young men psychologically, some beyond cure. As a child, Tove had already seen one such man in the shape of her father. Young and in love, her life was dominated by waiting, uncertainty and fear. Though not a great deal happened externally, within her it was a different story: 'I thought at first that this dreadful time was just a kind of existence – not real life. But now I've begun to wonder if life is only now making its approach and demanding that I take a stance: acceptance or rejection.'

Tove's love for Tapsa deepened as the months went by. She wrote with happiness that in three weeks' time she would have him home. He had been slightly wounded in the fighting near Petrozavodsk and was being treated in hospital. Her wait for Tapsa's visit was fraught. Tense with excitement, she complained of being unable to really concentrate on anything. All she could do was walk about and prepare for her soldier's arrival, as she suffered all the classic symptoms of being in love. She said that she felt like an idiot of seventeen. But being newly in love was wonderful and she was happy again – something not to be disparaged in a life overshadowed by war. In the same letter she said she had sold a picture for 1,000 marks at an exhibition, and that the family now had mushrooms, fish, lingonberries and flour from the island, so the winter was taken care of. Everything was fine. Even Samuli, who had got married, was 'starting to wake up' from his 'marriage trance'.

The early part of Tapsa's leave was wonderful, and Tove recalled the first day of it with nostalgia:

We [. . .] had it all to ourselves. He was here incognito, came straight to the studio with flowers, an icon, ersatz coffee, sugar, memories of the war. He was so tired, lay

The Girl and the Wardrobe. Self-portrait
in silk evening dress, oil

Tove in a red silk evening dress,
photograph by Eva Konikoff

*and slept while I sorted his clothes and boiled macaroni for lunch – I felt so strangely
domestic and idyllic. And happy.*

*We had a festive dinner with wine and your candles, Impi had cooked a bird. [...]
I wore my dark red silk dress and he – the only time he did so – a medal. It was all so
solemn that we hardly said a word. [...] To think that of the two hundred who set off
from Käpylä in June he is one of the ten who survived.*

Love was challenging, though. After that first wonderful evening Tapsa
neglected Tove, did not show up at all, and went off on his own business. He
aroused great interest in many women, and being rather susceptible to admiration, did not even try to conceal his other relationships. Where in the past
he had clearly been timid – at least where Tove was concerned – he had now
acquired courage. Perhaps the war had hardened him: 'I often have telephone
calls from women trying to reach him. He is now the way I wanted him to be –
that apologetic doggy look is gone, he doesn't beg and is not so obedient [...]
Now I love him.'

When one has been waiting and yearning and is so full of love, one has doubt-less put a strain on one's own resources too. And when hopes and expectations have been high and they are not fulfilled, it is extremely difficult to face the harsh reality. The fall was dramatic, and Tove wrote to Eva about what happened in several letters, reiterating the same points, the worst of which seemed to be Tapsa's absence.

Tapsa held passionate opinions, and his disposition was equally passionate. At times he went off the rails completely. In Tove's view, at least, he had too many friends. The fiancée of Nyrki Tapiovaara, who was killed at the front, said that she suspected Tapsa's friends of exploiting him and 'making fun of his naiveté, his sky-blue idealism, behind his back'. Tove's concerns about her lover were not unfounded, and she was not the only one to have them.

Tapsa had a compulsive desire for someone to write a book that would make a definitive statement about the war, but he did not want to do it himself. What he had in mind was not a story of battle and suspense, but rather something 'genuine, the kind of book that will help people and make it so it won't all have been in vain'. No one, not even Tove, understood exactly what he meant. Tapsa rushed around, obsessively searching for someone who would be able to write the book. Tove and Tapsa paid a call on Hagar Olsson. Tove described their meeting:

> One night we were at Hagar Olsson's: by turns he shook her and got down on his knees to her, begging her to promise to write that book before he went back – and she was half flattered, half irritated and thoroughly alarmed. That night for the first time he was drunk – his friends had been plying him with liquor all day and Hagar supplied the last of it. For the first time, I saw how terribly he suffered from all he had seen, from all the faces that followed him, how confused and helpless he was. Good Lord, what will he be like when I get him back next time? Now he's dashing around and talking, talking – talking too much – and I'm scared.

Hagar Olsson was a prominent and respected Finland-Swedish cultural critic and author whose sharp opinions were often resented. Her play *The Snowball War* (*Snöbollskriget*) of 1939 is about the threat of war, and a warning about the attitudes that lead to it. During the war and after it she was a leading socio-political analyst of her time, and her writings were marked by a deep pessimism. *I'm Alive* (*Jag lever*, 1948) is a programmatic collection of essays in which, among other things, she described the Nazis' concentration camps and crematorium ovens. She demanded that artists should be held to account for what they had done during the war, in which forces they had served, what they had defended

and what they had opposed. Her 1944 essay 'The Decadence of Authorship' ('För-fattarskapets dekadans'/ 'Kirjailijat ja maailman tilanne') was a kind of writer's manifesto, in which Olsson analysed the situation during the final phase of the war. The time when people stood face to face with the Devil was over: now the 'little man' himself was the main problem. What she advocated was a sort of 'blacklist' of authors. She thought it was not enough to ask someone what they had written – they must be asked whose side they had been on. Writers who had merely fulfilled their own literary aims were writing 'to the wind', and those who defended the indifference and political irresponsibility of such writers were the worst enemies of mankind.

In appealing to Olsson, Tapsa probably did the right thing, but his ideas seemed to be rather woolly and this was not helped by the fact that he was thoroughly drunk. The book never got written. In its intensity, the ambition was symptomatic of Tapsa's difficulty in comprehending the war, his own part in it and his justification of it in the light of his own world outlook.

Meanwhile Tove wrote about her own jealousy. She reassured herself that she was not interested in Tapsa's women – after all, what did it matter who Tapsa was with, the main thing was that he was happy. Three days later she wrote about how hard it was not to be bitter, to under-stand what things meant and yet not be afraid. Bitterness and fear were the main emotions with which she did not want to burden her life. She returned to the evening at Hagar Olsson's, writing that when they had left the apartment Tapsa suddenly told her he had been stupid and unfaithful. Even in the turmoil of her emotions, Tove remem-bered her resolve not to put pressure on him and to see to it that the short time she believed he had left should not contain one unhappy moment. In his usual male fashion (Tove noted with sarcasm), Tapsa explained that he had been drunk and also blamed the long period of sexual abstinence at the front. Angrily, Tove burst out: 'He could go to

Tove Painting, drawing by
Tapio Tapiovaara, 1941

anyone he wanted . . . I waited three evenings because he said he loved me [. . .] But I couldn't sleep, and that has never happened to me before. And I didn't dare to take sleeping pills – for he might arrive. [. . .] When the men stop their killing, I will have children – but they'll probably never give up.'

Tapsa had suggested that during his leave they should try to have a child. In the light of his behaviour, the proposal seemed strange and unreasonable. An acute need to make life carry on by means of a child was understandable, but had less to do with the couple's relationship than it had with the war itself. There was a general wish to pit new life against all the death, to replace the men who had fallen. For individuals, a child meant continuity, something that would remain of them now that death very probably stood at the door. But on the issue of children Tove had very clear views, from which she did not deviate. Tapsa said he had lived with a woman who had promised him a child. The thought made Tove furious, but at the same time she remembered that Tapsa had also asked *her* for a child – for he wanted her to conceive a 'little Tapsa' before he returned to the war.

The day before Tapsa left, Tove swallowed her pride and telephoned him. He promised to come and say goodbye. Tove described how she tried to be pleasant, grateful and forgiving by telling him that she understood him. She assured him that she was not bitter, but loved life and wished for God's blessing on everyone. But privately she thought that 'it felt all the time as though God were laughing at me . . . it went well, I said everything I wanted to say, but it was like theatre . . . then he said: "Listen, I'm not going to the front."' This caused Tove another storm of emotions. It was as though she had written an obituary and the deceased person had risen from the dead – it turned out that this was not the last time she would see him, after all. The news left her relieved and happy.

Then Tapsa said that he wanted to go out and have breakfast, and Tove said she would join him. He merely shrugged nervously, but off they went, hand in hand. At their destination they found a woman who had already been waiting for Tapsa for three quarters of an hour – a large platinum blonde with heavy make-up. As Tove described her, the new acquaintance seemed nice enough, and rather pathetic. Once again, being in love was hard. Tapsa's beautiful idea of their making a child together before he left for the war had run into the sand. A scene followed: 'I didn't understand it at all, and I was tired. I went to an exhibition and Tapsa followed me. I told him I wanted to know and was unwilling to wait any longer . . . his reply was: I'll always come back – in the end.' Tove demanded that he commit himself, choose between his women. She wanted to put an end to her own constant uncertainty and disappointment and described her own part in the episode: 'That's not good enough for me . . . you must close one door and then open another, you can't leave them ajar. Go away, and go for good, I said.'

Tove arranged to meet Tapsa in her studio at ten that evening and he arrived punctually. But it was all very gloomy, and there seemed to be no ray of light anywhere. Work was still her only chance for happiness. Tove had indeed been deeply wounded:

I was filled with dissatisfaction and sensed with dread how poor I had become. Instead of the warmth, the old, simple warmth that asked for and demanded nothing there were only bitter recollections, brooding and worry. [. . .] He was totally alien to me.

First I must understand, I said. [. . .] That his letters meant nothing, [. . .] that he loved me but still kept me waiting every night [. . .]

Tapsa said nothing. [. . .] I understood less and less. He fell asleep and I was terribly lonely.

Suddenly I thought that there ought to be only one thing that could make that which is ugly beautiful again and it was that people should love one another enough. Enough in order to understand – and not just forgive, but also forget. I woke him up and tried to erase everything from my brain and said: 'Tapsa, I've forgotten all about it. Let's just be happy.'

After all, it didn't matter so much what he felt for me and what he had done – the main thing was that I should love enough. He smiled at me and hugged me. Then he went back to sleep and I lay there trying to feel nothing but full of love. But there was no calm, I wasn't happy with myself. All the things that make me not want to marry came before me again, all the men I had seen through and despised [. . .], all of that loyally united and protected pedestal of male privilege, the glorification of men's weaknesses in as many inviolable slogans [. . .] I can't bring myself to admire and comfort and pretend that it's not just scenery! I feel sorry for them, yes – I like them, yes – but I don't want to give my life for a performance I have seen through. [. . .] I can see what will become of my painting if I get married, because in spite of everything I still have within me all these inherited female instincts to comfort, admire, submit, sacrifice myself. Either a bad painter or a bad wife. And if I become a 'good wife', then his work will be more important than mine, my intelligence will be subordinate to his, then I will bear children for him, children to be murdered in one of the coming wars. I don't have the time or the will or the means to get married . . .

In several letters to Eva, Tove returned to the meetings she had with Tapsa during his spell of leave. Meanwhile Tapsa had already returned to the front

Self-Portrait, oil, 1942

and all her joy and desire to get to grips with her life and work seemed to have vanished. One day she would paint again, set her life in order, and meet her friends. In her notebook she wrote of the things that Tapsa and she could have done together, like dancing for dancing's sake, dancing away the war and the suspicions, and then going skiing, visiting the theatre or exhibitions. And in spite of all her disappointment she was concerned about his 'naïve and sky-blue idealism'. She did not reject him, but wished for different ways to be with him, simply 'be together and not take responsibility for each other's work, life and thoughts . . . Then our life together would be more successful, perhaps.' But Tapsa's repeated assertion that she was some sort of freeloader or gatecrasher troubled her greatly. She seemed to believe in his accusations and made his shoddy treatment of her into her own fault:

> But can I talk about love, I – when my own business seems to be what matters most to me? Then I don't love enough. I don't pay anything, so I shan't receive anything. It all went round in circles, the hours passed – towards morning I fell asleep, only to be woken by the telephone while it was still quite dark [. . .] As usual, it was a woman asking for him. I felt it was all somehow dirty – and that God was laughing at me even more . . . In the evening he phoned and said in a very quiet, dejected voice: 'I was wrong, it's the front for me after all.'

Afraid of what lay ahead, Tove went to the railway station to say goodbye and tried to be cheerful. 'Then the platinum-blonde woman arrived [. . .] Perhaps I expected too much of the relationship?' Love was full of disappointment; she despaired of her own ability to love, and wondered if work and art could really replace it. Deeply depressed, she doubted her ability with those things too. But she tried to preserve the hope of something better and thought that an artist of genius could nourish people, even if her own works did not yet give enough. They did, however, offer her something and occasionally restored the joy she had lost. In the future she too would find joy, she would travel and experience success, and she hoped that one day she would understand this unhappy time. For now, she merely felt 'so tired. And lonely . . .'

A few days later, on 6 November 1941, she wrote again to Eva that she had regained her strength. She had chosen, and done so conclusively: she was going to be a painter, 'and only a painter, and I think that it will be enough for me'. Soon Tapsa began to write again as often as ever, but she no longer described him with the grand words and emotions she had used before his spell of leave. Life was hard and her depression obvious: 'The year grows so heavy with itself in November, and this is a War November. But I suppose it will get brighter!'

She had met Tapsa's 'husky platinum-blonde girlfriend', who said that she had tried to get him away from the front. 'By what means I don't know. But I hope she will succeed.' In December Tove was still musing about her relationship with Tapsa, and wrote: 'I wanted to burn my bridges, put all my trust in a feeling for once, and not leave the door open even a crack. [. . .] The radiance has gone – but I will give us something else instead, perhaps.' Radiance was the kernel of the vital energy in love, relationships and art. If the radiance died, nothing of real value remained. Everything sank into dull mediocrity, and she really did not want that. 'All those poor people who lose their radiance.'

In March Tapsa had two weeks' leave. The same problems recurred, and were much worse this time. Tove hardly ever saw him, and she felt that he viewed her as a duty and an obligation. Night after night she waited. On the last night, a drunken Tapsa telephoned from his girlfriend's apartment. They discussed their relationship in a friendly and ordinary way, as Tove described it: 'I asked if he wanted to be free, and he was touched and grateful [. . .] It's really strange, all this. That throughout the war we've maintained our joie de vivre with our letters, often writing every day, just telling each other about all the lovely things we'd do when we were able to be together; that he's loved me for seven years – and then as soon as he gets a spot of leave he goes to that husky painted blonde from Robertinkatu and says he's grateful to be free! But one thing I know: I've paid my debt to him. Haven't I, Koni?'[3]

Even after this, Tove tried to build a friendship with Tapsa, and she succeeded. Once the disappointments and the passion were out of the way, the times they spent together were calm and pleasant. He had been able to leave the front entirely and was now back in civilian life, illustrating a book that Tove was

3. From a letter to Eva Konikoff.

translating for him. There were parties with intoxicating drinks and waltzes, and the good intentions and firm resolutions about 'friendship only' were forgotten. 'Just this once, it doesn't count,' was how Tove described her thoughts. Waking up to everyday life and a reality where the old problems still remained was not a painless process. The loneliness felt ten times worse. Tove wanted to end the physical relationship, but Tapsa aspired to continue the 'cheating'.

In her next letter to Eva, Tove wrote that she feared she might be pregnant. Tapsa had once again accused her of being a freeloader, like someone who sits in the best seats in the stalls at the theatre without having paid for a ticket. Now everything seemed to be turned upside down, and quite badly so. If she were pregnant, then 'now it was time to pay, and with interest'. Ever hopeful, she thought it might possibly be a false alarm and was perplexed by her own passivity. She merely waited, but could perhaps have done something, though she did not specify exactly what. At the same time she wondered what she would do with the child. She hoped it would be a girl, and thought she might take it to a country that was more congenial than Finland. But the prospect of a boy frightened her – she did not want to give him up to the war. Just over a week later, she wrote that on this occasion there would be no little daughter and that she was most thankful.

Not even this stressful episode spoiled the friendship between the former lovers. In August, Tapsa spent five days with Tove in Pellinki. Though Faffan made no secret of his reluctance, he allowed the visit. On the island Tove and Tapsa reflected on life. Tove pondered its fundamental questions: what was important in life, and what was enough to meet a person's needs? 'Just living – quite simply? Is that enough? Are aspiration and ambition only misleading signposts? Are the encounters on the way so important that the goal becomes a minor matter? Perhaps it is just as important to "be able to" and "know how to" as it is to enjoy what others, with more skill and wisdom, have made and devised for us, to adapt ourselves to life as a small, linked, insignificant part of it, to watch the spectacle and let the sun shine.'

Tapsa's sociable nature was a source of wonder to Tove: he got along with anyone, was popular and charmed everyone on the island without exception. Tove felt very different from him. Now her relationship with him was calmer, though devoid of radiance, as she herself noted. They felt happy together – were used to each other, like husband and wife. She mused about her love and the loss of it, and considered that the two dreadful disappointments she had suffered during Tapsa's leave had killed it. At the same time she wondered whether she would ever be able to love enough. Her connection with Tapsa was marked by great understanding and tolerance: 'I have found a tenderness for him that is certainly not love – more something warm, good [. . .] Nothing he does can hurt as much as it did then, during those spells of leave.'

Tapsa needed a great deal of support, which Tove tried to give, though it was not always easy. At times he became unbalanced, and once again suffered a degree of obsessive behaviour. He claimed to be looking for the truth, but no one knew what he meant by 'the truth' or what he really wanted. Whenever she had not seen him for a long time, Tove would simply say rather sarcastically: 'He's probably looking for "the truth" again. I hope he finds her.'

During the years that followed, Tove saw Tapsa at rare intervals, faithfully reporting to Eva on his welfare. With sincere relief she wrote that he had met a 'really sweet and delicate little creature' and in 1945 he married the ceramic artist Ulla Rainio. Tove was pleased by the news that the young couple were going to have a baby, and she thought that Tapsa would be happy now, as he had long wanted a child. A daughter, Maria (Mimmi), was born in 1945, and a son, Jukka, in 1947. Her relationship with Tapsa somehow remained close and warm and she became godmother to his first child, Mimmi. Tove had a rare ability to forgive people and accept them. She could build a lifelong friendship with someone even after a passionate love affair that ended unhappily.

Later, too, Tove thought about Tapsa with warm affection and remembered how wonderful it had been to dance with him. She hoped that they would meet again in heaven, where they most certainly would ask the angels to play the Vienna Waltz – and they would dance again.

SELF-PORTRAITS, ALONE AND TOGETHER

Female artists in Finland have painted many self-portraits. These paintings often feel like a commentary on being a woman and a female artist – they display the process of ageing and highlight its many effects. Tove Jansson produced a number of such works. A large proportion of them are primarily studies of her physical and mental state. They are like reports on their creator, and narratives for the viewer, but they also contain many elements to which only she had the keys.

Despite the war and the heartaches, or perhaps precisely because of them, Tove immersed herself in her work. Life had to go on and she needed to pay the bills. Her painting, her illustrations and the writing of the Moomin stories

The Studio, oil, 1941

played an important part in sustaining her vital energy. Work created faith and hope amidst the dreariness of everyday life. Some of her major paintings were begun during the stormy interludes of love and traces of that emotional roller-coaster can perhaps be discerned within them. The painting *The Studio* (*Ateljén*, 1941) preceded Tove's final move away from her parents' home and was created in one of her temporary studios. The work came into being either during the wait for the Continuation War or just after the beginning of that conflict. Its atmosphere suggests an apathy and loneliness born of fear – whether caused by the war, by waiting or by a lover's betrayal. The artist,

Self-Portrait with Fur Cap, oil, 1941

a faceless young woman, probably Tove herself, sits by a window in her white artist's smock, her hands helplessly in her lap. Next to her stands an easel, and behind her is a row of paintings or stretched canvases stacked on their sides. A similar atmosphere exists in the painting *The Woman in the Window* (*Kvinnan i fönstret*) from the same year, which shows the same woman. The window is open, and the day so windy that the white curtain flutters freely. Outside it is summer, the trees are swaying in the wind, the grass is green and the sun is shining. The woman has turned her back to the viewer. A jug, the back of a bentwood chair, a mirror and flowers adorn the work, and are typical of their creator.

Self-Portrait with Fur Cap (*Självporträtt med skinnmössa*, 1941) also originated from the darkest time in Tove's love life. The painting is an odd one: the artist sits on a bentwood chair with what appears to be one of her Brittany paintings in the background. On the table beside her is a round vase with blue floral decorations, familiar from many other paintings, and a bottle. The woman's hands rest in her lap, her gaze is piercing and her expression demanding. She is wearing a large and rather strange fur cap and her waistcoat is also made of some furry material. Her blouse is a glowing red and her skirt chocolate brown – the warm colours of her clothes soften the sternness of her expression.

The large painting *The Family* (*Familjen*) is dated 1942, but was mostly composed during the previous year. In addition to being from the same period, another

The Family, oil, 1942

aspect the painting shares with the self-portrait is the way in which Tove's face is represented. In *The Family* it resembles a copy of the face of the woman in the self-portrait, or vice versa. It is as though the fur cap in the self-portrait has been exchanged for the large, black cloth hat in *The Family*. The woman's expression, the direction of her gaze and her facial features are almost identical.

The Family is a portrait of the Jansson family during the war. The war is present, though indirectly, and we can see how it casts a shadow over the family members. The composition consists of two groups: Faffan and Per Olov form a duo on the right, while Ham, Lasse and Tove make up a group on the left. Lasse is sitting on the bentwood chair. Trailing along the wall is a climbing plant in a floral arrangement, and next to it stands one of Faffan's miniature sculptures representing a naked female body. In the centre of the room is a mirrored bureau on which there are books and papers. In the foreground the sons are playing chess with red and white pieces on an octagonal table. The same bright red colour recurs on the bureau, and its strength and brightness stand out in the surroundings, which are otherwise drained of colour. The colour red, used as a symbol of blood, may be an allusion to war and death, as Per Olov is wearing his military uniform. For centuries, chess as well as various card games have been used in art as symbols of fate and its incalculable nature. In such paintings, mankind is playing its eternal game with death.

Tove has portrayed herself very dramatically – she is dressed in black, as if in mourning. Her large black hat recalls the mourning headdress common in Finland at the time. The hat also has a black veil that is drawn aside. Tove wears black gloves and is holding her hands in a strange posture, extended forward; she looks helpless. Her gaze is turned towards the viewer – it is serious and without expression. Ham is casually smoking a cigarette and her gaze is directed at Tove. The father looks away from the family towards the viewer, and like the mother he is wearing an artist's smock: they both appear to be taking a short break from their work. Lars is absorbed in the game and the chessboard, while his elder brother Per Olov looks into space, but also slightly above him. The work is mysterious: it is as though Tove were analysing not only the tensions caused by the war but also the currents of emotion within the family. Tove worked on the painting for a long time. It was the result of a 'truly great effort', as she enthusiastically described the working process. However, at the spring exhibition of 1942 the painting was received so poorly that she called it 'a real blunder'.

Tove was deeply depressed by the negative review – understandably so, as she had worked on the painting for a very long time and entertained high hopes for its reception. It usually took her some time to get over unfriendly reviews. She was already going through a difficult period, as her relationship with Tapsa was going wretchedly. Her despondence was made worse by a critical article written by Sam Vanni, in which this friend whom she admired censured her art for being 'graphic'. While Sam's review was influenced by his familiarity with Tove's already extensive output as a graphic artist and illustrator, it also expressed a justifiable perspective on some of her paintings, including *The Family*.

A 'graphic' quality in art is neither good nor bad. It is a characteristic, which a young artist might equally well have seen as a positive one, a stylistic idiom of her own that was hers to develop. But for an artist who strove for pure painterliness it could be a real hindrance. The reference to 'graphic quality' almost drove Tove frantic. She felt that in some way she was only half an artist and she admitted that Sam was right. The previous year Sigrid Schauman had criticized her paintings for being 'illustrative' and made clear that this was a bad thing.

When Schauman reviewed works that Tove showed in the 1942 Young Artists'
Exhibition (*Nuorten näyttely*), and a year later in a solo exhibition at the Bäcksbacka Art Salon, her criticism was that there were too many messages, subjects
and narratives in Tove's paintings. So hurt was Tove by this that she gradually
came around to the general idea that a painting should be purely painterly, and
that the narrative qualities of graphic art should not be imported at all into the
world of painting.

Later Tove herself took a negative attitude towards *The Family*, and considered that the composition in particular was unsuccessful. At the time of the
work's creation, the family was no longer together, so she had to paint all its
members from memory and then combine them into a whole. This may be one
reason why the work resembles a still life. The whole composition is like a stage
on which the characters are placed separately, like paper dolls. The work is not
painterly: it is not in the least impulsive, and is somehow too full – cramped
and clogged. Yet at the same time it is unquestionably a key work in Tove Jansson's career. In it one can sense the fundamental underpinnings of its maker's
art and perceive her artistic uniqueness and passion. At the Athenaeum Tove
had acquired a training that placed emphasis on painterliness, composition
and colour, aspects which Lönnberg and Vanni paid particular attention to in
their teaching. Yet in this work one can see Tove's deep predilection for story
and storytelling, at the expense of painterliness. A narrative that is important
to the artist emerges from the work and endows it with a literary dimension.
Tove had trained herself in the unity of image, word and story, and that was the
area in which she developed when she illustrated her own texts and those of
others. Although she wanted to keep the different sides of her talent separate
and preserve the distinction between the worlds of illustration and painting,
she did not always succeed in doing so. The things for which she was criticized
as a painter were the same things for which she received praise as an illustrator.
At the time she painted her family, she was also creating another family, that of
the Moomins, whose dynamics rather strongly recalled her own.

A WOMAN LIKE A LYNX

Tove recovered from the devastating criticism that greeted *The Family* and began
a new painting. It was a self-portrait and it shows her wearing a large, fluffy
lynx boa. In *Lynx Boa*, Tove also examines herself from the outside: 'I look like
a cat in my yellow fur, with cold, slanting eyes and my new, smooth hair in a

bun. And fireworks made of flowers. I don't know yet if it's good or bad, I just paint. Turn down drawing jobs that don't interest me. [. . .] For I've always taken everything too seriously.'

The painting seems to present a new Tove Jansson, looking calmly to her right, at her future. Her eyes are no longer piercing; painted in a single colour, they are expressive and almond-shaped. Compared with earlier self-portraits, her mouth is softer and more sensual, having lost its angry tautness. Her head is bare and her hair smoothly combed back. The boa's large, soft, yellow-brown mass frames her neck and covers the front of a sober, brown-striped suit. In one hand she holds an umbrella. The background is an attractive grey-blue, and on the right is a greyish, blue and white floral pattern. It is a bold and elegant painting, full of its creator's healthy self-esteem.

Courage was something the young artist needed. Her biggest test of the war years was her first solo exhibition, which she held in 1943 at the prestigious art salon owned by Leonard Bäcksbacka, a friend of the family. By then she was nearly thirty: relatively old for a first one-woman show. Two periods of training, the years of foreign travel and then the war had postponed her debut. It is also possible that the solo exhibition was not an easy undertaking for the sensitive young woman – but in the maelstrom of experience her self-esteem had grown. She wrote enthusiastically about her negotiations with Leonard Bäcksbacka – 'Bäxis' – and how the respected gallery owner had agreed to hold the exhibition. The days that preceded the show were filled with work, and Tove was full of ardour and confidence. The event opened in October 1943, in the middle of the war, and comprised some fifty works. It was well received, reviewed in several newspapers, and the reviews were universally positive. Sales of Tove's paintings increased, with around a dozen sold at the private view alone. Her career received the lift that it needed.

The negative reviews of *The Family*, combined with her own exhibition, took a lot out of Tove, and her stamina dwindled. In 1944 she wrote that she had not been able to paint for a year, and described with melancholy how she sat looking at her canvases, trying to remember all the things she had planned to paint. The paintings were not what she wanted them to be. In her mind now there were new ideas, unfamiliar paths and foreign horizons. And in them all were the images of horror: the events that were taking place at the front, on every front, on everyone's front, and right at that moment.

Tove often complained about her spells of depression. During them she wrote that she did not have the strength to paint and that this was a major disaster

Lynx Boa, oil, 1942

in her life. Nothing in the world seemed to be able to replace it. To be candid, it must be said that her output was at all times so extensive that this inability to work cannot have endured for long. Now and then she felt strongly that the war had taken away her inspiration and she declared that she was going to reclaim its years with interest when peace arrived. The war was dreadful, so dreadful that she could not even bring herself to think about it, let alone write about it:

> Later, people will say that we were privileged to live in interesting and important times. But I think that the magnitude of what is taking place around us is simply making us smaller. People don't have the strength to be grand if a war goes on for a long time. They shrink more and more, and see less and less, latch on to nationalist phraseology, slogans, old prejudices and principles, and themselves.

As for joy, she missed it so much that she said she was quite sick with longing. As impossible as it seemed, in spite of the war she wanted her paintings to 'be something that springs naturally from oneself, and preferably from one's sense of joy'.

Tove's desire to paint returned when she moved to a new studio. On Ullanlinnankatu she managed to rent a place that she loved and that fulfilled all of her needs. At one time the studio had belonged to Hjalmar Hagelstam, and in the early years of its existence the Free Art School had had its premises there. Although Hagelstam had been killed in the war, Tove thought that some of his 'cheerful love of adventure is still here'.

The studio had suffered many kinds of damage in the bombing, and in winter it was icy cold, but it was still essential to her and infinitely loved. 'The first time I entered the new studio the air raid sirens went off and the artillery welcomed me with a gun salute. I stood still and just looked, and was happy. The wind was blowing in through the broken panes.' The Ullanlinnankatu studio, with its large arched and vaulted windows, was as tall as a church. From them one had a splendid and expansive view of Helsinki. In addition to a room that measured almost eight by eight metres there was a small chamber that served as a bedroom or guest room. Tove acquired the large four-poster bed that has become familiar from many photographs, and there were also several of her father's sculptures, including some large ones, on the premises. The walls were hung with pictures by friends and by Tove herself, in particular a portrait of Sam Vanni, drawn by her. Tove fixed the place up, fought several attempts to evict her from it, and eventually succeeded in buying it. Now she was able to live and work in peace in a studio of her own. The fact that it became a part of her work and her everyday life was absolutely crucial to both.

Tove never abandoned the studio. In all her relationships, retaining it was a precondition of her tying herself to someone else and living with them. It represented much more than a work space that made her own art possible, though it was that as well.

ATOS WIRTANEN AND THE COURT AT KAUNIAINEN

Tove met Atos Wirtanen (1906–79) before the Second World War. They had many friends in common, including several of the contributors to *Garm* – Finland-Swedish literary circles were quite small. Tove said that at their first meeting she told him that she had read his collection of aphorisms with delight. Wirtanen lived in a rented villa in the small town of Kauniainen, near Helsinki: during the conflict his friends gathered there in order to avoid the bombing of the city and, above all, to talk politics and reflect on the war. In February 1943 Tove Jansson wrote to Eva with great enthusiasm that she had been to a party at Atos Wirtanen's villa. At this time Atos was still married, and this fact was almost all that Tove had to say about him: she certainly had no idea how important this man would be in her life.

At Atos's villa, Tove was given the task of mixing Manhattan cocktails for sixty people. The guests were literary folk, musicians and actors. Tove loved it all, and wrote that it was wonderful to meet people who were not 'artist snorks' (*konstnärssnorkar*)[4] in whose company one risked being 'struck down with mental scurvy'. She decided to continue to find her way into Atos's circle. And she succeeded. In the years that followed, she met people in this literary and political cultural elite who became close acquaintances and even friends, and in her host she found a possible husband. Tove's relationship with Atos was the most serious one she ever had with a man. It made her reassess the major and critical issues in her life: though still hesitant, at least

Atos Wirtanen

4. 'Snork' is a nonsense word in Swedish, though it is masculine and suggests sobbing. It was the original name for the Moomin figures; they were first called 'snorks' back in the 1940s. Tove also signed her paintings and illustrations for *Garm* with the word.

now there were times when she felt she was ready for marriage and children. Atos also played an enormously important role in Tove's future career: he was a kind of muse for the birth of the world of the Moomins, and he encouraged her to create the Moomin comic series.

Where Tove's previous lovers Vanni and Tapiovaara had been visual artists, Atos was above all a literary man. Most of his friends and working colleagues – his 'court' – were writers and journalists, the bright stars of their day, and they certainly had an influence on Tove's life. During her years with Atos, Tove increasingly managed to direct her interest and time towards writing. While in the past she had done a little, compared to her painting it had not amounted to much. Her years with Atos were a rich, creative and productive time.

Atos was one of the leading left-wing politicians and literary figures of his day, a true Renaissance man. He came from an Åland farming family of nine children, and received no formal education beyond elementary school. As a self-taught intellectual, though, he was extremely well read and learned. In his career as a newspaper journalist he had taken the long route – starting out as a typographer and typesetter, he moved to the paper's editorial office and eventually became its editor-in-chief. A hard-working writer with a particular interest in the philosophy of Nietzsche, he wrote the book *Nietzsche den otidsenlige* ('Nietzsche the Untimely'), which was published in 1945. Unlike so many others in Europe at that time, he did not worship Nietzsche's doctrines, though he was very interested in Nietzsche's philosophy – so much so that Tove said she often grew tired of the endless discussions of it. She waited for him to finish his book and free his mind from this obsession. Atos also wrote poetry, as well as collections of aphorisms and newspaper columns, and published biographies of Lenin and Strindberg.

Wirtanen was elected to Finland's parliament in 1936, initially as a Social Democrat, but in 1947 he moved to the left-wing Finnish People's Democratic League (SKDL). From 1948 he was chairman of the more moderate Socialist Unity Party (SYP). Atos was an active and internationally minded Member of Parliament, journalist and politician. He was chief editor of the Swedish-language *Arbetarbladet*, but moved to the newly established *Ny Tid* weekly, which was founded in 1944 as the SKDL's official mouthpiece. He served as its editor-in-chief from 1947 to 1953. He focused on cultural matters and gathered around him some of the most interesting writers of Finland's Swedish-speaking minority, including Eva Wichman, Jörn Donner and Ralf Parland.

During the Continuation War, Wirtanen took part in the so-called 'peace opposition'. At *Arbetarbladet* he was in constant trouble with the military censor, which eventually became so threatening that Tove tried to think of a suitable place for him to hide in case the situation became too hot to handle. According to the left-wing editor and author Raoul Palmgren, Atos Wirtanen was a unique figure: a brilliant journalist and columnist, and an original *Lebensphilosoph* who was also a most fascinating conversationalist and human being. In 1948 Wirtanen joined the *Kiila* ('the Wedge') group, where he was one of the few Finland-Swedish writers who espoused a socialist view of the world. Most of them were intellectual radicals who opposed fascism and war and were also highly individualistic – literary modernists who experimented with form and who even included some mystics. Through Tapsa, Tove had already met some members of *Kiila*, and through Atos she began, for the most part, to associate closely with its at least vaguely leftist Finland-Swedish wing.

At Atos's villa in Kauniainen, like-minded friends gathered to discuss politics, culture and art. Among the guests there were artists, cultural figures and left-wing activists, with much in common with their host. They included Eva and Eric Wichman. According to Tove, Eva Wichman (1908–75) was an enormously original and brilliant writer who also had many enemies. She was married to the author Ralf Parland, who also belonged to Atos's circle of friends. Parland was a respected critic and poet who took an active stance against war and fascism. Eva Wichman had once had an affair with Atos, and she and he were still good friends, even though they sometimes became irritated with each other's ideas. Tove said that Eva Wichman was the person for whom she had the highest regard after Ham, and she declared that no one could make her feel as calm as Eva in all her incandescent raggedness.

Wichman had worked in the field of applied art as a toy designer, among other things, but she later became a writer. She is best known for her poems, which are steeped in emotion, often filled with anguish and suffering, and gained depth from the war. In 1949 she showed a strong allegiance to socially committed and socialist literature, and wrote a great deal of poetry on political themes until into the

Tove, dressed for a masked ball, *c.* 1930

1960s. Other regular guests at Wirtanen's villa were Olof Enckell, Gunnar Björling, Tove's old friends Tito and Ina Colliander, Anna Bondestam, Eric Olsoni and Tove Olsoni. And soon they were joined by Tove Jansson. Tove had acquired a new set of social acquaintances and a new lover – perhaps also a love more in tune with everyday life than her love for Tapsa.

The war with the Soviet Union was over, but in the north of Finland the Lapland War continued into the spring of the following year. The ending of the war was, of course, a major event for all Finns, and also for Tove. Her life with Atos changed in other ways too, and she was able to see things in a very different light. After the declaration of the Moscow Armistice after the Continuation War, she wrote: 'I wake up in the mornings and remember – first, that the boys are alive – then that I have the Studio (and then Atos!)' The end of the sentence, the part about Atos, was added with a different pen, and later she continued: 'And I want to and will be happy. I am already, Konikova.' Tove wrote to her friend Eva about her new love without losing her mischievous sense of humour:

> You would like Atos Wirtanen. He is just as vital as you are. Full of an irrepressible sense of being alive, and with a brain that is sparklingly bright [. . .] He is no taller than I am, a tousled and crumpled little philosopher with a smile that is even bigger than yours. Ugly, cheerful and charged with life, ideas and utopias. And self-esteem. He is quietly convinced that he is just about the greatest intellect in Finland right now (why not the whole of the Nordic region? he sometimes wonders!). His great prophet is Nietzsche, about whom I have heard countless lectures and of whom I am starting to grow a little tired.

The theatre director Vivica Bandler has described Atos in much the same terms: 'Atos had many highly unrealistic social utopias, and many highly realistic affairs with women. He was so intensely alive that it made him attractive and popular, even if he didn't look very appetizing. In the "dangerous" times he dared to speak out for peace and reconciliation, and this was almost regarded as treason.' Many other contemporaries of Atos have said that he was bold and uncompromising in his views, even to the extent that those views threatened his freedom. After the war, during the so-called 'years of danger', the fear of Communism and of interference by the Soviet Union in Finland's affairs was widespread. It persisted into the early 1950s, when one only needed to advocate peace in order to arouse suspicion. As Bandler said, there were even insinuations that Atos had himself been guilty of treason.

From its very outset the relationship between Tove and Atos was far from free of conflict. Atos loathed sentimentality and was ungenerous with the words of affection – or at least the proof of his feelings – that Tove needed. He had not even told her that he liked her, let alone loved her. She sometimes found it hard to understand her role and to position herself in his life and on the map of the people who surrounded him. As she moved among the other guests at Kauniainen, she wondered whether she was his girlfriend, fiancée, guest or close friend, or possibly only an acquaintance.

The relationship was not made any simpler by the fact that Tove herself was living a double love life. She had another man, and that relationship was important to her, especially because of its strongly physical and erotic nature. This relationship with the man whom she called the Seascapist (*Marinmålaren*) had begun after her affair with Tapsa, and had flared up during the heavy bombing of Helsinki, when the man had returned home from the front, tired, hungry and miserable. Although they clearly had painting in common, Tove was a professional artist while the man was only at the beginning of his path towards art. Tove described the affair as a 'Pan episode', and said that their relationship was a passionate one, even though intellectually they were far apart. Body and soul did not meet. Even so, she realized that she was 'strangely dependent' on the Seascapist. She found the task of balancing the two relationships a nerve-racking one. Although in wartime it was probably easier to live a double life, it was still hard. She was forced to choose. She confessed the man's existence to Atos, and was astonished to receive proof of Atos's feelings for her – or at least that's how she interpreted it. To her enormous surprise, 'he became very unphilosophically jealous and quite wild with fury, and for a couple of days I thought I had lost him. However, after that he came closer to me – strange. But I'm happy.'

The process of giving up the Seascapist did not go smoothly. While she was deciding, Tove was affected by a severe nervous attack during the housewarming party at her studio, and in the midst of the celebrations had to be given morphine, as was the custom of the day. Left to celebrate without their hostess, the guests continued to have a wonderful time until the early hours. One love was dead, but the melancholy remained: 'Just occasionally, ever more seldom, I have a powerful longing for those dark, dangerous years, it glides swiftly over me like a black cloud.' This was apparently a reference to the Seascapist and the war: they had become woven together with their own blend of fear and eroticism.

Tove's love for Atos was a cheerful love. Her letters to him are full of light, warmth and humour, even though the things she writes about are often thoroughly mundane. She would write that she had pickled a hundred kilos of mushrooms, or how concerned she was about her brother Lars's spiritualist séances in her studio when she was away travelling. Such comments were always accompanied by details of the progress of her latest books. But the letters also contain admiration and statements of love. Tove often repeated that Atos was the warmest, bravest and wisest person she knew. She described her love for him by saying that she was full of words and poems, and felt like a dance tune that was all about him. She wanted to give him this tune as a springtime present, to be sung in the sunshine with lyrics and music that were always new.

During her years with Atos, Tove wrote and illustrated her first five Moomin books. In 1947, after an idea that came from him, she drew the first Moomin comic series for *Ny Tid*, of which he was editor-in-chief. Based on the adventures in the book *Comet in Moominland*, the series appeared every Friday in the children's section of the magazine, and was boldly named *Moomintroll and the End of the World*. Atos took a sincere interest in it, reading manuscripts and offering constructive criticism. Even after the end of the relationship, he investigated the possibility of distributing the Moomin series internationally, though they could no longer be published in *Ny Tid* as they were judged to be too bourgeois. After all, poor Moominpappa read a monarchist newspaper.

FAR, FAR AWAY – A COLONY IN MOROCCO

The lovers shared many plans and utopias: both were creative personalities, iconoclastic in their outlook. In 1943 Tove asked Atos what he thought of the idea of founding an artists' colony in Guipúzcoa in Spain's Basque country. In Tove's view, the place was suitable, though the society and landscape of Morocco interested her more. Her letters included sketches and drawings of houses and tents in the Moroccan colony. For Atos she planned a tower house that clearly resembles the Moomin house, and may have been its prototype – in time and appearance they are not so far apart.

The founding of an artists' colony became the lovers' mutual dream. They planned to buy an empty villa near Tangiers that belonged to the Finnish anthropologist and philosopher Edward Westermarck. The house stood on a magnificent site, on a slope facing the sea. Tove wrote that she had never planned and

The colony in Morocco, Tove's drawing in a letter to Atos Wirtanen, 1943

dreamt so much as during that year: 'Not as a pastime – but as an absolute need. Travelled around the world and stopped in Morocco, where Westermarck's villa overlooks the sea. Warmth, colour, Eva! There Atos and I would found a colony for artists and people who write [...]'

In addition to Atos's tower and hanging gardens they intended to build several studios, a special house for those scheming artists and another for those who were homesick. They planned to invite writers and artists who in Finland could not find peace and quiet for their work. Sam and Maya Vanni were the first travellers to receive invitations. To support the project, money was collected – money that later had to be used for quite different purposes. The idea for the colony lived on for many years, but was then shelved and forgotten. Only some six months after an enthusiastic letter to Eva, Tove wrote with disappointment that it seemed the Morocco plans were not going to be realized. Atos was tied down for several years by his work in parliament, and in any case did not appear to be particularly eager, as he 'made absolutely no attempt to contact Westermarck's heirs in order to buy the villa'. Tove sought reasons for this in the political situation: just then, no one seemed to be interested in money – 'they only want land, jewels, furs, butter, furniture ...' Although this may have been one factor, it was not the only one. Atos doubtless found it just as hard to commit himself to a house in North Africa as to a marriage with Tove.

Many years later, Tove wrote about Atos and her Moroccan dreams in her story collection *Fair Play* (*Rent spel*), in which Atos appears as Johannes. Reality and fiction are close enough, except that Morocco has become the South of France: 'And that time we collected money to buy an abandoned house in the South of France and were going to invite friends who wrote or painted and needed to work in peace – but every time we managed to scrape something together he would give it away to some strike fund . . .'

Founding the Moroccan colony was not the only dream that Tove had. Alongside it, before and after it were many other places and addresses that formed the subject of her dreams. Among the alternatives were Guipúzcoa, the Pellinki islands, the houseboat *Christopher Columbus*, and the island kingdom of Tonga. Building and planning were central to Tove's life. Houses and apartments were symbols of life changes and choices. She hoped that by going away and settling down in an unfamiliar place she might discover a new and different life that was happy and creative. Especially during the war, such dreams and plans offered an essential psychological refuge, helping her to escape all the ugliness, suffering and fear, at least for a moment. Through them she was able to live from one day to the next, preserving at least some positive energy, and enabling her to endure the anxiety and the gloom. Although the dreaming and planning brought no results, there was some point in it – indeed, it was essential for coping with daily existence, as she noted herself.

In her painting *Garden* (*Trädgård*), begun in 1943, Tove turned her dream into reality, at least on canvas. The garden is in some southern land, and its large palms and flowering trees are like a cheerful breath of wind on a summer's day in a courtyard that is already full of cheerful colour. Persecution, quarrels and the treacherous world were far away, replaced by colour, warmth and feelings of happiness. Just to paint with these blossoming colours was a welcome antidote to the fear and greyness of the war.

Tove's self-portrait drawn in a letter to Atos Wirtanen, August 1943

The colony in Morocco, however, clearly looked as though it would remain a dream, for Atos was not the right man to share the project with Tove. Yet he was still the man in her life. She said that their two years together had greatly enriched her, made her warmer and more intensely alive in a completely new and calm way. Now united with Atos, she hoped with all her heart that 'no one else is ever by my side. He has changed me so much so that now I would willingly marry him. I would keep my own studio, of course.' Not even the idea of a child seemed excluded, though she was worried that the

Garden, 1943, oil

studio would be too cold and the baby would catch a chill. 'But I'm not afraid any more. It would be very nice to have a little one.'

Tove had settled down. Her fears of tying herself down and becoming a mother had levelled off and were now more subdued, if not completely resolved. Everything seemed possible. A letter to Eva contained many earth-shaking pieces of news and Tove spent several months – until midsummer 1945 – writing it. In the final sentence she expressed what was no doubt the greatest reason for happiness, one that was shared all over the globe: 'Eva, there is peace in the whole world now!!!!'

III

Work and Love

Wolle [Weiner] called in the middle of the night and said that peace had been declared.
*   I went back to bed and lay there in the dark, thinking only one thing: Per Olov can*
come home. We can keep him, his girl can keep him. Lasse won't have to go to the front.
All the men who have been fighting out there for more than four years can come home.
It got light. And only then came the joy, like a wave. And with the wave came joy and
desire and strength for anything. But I knew for certain that I would never allow myself
to forget. Never ever to forget.

Tove recalled the horror of the war years and how hard life had been throughout them. Later on she would refuse even to talk about those years and described them as lost years. Yet they were not lost at all – quite the opposite. In those years Tove created works and sketches for works that proved to be highly significant in the context of her career as a whole. Many things also happened in her personal life and the young Tove's emotions ranged from extreme happiness to days of despair and depression.

Tove's youth and her attitude towards her own life are perhaps best illustrated by the *ex libris* motto she created in 1947, and used from then on. The Latin phrase – *labora et amare* – is not quite correct grammatically, but its intended meaning is 'work and love'. It was characteristic of Tove to put work before love. Most young women would have put them the other way around. The small *ex libris* drawing contains a large number of motifs, including sea, anchors, roses and thistles, and grapevines winding around Greek columns. Right in the centre of the drawing is a burning heart, at the top right is a naked woman, and on the top left a lion king with a crown, brushes and palette. Tove's astrological sign was Leo. Along with representations of all the things that she loved, the drawing also shows her own symbols. The large number of different elements makes the small picture area rather crowded, rather like the life of the artist who is just starting out, a young woman in quest of independence and great love. Later she drew another *ex libris* in the form of a large sea wave. Her last essay in the genre was illustrated by Ham, and based on Tove's initials.

The peace had been signed, but life was no easier for it. Finland's economy had been ruined, and there was a shortage of everything: food, clothing and housing. It took almost thirty years for the economy to regain the level it had attained before the outbreak of the Winter War. For a long time during the war years manufacturing remained at a standstill, and this caused universal scarcity. The payment of war reparations required an enormous amount of labour and material resources. There were large numbers of poor, sick and homeless, many houses had been bombed, and the people from the areas of the country that had been ceded to the Soviet Union now needed accommodation. The housing shortage was acute and there was no wood or other fuel for heating. People shared, repaired and built new homes. Many families with young children were forced to live in bomb shelters, attics and a variety of temporary accommodation. There were large numbers of disabled war veterans and people who had been mentally scarred by the war. Due to the shortage of clothing, many men continued to wear their grey army uniforms. Food was rationed and the rations were not really enough to live on, but there was nothing else, only constant hunger. The black market flourished, but it helped only those who could afford its prices and had the courage to buy. In a situation where everything had to be fought for, there also seemed to be a lack of humanity. The poor were not friends of the poor. Tove wrote to Eva that loneliness was the greatest curse of the times – people's gloomy, silent loneliness: 'In how many eyes have I read the longing for real intimacy, real contact. If I, with so many loved and loving people around me, sometimes feel that longing, then what about those who have no friends or family?'

Tove analysed the war in depth and in very critical terms. Within the Church and among religious believers the war was frequently seen as God's punishment for the sins of mankind. It was thought that God sent the war and that only He could take it away, that it was the wages of sin, the penance imposed on the wicked. Tove wrote to her friend the artist Ina Colliander about this in categorical and rather heated terms:

> I've been thinking about what you wrote about how God sends war, pestilence etc., in order to try us. That it's something we need. But I don't think you are right. The war is a condensation of all our own wickedness – not something He has given us. Free will, that is what He has given us. One can see it! I have often prayed that Peo would

come back, but never for victory, not even for the war to end. The way I see it, God
has nothing to do with our war, even though He may protect individuals. We must eat
our own shit, as the Chinese say. But do you really think we are better for it? On the
contrary – all I have seen these past years is increasing hardness, meanness, hateful-
ness, bitterness, selfishness. War is so thoroughly negative that it cannot give rise to
anything good. [. . .] There may be those who rise up from the mess purified, praising
the Lord – but alas, I haven't seen them.

The life of a young woman always has room for a young woman's desires,
joys and dreams, and fortunately no war can interfere with them. All Tove had
to do was to cope, and obtain work for herself. She had agreed to hold another
solo exhibition at the Bäcksbacka gallery in 1946, and was now concentrating
on preparing the work for it. She felt she had the arrival of peace to thank for
her new style of painting: 'Gone now is that grey-on-grey tendency, and instead
the colours have come to stay, and stay permanently,' she wrote, adding that
'my paintings are freer now and their colours are brighter.' She considered that
the illustrative quality for which she had been criticized, and which had led
her to assess her own work too critically, was also gone. It should be said that
many of her wartime paintings are full of colour – they are anything but 'grey-
on-grey'. Like most artists she simply wanted to create something better and
wrote humbly but with optimism of her paintings: 'They aren't good, but they
improve with every show. The rest of it doesn't bother me. Perhaps I paint too
much with my brain (though with every picture my heart is in despair).'

After the years of austerity, everyone longed for joy, colour, beauty and, of
course, food. Tove was no exception. From the United States Eva sent parcels of
old clothes that were used but still wearable, jewellery, belts, shoes, coats, skirts,
blouses, wool socks, as well as gathering together powder, soap, skin cream, ear-
rings, hairpins and tobacco: everything that was essential for a young woman's
joy and beauty. The parcels even contained a necktie for Atos and a purse for
Ham. Tove rejoiced at each single item, however small, and thanked her friend
effusively.

BROCADES AND PERFUME

Tove was lucky enough to be able to visit Sweden as an exchange student. Time
in a country that had been spared the war was to her like a visit to Paris, or a
momentary return to the time before the nightmare of the conflict. She received

no funds for the trip, but as she could stay with acquaintances and relatives it could all be arranged quite cheaply. Atos also came to Stockholm for a week for a conference, so the separation was not too long. Stockholm was a perfect wonderland for the young Tove, who enjoyed the atmosphere and eagerly absorbed the joy and the colour.

After stewing in one's own juice for six years it feels quite wonderful to come out into the open air again. For the first few days I simply walked and walked round the city, semi-intoxicated, enjoying the neon lights, the hustle and bustle, the fantastic shop windows, looking, sniffing and breathing in a thousand new impressions, discovering within me bottomless wells of female vanity that have been dammed up for so long! Have you any idea what joy it was to be able to buy footwear at last? Little high-heeled boots in soft leather, the prettiest I could find. And a flaming red raincoat (Faffan will probably say it's Bolshevik!), an overcoat and a new handbag, small, coquettish and impractical! The Swedes think we are frivolous for wanting to buy brocade and perfume rather than milk powder and wool knickers – but they don't understand that radiance and finesse are what we've missed the most! So I have bought silk stockings and new clothes for everyone back home – the gold has run out and I had to make do with window-shopping and wishing for a hundred more adorable things. Everyone has been so incredibly nice to me, and I have not found a trace of the much-reported nonchalant superficiality of the Swedes.

In Stockholm Atos stayed with his sister. Tove could also stay the night there, but only in secret, when the sister was away. Atos had introduced Tove merely as a friend. Despite all the subterfuge, everyone guessed the true nature of the relationship and Tove was hurt by the wry smiles people directed at them behind their backs. On those grounds alone she would have liked to tie the marriage knot. Life was easier in Finland, especially in artistic circles, and she snorted to herself: 'I seem to be more bourgeois than I thought.'

Tove stayed in Sweden longer than Atos and had great expectations of their time apart, expectations that were focused on the possibility that he might realize he missed her. For herself, she would have liked to achieve a sense that life could go on without him, at least for a while. In fact, the distance between them may indeed have made him miss her and express his feelings, for in a letter he called her 'Sticky Catchfly' and 'Shell Dancer'. Tove replied that these pet names were much to her liking. In summer the archipelago was red with sticky catchfly, and she loved seashells. At home she always surrounded herself with them, and they were a recurrent motif in her stories, illustrations and paintings.

In addition to his political and historical books, Atos wrote and published many collections of aphorisms. Of these, one that stands out is his personal motto, which sums up his philosophy of life, at least according to Raoul Palmgren: 'If you speak the language of tomorrow, beware of your contemporaries.' The relationship between Atos and Tove would cause no scandal nowadays, but back then 'living in sin' was met with condemnation, even contempt – though only towards women. Women were held to be the guilty ones – they received society's opprobrium and were regarded as 'bad'. For men, freedom in sexual relations could be a source of respect. Even today, a similar concept of the 'bad man' does not exist. If one talks about a man being 'bad', it means something else entirely.

Atos did not want to marry. Perhaps, as Tove surmised, he had been frightened by his first experience of matrimony, which had lasted only a few months. But cohabitation was difficult. Because Tove and Atos lived quite openly in a marriage-like relationship, people gossiped and talked about them behind their backs. Faffan was angry, but Ham showed understanding and said nothing. Even Sigrid Schauman, known to be very liberal in her views, reprimanded Tove and urged her to formalize the relationship, wondering what she and Atos were waiting for. Tove replied: 'Actually, I don't think it would be all that hard for us to ignore [. . .] the implicit chatter that is bound to arise,' but admitted that living together as an unmarried couple was far from easy. If in the morning she received an unexpected visit, she had to conceal Atos's presence and could not simply offer the excuse that her husband was still asleep. Travel was also difficult, starting with the booking of hotels. As an unmarried couple they had to stay in separate, single rooms – if there were any. Most complicated of all was the purchase of property which they intended to share – such as Westermarck's villa in Morocco, a boat, or an island in Pellinki. Nevertheless Tove was proud of Atos and she enjoyed his company.

After the war, Tove's relationship with Atos grew deeper. She could have obtained a stipend from the French government to study in Paris, but did not want to go because she could not even think of leaving her lover. She was able to look at herself from a distance, worried about what he saw and feared that her intellectual independence was at risk. She wanted them to marry, at any time that was convenient, but the 'philosopher' was unwilling. In frustration, she burst out that she was tired of half measures and her own half-heartedness, and said that she would even agree to a secret marriage. She joked about being an 'unmarried woman' and if they had a child what its surname would be. Everything would be so much easier if they were married: travel, parties, everything. She loved him 'so much that [. . .] it hurts'.

Their marriage would not change anything: they would each be able to retain their own apartment and studio, and the only difference would be that their everyday lives were easier. Tove saw Atos as 'a genuinely unique phenomenon, something comet-like and absolute', and believed she had the ability to recognize this after 'all [my] 101 love affairs'. In a relationship where the other person was afraid to commit himself in any way, her own deep devotion frightened her. Yet she felt it impossible to leave Atos: '[A]fter him it would be very hard to fall in love with anyone else, and impossible to marry anyone else after knowing his joy, free spirit and intelligence. This frightens me, but also makes me proud and confident.' She had discovered what may have been the main reason for Atos's reluctance to commit himself: 'I know that he cannot really love in the sense that we mean when we use the word. He likes me in the way that he likes the sun, the earth, laughter, the wind. Likes me more than that, but in the same way.'

Atos was a driven, passionate politician, preoccupied with world issues and ideologies. He does not appear to have had much time for Tove. She complained that whenever they met he was so tired that he slept most of the time: 'He goes like a machine round the clock, you see. I just hope it doesn't break down.' Her hopes of receiving confessions of love or even small romantic gestures remained unfulfilled. Atos once bought her a present – a ceramic brooch in the shape of an ox. Not exactly the height of romance, and certainly not the ring that she wanted. 'The dear donkey,' a disappointed Tove wrote to Eva about Atos and his choice of present.

The following year, 1947, marked a turning point in their relationship. Shortly before midsummer, Tove wrote that now they only talked about general matters, though in a way that was personal and interesting. There was not much tenderness between them, but Tove said: '[h]e has become a very good lover, and I don't long for expressions of love any more, for I no longer feel love'. But much was to happen before they reached that point.

VIVICA BANDLER AND RIVE GAUCHE

Tove's life progressed calmly: it was filled with work for the upcoming exhibition, and with concern for Atos. Soon all that was to change. One week before

Christmas 1946 Tove wrote Eva a long, intense letter that brimmed over with a new sense of being alive:

> [S]omething has happened, and I realize that I must tell you about it. I'm so happy and pleased, and so relieved. You know that I feel like Atos's wife, and probably always will. But now what has happened is that I have fallen madly in love with a woman. And it feels so absolutely natural and real – there are no problems at all. I simply feel proud and boundlessly happy. The last few weeks have been like one long dance [. . .]

The object of the new love, Vivica Bandler, was the daughter of Helsinki city treasurer Erik von Frenckell and the sister of Lasse's classmate and girlfriend, Erica. Vivica was three years younger than Tove and married to Kurt Bandler, an Austrian of half-Jewish descent who had fled from Nazism to Finland. There, he had taken part in the war as a volunteer. At the time Tove and Vivica fell in love he was living in Stockholm and Vivica mostly in Finland, though her frequent travels also took her to Stockholm. Tove was living with Atos, who was constantly going on business trips.

Vivica Bandler described her first meeting with Tove in 1946 as a flop. Lasse and Erica had arranged the meeting for their older sisters. Tove was almost terrified of Vivica, who in turn thought Tove looked ridiculous with her little curls, frills and flounces. Their next meeting happened by chance. In post-war Helsinki hardly anyone threw parties, but on this occasion someone had done so. People's lives might be filled with poverty and deprivation, but they were still allowed to dance – and dancing was Tove's passion. Tove and Vivica found each other after the other guests had gone home. And they danced until dawn. 'That's how we became friends. Probably while we had hangovers after too much Jallu [cut brandy].' That, at least, is how Vivica Bandler recalled that crucial night in their lives.

Tove described her new love as rich and warm. It was like a voyage of discovery to new landscapes, destinations of unbelievable beauty. 'Like finding a wonderful new room in one's old house one thought one knew inside and out. And just entering it, unable to conceive that one never knew it existed.'

For four days they vacationed at Vivica's family's farm. Tove was radiant with happiness: 'Such conversations, Eva! Like rediscovering the best in oneself, refined and transfigured [. . .] Do you know, at last I feel that in love I can experience myself as a woman [. . .] That I can talk about everything and not be ashamed any more. That my friends are staring at me and asking what has happened to me. I'm completely new, relieved and happy and free from feelings of guilt.'

Tove's love for Vivica allowed her to discover herself, given her an awareness of her own femininity and a greater professional self-esteem. Tove wrote that she no longer felt like the poor woman who had to watch the sun rise, knowing that it only happened because of a man. For the first time she felt that she was the sun, even though it would only really begin to shine when Vivica returned to Finland in the spring.

Tove did, of course, feel apprehensive and even surprised at the realization that she was not completely heterosexual as she had believed. Yet she was not afraid, at least not judging by her letters. She reflected calmly on her sexuality, doing so on her own terms and in the context of her own life, perfectly aware of the condemnation and slander the love affair would bring from her social milieu and the pain it would probably cause, but ultimately she was indifferent to it. It was counterbalanced by a true love and the happiness it brought:

I don't think I'm completely lesbian. I feel very clearly that there can't be any other woman besides Vi, and my attitude to men has not changed. Has possibly improved. Simpler, happier, less tense. Atos has been out of town, returns tomorrow. And tomorrow Vi is travelling to join her husband in Stockholm, and then they go on to Denmark and Switzerland, where his parents live – and will spend the whole of the spring in Paris where she is going to direct a film.

It's dreadful for us to be parting just when we have found each other, but we have our work and can wait with trust. Life may be very difficult for us in the future. Other people don't understand – they haven't experienced it. The slander is already sneaking about. But I don't care. I may even lose Atos now. [...]

I just live in one big state of joy and torment. Eva, life is so immensely rich!

Their love was extremely passionate and physical, and their intellectual relationship went deep as well. As they had previously agreed, Vivica travelled to Sweden, Denmark and Paris, and the lovers parted at the most intense moment of their love. Tove tried to obtain a permit for a visit to Paris, and Vivica made attempts to arrange an exhibition for her there, but neither venture met with success. Travel was not easy at that time: it required not only money, but also permits of various kinds. However, the separation gave rise to a large volume of truly passionate and extensive correspondence, and it has been kept for posterity. Tove's relationship with Atos survived. Her love for Vivica had extinguished her love for him, but her respect for him remained, as did their friendship. The relationship even seemed to have improved: 'And suddenly we have much more to talk about than before, much more to laugh about, think about ... Perhaps it's the best kind of friendship. Sex matters so little just now. It's as if I were asleep. I don't feel anything and I don't even miss doing it. It's as if I were concentrating on some major job, but there's also something else. My heart is with you, and without it I have never been able to love.'

Vivica considered that it was the intellectual side of their love that made it unique. While normally her heart had been the governing force in her love affairs, now her brain was involved, too. And in a letter she asked Tove: 'Do you want my head on a plate? You can have it, because it's yours.' Likewise Tove underlined the completeness of their

Tove as Moomintroll, drawing in
Tove's letter to Vivica, 1947

love when she wrote to Vivica that her intellect loved Vivica's intellect, and her heart and body loved Vivica's too. The love of the heart was the greatest love. So great was Tove's love that her heart was sick with longing when they were apart, but it danced for joy simply because Vivica was there and because Vivica loved her. Her love was powerfully present during the day, and at night it also encroached on her dreams in the form of nightmares about losing Vivica. So dominant was it that for the first time the desires of Tove's heart took precedence over her work. Previously she had not avoided her duties but had kept strictly to the schedules she had agreed to. But love also benefited her creative work: she saw that her work had been enriched and now she was also rid of her annoyingly excessive ambition. And she felt calmer in general. At any rate, so she thought.

Tove's days were filled with painting Vivica's portrait in a fresco. Her only desire was to procure the return of her beloved model. Since that was not possible, she had to paint from memory. During this time she began to write her third Moomin book. In *The Magician's Hat* two new characters were added to the world of the Moomins: Thingumy and Bob, who also brought with them the Groke. Thingumy was based on Tove, and Bob on Vivica. Tove began to sign her works 'Tofslan' (Thingumy), and sometimes she even used both names. Her letters to Vivica were often addressed to 'Vifslan' (Bob). In the book, these creatures speak a language of their own which outsiders sometimes find hard to understand – exactly as in real life, where Tove and Vivica had to use secret codes for things that were taboo.

Tove wanted to be open, and told her best friends, like Sam, Maya and Sven Grönvall, that she had fallen in love with Vivica, but was disappointed when this got a rather mixed response. Although her friends were unable to share her new happiness, with her mother she could talk about how fond of Vivica she was. Ham was certainly fully aware of the relationship, but was concerned because of Atos, whom she liked a great deal. For her part, Vivica worried that Ham might be upset about the affair, because of her silence on the matter.

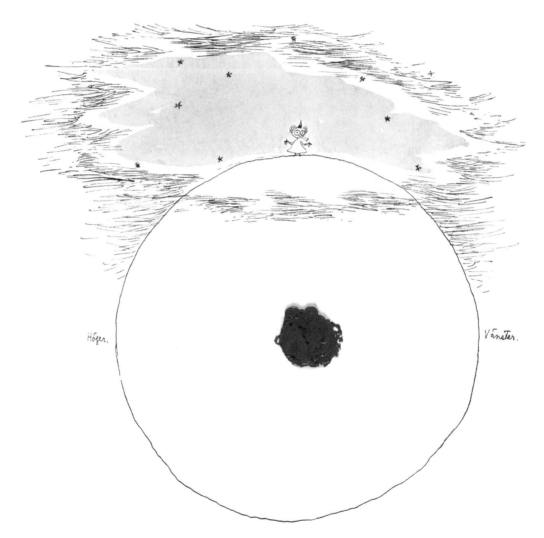

A lonely Thingumy, painting from a letter to Vivica, watercolour, 1947

At the time, homosexuality was banned by law in Finland and classified as an illness. It was also a sin – one of the very worst. Tove and Vivica had to be careful. Vivica in particular advocated caution, partly because her husband, Kurt, did not know about the relationship and Vivica wanted to go on hiding it from him, but mainly because of public opinion. And initially, at least, Tove did not tell Atos about her new love. She wrote to Vivica that she had always found it hard to be unfaithful and did not want to be unfaithful now.

When Tove telephoned her from abroad and asked her if she still loved her, Vivica was genuinely afraid. But Tove was merely talking as people in love normally do. Vivica explained her fear by the fact that she had been on the Gestapo's lists – even after the war was over she suspected that her conversations were being wiretapped and recorded. She wrote that she did not want Tove to get into trouble and so they must be careful. For the sake of security they developed their own private language to express their forbidden love. 'But it's probably best not to say that dangerous word – love,' Vivica wrote. When travelling, Vivica lodged with families and therefore had to take care that letters and telephone conversations did not arouse too much attention on the part of her hosts. She asked Tove to write often, and they did indeed write to each other almost daily – but Tove had to post many days' worth of letters in the same envelope. Viewed in hindsight, this degree of caution may appear excessive, even slightly paranoid. It needs to be recalled, however, that in large parts of Europe only a few years before this, people were being sent to the gas chambers for homosexuality. In Finland one could be put into a mental institution or sentenced to a prison term, and this was still happening to women in the early 1950s. Homosexuality was a crime in Finland until 1971, and classified as an illness for even longer, until 1981.

Against the background of the major afflictions that people suffered during the war – death, hunger and destruction – homosexuality caused less concern. With the arrival of peace there was a hardening of attitudes, and the pressure to conform increased. Yet homosexuality was not accepted in the towns and cities. Lesbian women were slandered, gossiped about and made objects of negative stereotyping, both at home and at work. Vivica felt depressed after hearing one of her husband's friends insult her, calling her a 'skirt-chaser' and 'pig' who would sleep with anyone, man or woman. 'Everyone had a private hell of their own,' she said. There was every reason to be cautious, and so people often entered into so-called 'sham marriages', in which one or both of the parties were homosexual. The aim was to give the appearance of a 'normal' heterosexual union and keep one's dreadful secret hidden. This could lead to tragedy if one of the pair was heterosexual.

Male homosexuality and lesbianism were not generally referred to as such: instead, people used various codes, as well as euphemisms of a more everyday kind. Initially Tove called her homosexuality 'Rive Gauche', after the Left Bank of the Seine: to choose 'Rive Gauche' meant to choose lesbianism, though she often used the latter term as well. In later years, when speaking of her choice, she tended to refer to her 'new line', and her 'attitude'. As early as 1952 she wrote that from now on she was going to describe herself as a 'ghost' (*spöke*), a word widely used in lesbian circles about lesbians. Sometimes the Swedish slang verb *mymla* was used in relation to lesbian sex, but Tove used it to mean love-making in general. Birgitta Ulfsson remembers her saying, 'Oh, look at them, they're obviously mymbling with (*mymlar med*) each other' when she saw a couple making love.

The social conditions of the time did not make things easy for the lovers, and this love story was not a simple one. When Vivica returned from Paris, Denmark and Sweden, she said she had met a new love in Paris, and she also seemed to have found another in Finland. Tove understood, but suffered. Her life with Atos continued unchanged, and her love for both of them ran in parallel.

Solemnly she wrote that after Atos there would be no other man in her life, and no other woman after Vivica.

YOU I HAVE PAINTED THE SWEETEST

After Vivica had gone, Tove stayed behind and painted murals for the restaurant in Helsinki City Hall. The artist for the assignment was not selected on a competitive basis – Tove received the task as a direct commission. The original request had been for something on a relatively small scale, a few 'darling vignettes'. But Tove was ambitious. Encouraged by Johannes Gebhard, formerly her teacher at the Athenaeum, she wanted to make something larger, and deliberately exceeded the desired specifications. The deadline for completion remained the same as in the original plan, though, so the schedule was really tight. Many people warned her against this, including Vanni, who told her she was a fool if she thought she could complete the task by spring. The rush and stress were caused by Tove's own ambition, and thus were self-inflicted.

These were bleak times in the art world, and the competition for work was acute. Some may have thought that Tove got the job through personal

Painting from a letter to Vivica, 1947. Tove as Moomintroll
says that painting frescos is hard work but fun

connections – or with the help of Vivica's father. But because the task had originally been quite a modest one, a competition would have been unnecessary. In
spite of her youth, Tove was already an accomplished decorative painter with
substantial works to her name. She had produced brilliant large-scale paintings,
including stained glasses for the Tullipuomi restaurant on Mannerheimintie in
1941 and for the Apollonkatu girls' school in 1944, as well as two murals for the
staff dining room of Strömberg's electrical factory at Pitäjänmäki in 1945. So
she was well qualified, and had experience of similar work. The new commission
did, however, concern a valued public space, and many other artists would have
liked to have it – no wonder that her colleagues were wild with envy. While Tove
was creating the paintings, she could feel the hostile crowd of artists behind
her back – which made her exert herself to the utmost, for in this enterprise
she could not afford to fail.

The Helsinki City Hall frescos are a direct continuation of the fairytale landscapes and depictions of Paradise she had painted in the 1930s, and in most
cases the fairytales also concern Paradise. *Country Celebration* (*Fest på landet*)
shows the countryside in every possible facet of its loveliness, and in *City
Celebration* (*Fest i stan*) the festivities are marked by urban culture. This official commission from the city of Helsinki required of Tove an almost manic
absorption in the work. Yet she was preoccupied with her love for Vivica, who
had gone to Paris. The pain of the separation and perhaps the premonition or
fear of future disappointments gave these days a dark nuance of their own.

99

Envy and gossip on the part of her colleagues about the women's relationship also gave the work a bitter flavour.

Nervously, Tove presented her sketches to the architect and then to Vivica's father, and they were accepted. When she had completed the full-size sketches on cardboard, the most demanding part of the work was over. Now she could be sure of success. Happily she wrote to Vivica:

Good morning! Beethoven's fifth is playing solemnly and joyously in the studio, Atos brought the record from Stockholm. I'm not working today, can't even be bothered to light the stove and cook. Last night I finished the cardboard sketches in colour and now I don't feel like bothering about Art for a whole day. I want to think about you, listen to music and be outside of time.

Tove's two truly large paintings were ready on time. The first of them she created with Niilo Suihko, who in his capacity of skilled professional restorer had mastered the fresco technique. The second painting she wanted to do on

Fairytale, oil, 1934

her own. One painting depicts a heavenly pastoral idyll in which people happily rest in natural surroundings in the midst of flowers and grapes. Everywhere there is perfect happiness and fairytale-like beauty. In the other painting, which shows a Paradise influenced by culture, people in evening dress dance their cares away on a terrace bordered by Grecian columns. White doves fly on the horizon, and wine bottles and glasses stand temptingly on the table. The ball is like a pictorial representation of the artist's life at that moment. The central figure is an elegant, dark-haired woman in pale clothes who is dancing with a tall and well-built young man, making her skirts flutter. She is fully recognizable as Vivica.

Tove has placed herself in the foreground of the picture. She sits smoking and looking contemplatively to the side, partially obscured behind a vase of flowers. Two Moomintrolls have also been included in the paintings. In the pastoral idyll there is a troll on the left, at the foot of the picture, among the flowers. In the dance fresco, the troll is close to Tove's elbow, next to a glass of wine. When the frescos were completed, Tove wrote to Eva with relief that the big job was finished, and that 'I think they went well'. When the City Hall was given a thorough refurbishment, the restaurant was renovated and the works were moved to the Swedish Workers' Institute in Helsinki, where they are still accessible for all to see.

Painting Vivica was a declaration of love. In the fresco, their love would be preserved and the picture would constitute a memory of the time when they loved each other. But it was also a picture of courage. Tove painted the object of her unlawful and secret love as a central figure in such a way that all the artists and everyone in her intimate circle could recognize her. By so doing she showed her indifference to the gossip and slander of her contemporaries. She wrote a long love poem to the Vivica in the painting about all the things she wanted to tell the people who looked at it.

Blue, blue I painted the sky,
yellow as sun your dress
beautiful your smile.
You I have painted the sweetest
I painted you on the wall,
there you shall remain
as you were
when you loved me.

There was a great deal of love, but there were even more disappointments. Joy was hard to come by, and Tove wrote that 'sorrow sits in the studio's walls'. In July Tove wrote sadly to Eva that Vivica was going abroad, sailing, with her childhood friend Göran Schildt. Tove confessed to Atos that she no longer loved him. In addition, she had money worries. During 1947 she only sold two paintings.

The reasons for the death of Tove's and Vivica's relationship are somewhat obscure, and maybe that is for the best. According to Vivica, both of them had suffered from enormous insecurity in their youth. It was not just the war and the misery it brought with it, but the fact that '[y]ou see, there are people in this world who are afraid. Many of the Moomin books are a sort of overcoming of fear.' They were friends all their lives, and really good friends at that. Vivica said: 'Loneliness, insecurity and fear in its naked form are a solid basis for friendship . . .' It was, perhaps, not the best possible basis for a love that was passionate but condemned by society's norms and laws.

City Celebration. **One of the frescos in Helsinki City Hall, oil, 1947**

Tove did not explain what really lay behind the break, but simply described her own moods. The most important thing was to avoid hatred and bitterness. Even so, everything felt quite meaningless. She saw the whole love affair as unnecessary – it had simply torn her apart. In the same letter she reflected honestly on Atos and her relationship with him, as well as her tormenting love for Vivica. Tove was ready to show almost limitless understanding to Vivica and her affairs with other women, and even made friends with her new lovers. Vivica has described the beginning of their affair and the reasons for its ending:

> *Tove Jansson and I met when we were 30. She gave me the courage to become an artist, and I gave her the courage to develop as a human being.*
>
> *It's like being hungry all one's life and then suddenly being given dessert, nothing but dessert. For the first time I received more than I could give back, and I couldn't cope with it. It was all so good that I couldn't stand it, I was used to things always going wrong, and when they didn't I made them go wrong myself.*
>
> *I've regretted it. Not all my life, but half of it.*

Tove's love for Vivica resulted in the creation of the small creatures Thingumy and Bob in Moominvalley. These creatures and the elegant Vivica dancing in the mural remain as the memory of a love that had been so good and beautiful that it must not be forgotten. Vivica's estate has been found to contain a letter to Tove, probably written in the late 1960s, in which she confesses her love for

The monkey sitting in the sea in Pellinki, 1940s

her. Vivica wrote that Tove had been the best thing on earth for her, even sur-
passing her mother, whom she loved greatly. Tove's existence had been a great
comfort in times of despair. She ended the letter by saying: 'You were the great
love of my life. Every time I hear your voice, see you, or even just hear you, a
trembling passes through me. I believe not in God, but in you.'

THE THOUGHT OF MARRIAGE

The City Hall restaurant frescos were completed on time and Tove recovered
from the fatigue brought on by the work. But her love for Vivica continued in
despair. She found an outlet for her disappointment by building a new house
on the island of Bredskär in Pellinki, which she called the Wind Rose House.
Tove's love of work was like an 'atavistic instinct' of the blood, as she put it.
The island was a big part of her, as she wrote to Eva, 'the best thing I have
ever wanted'.

When Tove built something, the result was always what she had planned and
intended – unlike when she painted, when the finished work never wholly cor-
responded to what she had planned at the outset. She simply built, wearing out
her sorrows with physical labour and living on the island until late in September.
She slept in a tent and enjoyed the beauty of the landscape: the red new moon,
the pine branches that she could see like a lace pattern through the mosquito

net. And she wrote long letters to Eva, who did not seem to understand the relationship with Vivica. Tove defended her beloved to Eva, who had belittled her:

> [*Vivica*] *whom you call 'that person' has given me infinitely more than the bitter fruit one obtains from an adventure in which one gets one's fingers burnt. [. . .] and I think that prim spinsterishness has left me somewhat thanks to her. And that whining concern in and out of season, that fear of not being popular. I have acquired a new freedom through her, I think. And if that is so, then all our agony was worth it.*
>
> *I thought I had felt as intensely as I was able to, but now I know that there are further possibilities, endless ones. Both of happiness and suffering – and of expressing them. Probably I have been afraid all my life. Now I know that I can be brave. [. . .] She is so rough-edged [. . .] she is not spoiled [. . .] Do you know what Vivica used to say when I came out with some remark that was sentimental and spurious? She would utter a mocking 'meow'! It felt terrible, but it was better than when Atos looked uncomfortable and bored and just said nothing.*

Waiting for her in Helsinki was Atos, who was working and travelling, 'looking after the people's welfare', as Tove said sarcastically. But he had also managed to visit the island – only for one Sunday, it was true, but it proved to be a very successful day. In the winter Tove had suggested that they separate, as she did not think there was love between them any more – just habit and friendship. Even so, they got along well together, something that Tove set great store by. Atos made no response to her proposal that they separate, but went off to Poland on a business trip. Tove reflected on her feelings and said that life was strange. When one finally realized that one needed to be genuine and honest, one did not know what the truth was.

She met up with Vivica, who had come to Helsinki, but their meetings were overshadowed by quarrels, misunderstandings and suspicions. Was it the case, Tove wondered, that in a relationship between two women there were no opposing forces? The similar reactions of the two partners merely strengthened one another and led to excesses. She wanted to be free of the relationship, but did not want to give up their friendship. It was too strong for that. She even accepted the heartache, and felt indebted to Vivica for making life richer and more intense. Tove wrote: 'What does it matter that one isn't happy, if one sees and feels and thinks more strongly?'

But she could not mourn for ever. She wrote to Vivica that she had hoped their love was over, but unfortunately it was not. Nevertheless she suggested that they should stop seeing each other, as '[t]he thing is that I can't go on being unhappy any longer'. At the same time she sent Vivica a large bundle of poems she had written to her.

Tove apparently sought security in the life to which she was accustomed, and she decided to propose to Atos. If he said yes, and they married, she planned to close the door for ever on that other world, the Left Bank, and be exclusively heterosexual. She desired clarity in her life and her emotions, as it was so hopelessly difficult 'to remain suspended in the air, between woman and man'. In her letter she told him first about the situation regarding the Moomin books. She had just delivered a manuscript to her publisher and said she was now painting and thinking. And as if something had suddenly occurred to her, she then suggested: 'So I wonder if you think it would be a good idea for us to get married? It wouldn't change our way of life, I think. If you don't want to, we can talk about something else when you come back.'

She ended the letter 'Like you very, very much' – words that were perfectly appropriate but rather lacking in passion. Marriage was important to her – it was an institution that she hoped would resolve her severe inner conflicts: 'I imagine the "symbol" would mean a lot to me. Why, I don't know. [. . .] But perhaps I should be calm, and able to work. And stop yearning for "la Rive Gauche". So much for that.'

When Atos returned from his trip, he pretended to be surprised: '[I]s it true that we're not married yet? I thought we were. [. . .] We must really do something about it, otherwise people will begin to suspect that we don't get along together.' Tove began to plan the wedding. As witnesses she wanted to have her best female friend in Finland, Eva Wichman, her brother Lasse, and, of course, Ham. But not her father, as she thought he would not accept his daughter's choice of husband if it meant him acquiring 'an almost Red son-in-law'. Tove asked Eva: 'Don't you think I'll make an amusing politician's wife?' However, she doubted that Atos really wanted to get married. He did nothing before the wedding, did not even get his birth certificate from Åland, putting the blame on the busy pre-election period. The wedding was to have been held in the spring of 1948, but it never took place.

Tove was understanding, and said that Atos should not be judged by the same standards as other people, as he was special and unique. At around the same time Atos's ex-wife died in Paris in circumstances that were very unclear. Although their marriage had lasted no more than a few months, Atos was beside himself with grief at her unexpected death. It may have been that the event affected his willingness to commit himself to a new marriage. Though one might have expected her to have feelings of disappointment, Tove did not express them in her letters at any length. She tried to get on with her work and regain her enthusiasm for painting.

IN SEARCH OF JOY AND DESIRE

In 1948, Tove travelled to Italy with Sam and Maya Vanni in order to gather her strength, and above all to regain her desire and will to paint again. Sam had always been an inspiring friend. Now, once again, Tove wanted to achieve creative joy with his help. And their work was successful. They gave each other peace, worked separately and hard, yet in several of the paintings they produced during the trip their mental proximity is evident – these works are very much alike. Sometimes it is hard to tell which artist painted which work.

Travelling as a 'third wheel' with a married couple was not at all easy, especially in view of Sam and Tove's shared history. The love between them had not died, simply changed its form. There were many emotions, and each of them enjoyed the other's company. They had endlessly long conversations about art. Tove appreciated Sam's criticism and support and loved to wander around town with him. Sam was in the habit of buying sausages and wine at street stalls, which Tove also liked. Maya was reserved and did not take part in these activities. But there were too many emotions, and to some extent they were contradictory. It became clear that getting along as a trio would be too difficult, and Tove went off alone to Brittany to paint.

In Brittany she got a letter from Vivica that made her almost delirious with joy. Vivica boldly proposed that they should stage a Moomin play at Helsinki's Svenska Teater. The play would be based on *Comet in Moominland*.

During the trip Tove wrote to Atos and congratulated him on his success in the elections. But the earlier emotion was gone, and the letters were now friendly and matter-of-fact in tone. Tove hoped they would meet, but said that she planned to go to the island as soon as she could. She wrote that she missed the island, but not that she missed Atos. Her life with him continued slowly, but it was clear that they would no longer discuss the wedding. At the very end of 1948 Tove wrote in a letter about how Atos had explained his emotional life, and the rationale behind it. As a young man he had been deeply depressed, and his life had been one of suffering and misery. He had been filled with all the typical things a young man suffers from – longing, loneliness, unhappy love, fear of death. At the time he had thought he could no longer go on living 'subjectively'. Suffering was the price of feelings and sensitivity. He had suffered from bottomless depression and had thought of shooting himself. Luckily he had only succeeded in taking the life of the subject, the 'I' in himself. In the night he had cried out 'I am nothing' and believed he had managed to kill his ego. Love and commitment were not a part of the new 'I'. He had begun to live 'objectively' and no longer allowed personal feelings to guide his life. He wanted to love mankind, not any individual woman.

'It's true, that is what he is like. He doesn't know how to hate, or love, he cannot feel sad or afraid, he truly longs for nothing at all. It's wonderful to be with a superman [. . .] But oh, how I sometimes shiver. I think I am angry with him because I haven't managed to love him more. That is really nasty of me.' Tove also thought about her attitude to him: 'Peace and quiet are exactly what I've been looking for in recent years – so I ought to be glad that Atos is the way he is.' Atos's new objectivity meant a form of freedom from her own deep feelings. Her self-critical comment that a man like Atos was right for her hit the mark. She invariably found his company intellectually stimulating, he gave her a great deal of mental space, and he did not disturb her passionate work. The only drawback lay in the fact that the emotional price of this was high.

Later, in 1951, Atos tried to approach Tove again, but by then it was too late. During the intervening years their relationship had continued as a friendship only, and from time to time as a physical affair. It resembled marriage on a low flame. Tove's life had already changed. Atos was 'like my "ex", but without the radiance and risk there were during the seven years I loved him. Now he wants us to marry, but I no longer feel desire. I shall always like him.'

Tove was preoccupied by lesbianism – the idea was still new to her and she needed to get used to it. For several years she pondered it in her letters, even though their recipient, Eva Konikoff, reacted quite negatively to this new turn in her life. Sometimes Tove wanted to leave lesbianism behind completely. Certain things about it troubled her, and she condemned the homosexual relationships of her male acquaintances, their inner tensions and quarrels. She drew the conclusion that it was harder to create comfort and sustainable peace in those relationships than in heterosexual ones. Perhaps that was nature's way of taking revenge, she reflected sadly.

GARM AFTER THE WAR

Although Tove was uncompromising in her espousal of art for art's sake, that did not apply at all to her work as an illustrator for *Garm* during the war. When peace came, the wartime caricatures of Stalin and Hitler and the polemics about the horrors of war in general were replaced by pictures that showed bleak landscapes charred by bombs. She depicted the central problems of the new era of peace – the shortage of food, the rising prices and the eternal rationing. In the same way, she described all kinds of everyday things that irritated people and dealt with these subjects by means of satire and humour, as in the picture where a poor little wage-earner wonders how he will manage when he has not enough money. Taxation, travel, food and just about every essential item had become so much more expensive. She also portrayed the greed, materialism and indifference of the new generation, and a country that was rapidly growing more international. She seemed particularly amused by people's bewilderment at seeing visitors of different foreign ethnicities during the 1952 Olympic Games.

With the arrival of peace, the war trials began. Even among ordinary citizens, the wartime actions of people one knew or did not know were dug up. The principal accusations were of fascism or of having been on the wrong side and holding the wrong opinions. Everyone had to defend themselves, and it was human nature to attempt to deny or whitewash one's own history, earlier activities and opinions. Shame and guilt were harsh and merciless feelings, and political recantation was forced on many who had joined the losing side. One of Tove's most interesting drawings was a picture published in *Garm* in January 1945. Its theme was tergiversation – the attempt to cleanse oneself of the past and its defeated and condemned ideas. Tove drew an enormous machine bearing the words 'AB Metamorfosicum OY' and 'Wind direction of the day'. A gang of renegades with black faces and swastikas or Q-signs on the backs of their overalls are climbing into the bowels of the machine. The swastika represented fascism, of course, while Q stood for Quisling, the leader of the fascist puppet government in Nazi-occupied Norway, whose name was already a symbol of treachery. A coal-black Moomintroll has also walked into the machine. The apparatus is puffing, and spewing out soot and ash. Out of the other end emerge pure figures in dazzling white robes, playing harps and carrying flowers. With halos above their heads they are as innocent as saints. Although the picture is comical, the search for war criminals and 'heretics' and the harsh judgement of post-war society were perfectly real phenomena, and far from amusing.

Garm's cover for August 1946 alluded to nuclear war. It was then exactly a year since the bombs had dropped on Hiroshima and Nagasaki. In the picture. a pensive angel of peace sits on the wing of an aeroplane. Down on the ground a black-clad man stands looking up at the angel amid flowers that look like

orchids and carnivorous plants. Black bats flit around ominously. The man is holding a briefcase on which are the words URANIUM 135.

Many of Tove's illustrations take a stand on current political issues. Their content is often hard to interpret decades later, now that the political figures and the ideas they represented are long forgotten. The drawings in which she portrays man's relation to nature and the new superabundance of material goods form a unique whole that is still topical. There are too many gadgets, people are uncaring about their environment, throw rubbish around and contaminate nature, destroying it. Tove commented on this, for example, in the issue for Midsummer 1952. The cover illustration shows the scene after a party, resembling the aftermath of an air raid. Birch trees have been cut down and there are empty bottles, broken glass, remains of food and bits of paper everywhere. Instead of human beings, we see only their traces, some rubbish and a smoking midsummer bonfire.

THE ART FOR ART'S SAKE SNOB

After the closed secrecy of wartime, Finland opened up to new ideas and views which rolled in as if into a vacuum and presented a challenge. Atos's friends were culturally demanding, and they were important to Tove. But socially and politically Tove was no Wirtanen clone. Long before they had begun their affair she had created her perceptive and influential political drawings of Hitler and Stalin for *Garm*. Yet in order to fulfil the political and cultural demands of Atos's circle she had to actively follow the trends of the times and broaden her knowledge. This was also essential if she was to be able to continue devising hard-hitting cover illustrations for *Garm* and other publications.

Surrealism and Existentialism were popular topics of discussion in the magazine *1940-luku* (1940s) and among Atos and Tove's circle of friends. Socially committed art and Socialist Realism (according to many, the only true art) sparked heated exchanges of views. Everyone had to have an opinion on these topics. For a while Atos was a member of *1940-luku*'s editorial board and, like many of their friends, was very active in the Kiila ('the Wedge') group, which certainly influenced his contribution to the great debate that was taking place about art.

Surrealism aroused strong feelings, and the left was divided in its view of it. Jarno Pennanen was its ardent defender, but many other critics condemned it outright. An influential public speaker, Pennanen worked as editorial manager of the left-wing *Vapaa sana* ('Free Word') newspaper from 1948 to 1949, later becoming its editor-in-chief. He was active in the Wedge, and in the 1930s served as editor-in-chief of the radical *Kirjallisuuslehti* ('Literary Gazette'). He and Arvo Turtiainen were enthusiastic journalists and commentators in the country's Finnish-language media in the same way that Atos was in their Swedish-language counterpart.

Eva Konikoff had written to Tove about what she had seen in the United States, especially an exhibition of Surrealist art, which had made a deep impression on her. In her reply, Tove condemned Surrealism and said that it was just a passing phenomenon that had arisen from new ways of studying the human mind, like psychoanalysis. She compared it to a sensational dress that one could not wear for more than one season as it was too eye-catching. Surrealism would not have more of a future than such a dress. She called the Impressionists her masters, singling out Cézanne in particular, whom she found much more moving than 'the most high-flown colossal painting or crucifixion scene'. Tove stressed the importance of freedom and joy in creation, and thought that art could not be based on duty or feelings of responsibility. Art must contain despair, but also desire. She valued independence; she was very ego-centred in her view of art and also took a critical stance on dominant new ideas. Her uncharitable view of Surrealism appears strange – for with their irrational moods and fairytale-like character, her own early paintings were close to it in spirit.

After the Rites of Midsummer. Cover illustration for *Garm*, 1952

Existentialism was an important philosophical movement after the war too. In Finland, its main proponents were Jean-Paul Sartre, Simone de Beauvoir and Albert Camus. It came to Finland via Sweden, largely through Sartre's philosophy, and so Swedish-speaking Finns were able to acquaint themselves with his books relatively quickly. Sartre's writings were also published in the Finnish-language *1940-luku*. Raoul Palmgren in particular received much inspiration from Sartre and met him at an event that was arranged in Sweden. Existentialism was naturally the subject of debate at the gatherings in Atos's Kauniainen villa. Tove wrote with irritation that

The Angel of Peace Leaves the Earth and Nuclear War. Cover illustration for *Garm*, August 1946

15MK
75öre

GARM

AUGUSTI·1946

an anonymous 'coryphaeus' (*koryfé*) was horrified when he realized that she had not read Sartre – he thought he had been talking to an ignorant 'parlourmaid'. Afterwards she said that in pure annoyance at the incident, or rather after the way the man had looked at her, she had gone away and read Sartre. Sartre's concept of freedom certainly meant something to her, as one or two thoroughly Sartrean ideas may be seen throughout many of her works.

The central issue of the day was the role of art in society. Whom should the artist serve, or should he serve anyone at all? Tove and Tapsa had discussed these questions during their years together when they had studied at the Athenaeum, when Tove called him 'our Communist, Tapsa'. Tapsa introduced her to people like his friend Arvo Turtiainen, a brilliant left-wing poet of his time. Tove's own best personal friends were also prominent left-wing dissidents, like Eva Wichman.

FREEDOM IS THE BEST THING

Tove's close friends strongly influenced her world view and her creative work. Vanni and Tapiovaara, as visual artists, were important conversation partners for her. For decades Vanni was her principal critic, apart from the members of her family. Through Atos her interest in literature and writing grew and became more diverse. The cultural milieu of Kauniainen came to be highly significant for her in many ways. Through Vivica Bandler she formed an acquaintance with the theatre world, and theatre became an increasingly important art form for her.

Common to Tove's boyfriends Vanni, Tapiovaara and Wirtanen was a wish to influence her opinions and values. They were all highly charismatic men, schooled in self-publicity and accustomed to being listened to, admired and believed. With Sam Vanni, Tove had discussed questions that affected the essence of visual art and the philosophy of art. Their thinking was limited to art-related issues; Vanni was not a politically active person. On the other hand, years of intensive association with Tapiovaara and Wirtanen and their respective social circles had planted Tove among Finland's most prominent left-wing intelligentsia and its culture. Through them she met artists and activists who were politically inclined, and she also took part in events organized by the political left. The young Tove's most active contact with politics came with Wirtanen, who did more than anyone else to broaden her cultural environment. Tapiovaara urged her to reflect on the function of art and the responsibility of the artist. She was forced to take a stand on the strongly left-wing artistic politics he represented, where the morality and justification of art was determined by how well it served the people. Art had to be subordinate to larger social issues.

The Wedge was a very active and broadly based left-wing writers' association in the post-war period. The Finland-Swedish writers and artists became a problematic group for the Wedge, as it was hard to engage them in the association's activities. Raoul Palmgren describes a meeting in November 1948 that resulted in many Finland-Swedish cultural figures joining the organization. Among the new arrivals he mentions Mirjam Tuominen, Eva Wichman, Heidi, Heli, Oscar and Ralf Parland, Thomas Warburton, Sven Grönvall and Atos Wirtanen. While the last two represented the left's socialist wing, the others were mainly intellectual radicals and writers who opposed war and fascism. In addition to Atos, Sven Grönvall and Eva Wichman were close friends of Tove. She met Warburton, then an editor at the offices of the publisher Schildts, when she brought him the manuscript of *The Magician's Hat* (*Trollkarlens Hatt*, known in English as *Finn Family Moomintroll*). Their professional relationship proved to be intensive. Warburton became Tove's editor and friend, and he also translated four of the Moomin books into English. Atos's Kauniainen circle seems to have been well represented at the Wedge meeting.

It appears that Tove attended the 1948 meeting that Palmgren describes. In an undated letter to Eva, Tove says that Atos took her along to the meeting at the Wedge. Attempts had long been made to convert her to socially committed art, and now the Wedge was exerting every effort to add Finland-Swedish artists to its membership. The social democratic activist Jarno Pennanen gave a fiery political speech in which he said that people should not be afraid of politics and urged the artists to be open about such matters. So ardently and loftily did he speak about culture that Tove began to have doubts about his view of it. In her sarcastic way she said that she was always suspicious when people proclaimed they washed themselves, for it made them seem a little dirty.

Tove took a cautious view of the opinions that were presented, and did not allow herself to be swept along by the spirit of the meeting. As ever, she was careful not to lose her independence. She described how the Finland-Swedish artists at the meeting, true to form, stressed their desire to be individualists who were self-determining and could write in peace. They were afraid of being marked with a political label and they renounced nationalism, or as Tove put it, stuck to their old values. During the debate at the meeting, the divide between the two language groups grew wider. But in the end, after much antagonism and argument, a large group of Finland-Swedish artists joined the Wedge. Giving their reasons for this surprising show of support, they merely said that it would have been impolite for them to refuse. Tove found this amusing. The meeting was reported in the newspaper and Faffan was furious when he read that the Finland-Swedes had taken part. Tove commented in her roguish way: 'If he only knew that I was there, too.'

The Finland-Swedish writers had trouble in finding common ideological ground with the members of the Wedge, and little by little many of them left the movement. Tove also found it hard to embrace ideology of any kind. In spite of all the attempts by Tapsa in their student days, or by the members of Atos's *Ny Tid* group and his friends in Kauniainen, Tove remained a steadfast opponent of so-called 'tendency art' and was given the nickname *'l'art pour l'art snob'*. Even Eva Konikoff seems to have criticized Tove for this belittling of socially committed art, and Tove replied that she did not think of anyone else when she was painting, that she worked for herself – who else should she paint for? She said that she loathed 'tendency' in art. The war had brought nothing but dingy colours and nationalism. All artists portray not only themselves, but also the times in which they live, Tove wrote, adding that her art had been criticized for being controlled and unfeeling.

She was unable to share the values of her friends, or to believe as strongly in political causes as those nearest to her expected. All of this tormented her. Year after year she restated her view that the meaning of art lay in the concept of art for art's sake. Art should not be used for extraneous purposes or made subordinate to them. It was not an instrument of revolution – nor even a means of instituting social welfare. Its justification lay in itself. Later she wrote about this in a short story based on her own wartime letters and notes:

> And now let me make it perfectly clear that I had to listen more than enough to them going on about 'social responsibility' and 'social consciousness', and 'The Great Masses', and I may as well tell you straight that I don't believe in that social 'tendency art', I believe in l'art pour l'art, and there's an end of it!
>
> Tapsa says I'm an art snob and my paintings are anti-social. Is a still life with apples anti-social!? What about Cézanne's apples, they are very Idea of the Apple, the definitive observation!
>
> Tapsa said that Dalí only works for himself. Who else should he paint for, I ask? While one is working one doesn't think about other people, mustn't think about them! I believe that deep down every canvas, still life, landscape, whatever, is a self-portrait!

Tove found party politics repellent. She reflected on her attitude to collective strength, and said that mass meetings of any kind frightened her. And she did not understand why being an individual was thought equivalent to being anti-social, or why it was viewed negatively. She often declared that she not only hated 'tendency' in art, but also all kinds of gatherings, societies and associations.

The opinions of Tapsa and other left-wing artists continued to become more uncompromising with the years, and the various prevalent views of art acquired a political tinge. Tapsa and Sven Grönvall were the chairmen of the Wedge during the 1950s. The new trends in art aroused mistrust, and became entangled with politics in a rather peculiar way. The modern currents in painting arrived later in Finland than they did in the rest of Europe, and were the cause of much debate. Abstract art in particular was often condemned as American propaganda and said to contain the 'Cold War weapon' against Socialist Realism. Tapiovaara made a point of stating that 'an artist's world view should comprise ethics and aesthetics in equal balance' and that abstract art was an American conspiracy. Tove later had to confront these views when, in the 1960s, like many other Finnish artists, she adopted an abstract or semi-abstract style of painting.

In the last analysis, Tove's attitude to the world view of the left, the Social Democrats and the Communists remains unclear. On the basis of her letters and notebooks, she seems only to have been interested in the way in which the various ideologies related to creative art, and above all to her own work. And she was concerned about her artistic freedom. It was almost as though she felt sorry and wanted to apologize. In 1948 she wrote that all her life she would be 'an anti-social = apolitical painter, a so-called individualist who paints lemons, writes fairytales, collects strange objects and hobbies, and despises mass meetings and associations. Looks ridiculous, but that is how I want my life.'

Socially committed art, like art in general, was of course only a small part of the left's ideology. But in her letters to Eva at least, Tove did not comment on current political matters. Her political opinions were close to those of the Finland-Swedish intelligentsia and mainly espoused tolerance, with an accommodating approach to the different views and alternatives offered by human existence and society. But the ideas of the left cannot have been far removed from her own values. Her affairs with men like Tapiovaara and Atos Wirtanen would not have been possible otherwise, and neither would her friendships with left-wing figures and the social circle represented by the left-wing intellectuals at Kauniainen. She also had the courage to declare her political views in pictorial form.

Although during her life Tove kept a very open mind about everything, there was not a trace of her tolerance when it came to the matters of war and fascism. In those she was an absolute and dedicated pacifist and anti-fascist. In her ideas and lifestyle she was a feminist before her time, though she would never have used that word about herself. Her open-mindedness also meant a great deal to the Finland-Swedish sexual minorities. Though she did not take to the barricades on that issue either, the open and natural attitude she adopted towards it in her life and books had a significant effect on the secretive and scandal-laden atmosphere of the time.

As a young girl Tove had drawn the first Moomin-like figure on the wall of the outside lavatory at the summer cottage in Pellinki, a figure that looked like Immanuel Kant. Beside it she had written 'Freedom is the best thing'. She was preoccupied by freedom in its various forms, and its study became a major theme throughout the whole of her work.

In art she stressed that she wanted to be free, and this was also important in her personal life. A strong belief in ideologies and the collective goals they entailed was far removed from her world. The prohibitions introduced by man and society are most clearly visible in everyday life, and in her books Tove took an openly negative attitude to them. School, with its rules and regulations, had already filled her with intense dislike. In Tove's world, disobedience was not a grave sin. In her own life she acted according to her own views and her own morality and did not yield to public opinion, even on major issues, but she did not make too big a deal of it. Her literary characters were not always law-abiding, and her early plays and books met with disapproval, as it was feared that they would lead children into bad habits.

Tove had perceived the restrictions on the place of women in society when as a child she observed her parents' marriage. In her own life, she also had to be constantly on guard – with strong men – in order to preserve her freedom. With her father she had had to fight for the right to have her own opinions. Unconditional love was scary. Vanni had warned her not to lose herself by remaining in another person's shadow. She had noticed that in the intense phase of a love affair the risk of losing oneself was considerable, and she was aware of her tendency to submit in relationships. And in such situations she reacted strongly, for she had witnessed her mother's fate at the side of a strong man. During the war, when her relationship with Tapiovaara was at rock-bottom, she wrote that she could recognize within herself all the female instincts – the tendency to admire men, subordinate herself and renounce what was her own.

In her love affairs Tove lived without the sanction of wedlock demanded by the times, and she stood up relatively well to the judgement of her social surroundings. For her, marriage may have been an institution that placed too many restrictions on her freedom. Perhaps subconsciously she chose men who set great store by freedom, and thus even though she might have wanted to marry, it was a step never taken.

Great admiration limits freedom. Freedom is valued, and it is an ideal, even the most important goal, in many people's lives. Yet in the end freedom may not always be what it seems, as Moominpappa is forced to admit of the Hatti-fatteners: 'I thought they were so wonderful and free – simply because they didn't say anything and just kept going. They had nothing to say and nowhere to go . . .' The contradictions of freedom and independence, and their parallel nature, form one of the fundamental questions in Tove's books, and the same was true of her personal life.

Motherhood is always the strongest bond, and for Tove it was the most difficult and frightening one. It, too, was contradictory: there were times when she feared getting pregnant, and times when that was what she wanted. Responsibility always limits freedom. The question of whether to have children or not was therefore a difficult one for an artist who passionately cherished freedom. A certain paradox may also be seen in the fact that a woman who had opted for childlessness became loved by millions of children.

Tove's studio was to her a symbol of freedom; it was like Virginia Woolf's 'room of one's own', a place where a woman could create and maintain a sufficient portion of independence. It was a space she was not prepared to part with, not ever and not for anyone. It guaranteed her freedom to the maximum extent that was possible in the world. No love and no relationship would have been able to make her give up her own workplace. Ultimately, to her, work meant freedom and real existence. Only deep depression was sometimes capable of interfering with the joy that it brought.

IV

The Moomin World

THE BIRTH OF THE MOOMINS

Tove had more than enough illustration work, and now and then she became quite concerned about it as it distracted her too much from her painting. So why, as a gifted and dedicated artist, did she start writing the Moomin books? It cannot have been for financial reasons, for she certainly did not envisage making much money from them. At least to begin with, she wrote them for herself. Through them she escaped from the war and the harshness of the world. At home and at war, many Finns were numbing their senses with drugs and especially hard liquor. Writing about Moominvalley offered Tove an alternative escape from a life that was too cruel. Initially, it seems to have played a similar role in her life as her plans for the artists' colonies in Morocco and Tonga.

Perhaps we have the war to thank for the Moomins. She had already explored these characters previously, but it was not until the middle of the war that Tove created an entire world for them, one in which the author, too, was shielded from the horrors of reality. It was really just an escape from the ugliness of the real world. Tove said of the origin of the stories: 'I am really a painter, but in the early 1940s, during the war, I felt so desperate that I began to write fairytales.'

Tove found her hiding place in Moominvalley, but it was a place from which she could always return. She confirmed this in 1991. In the Preface to a new edition of her first book, she described what it felt like to write:

> It was the winter of war, in 1939. One's work stood still; it felt completely pointless to try to create pictures.
>
> Perhaps it was understandable that I suddenly felt an urge to write down something that was to begin with 'Once upon a time'.
>
> What followed had to be a fairytale – that was inevitable – but I excused myself by avoiding princes, princesses and small children and chose instead my angry signature character from the cartoons, and called him the Moomintroll.

Black Moomin Rowing, detail, watercolour, 1930s

The half-written story was forgotten until 1945. Then a friend pointed out that it could become a children's book; just finish it and illustrate it, perhaps they will want it.

This friend was Atos, and it was with his support that she continued to write and illustrate the book.

The Moomins were born with the writing of the very first book. While it was true that Tove had drawn Moomin-like figures earlier, in the 1930s they were mostly only vignettes, small puzzle pictures or parts of her signature. They were separate and isolated, without their own narrative world, and were often black-bodied, red-eyed and skinny, with horns and long noses – the kind of creature you would not want to run into at night.

It is thought that the first picture that looked like a Moomin resembled a portrait of Kant that hung in the outhouse of the cottage in Pellinki. It was followed by the angry-looking signature figures in Tove's caricatures, which also lack the plump, white softness of the future Moomins. Only much later did these figures acquire a lighter colour, put on weight and become chubby, easier for everyone to identify with. Their eyes moved lower down in their faces and became more human, while their mouths disappeared.

Tove's own recollections about the origins of the Moomins vary. After being subjected to constant interviews, she would come up with a slightly different version of the story depending on who she was talking to. She seems to have developed a stock of ready answers to the questions she was most frequently asked. The story often harked back to her early childhood, when she stayed in the home of her mother's relatives in Sweden. There she often crept into the pantry at night, prompting her uncle to warn about 'moomintrolls' that lurked in the dark. Even the name 'Moomin' contains a note of warning: it is a sound that comes from deep in the throat, with a long 'm' and an even longer 'oo', and has a threatening air well suited for frightening a small child looking for treats in the night.

In the 1930s, these creatures were frightening. In Tove's paintings of that decade, they sometimes appeared, for example, at the foot of sickbeds, and were undesirable in much the same way as head colds and angry concierges. She sometimes described them in her diaries as strange, ghostlike and scary creatures which the darkness of night had released from the shadowy forces of the subconscious.

In 1950 Tove gave an account of the birth of the Moomins in a letter to Eva, who had been given the task of trying to get the books published in the United

States. In the letter Tove said she had been struck by the sight of a wintry forest in which the tree stumps were covered in thick, soft white snow. The round formation of the stumps often had a projecting part that hung down like 'a big, round white nose'. This story of the origin of the Moomins' noses may have been partly inspired by Arctic exoticism, which was popular overseas.

Fairytales are important in the life of a child. Tove often said that the stories her mother told were unforgettable, and they certainly did much to stimulate her interest in writing stories herself. In her book *The Sculptor's Daughter*, she described the storytelling sessions, which were carefully planned and full of atmosphere:

> We turn out the lights in the studio and sit in front of the fire and she says: Once upon
> a time there was a little girl who was terribly pretty and her mother was terribly fond
> of her ... Each story must begin the same way, but after that it doesn't really matter.
> A slow, gentle voice in the warm darkness, one gazes into the fire and there are no
> dangers at all ... Everything else is outside and can't come in. Not now and not ever

Writing activated Tove's childhood feelings of happiness – of being a small child close to her mother, listening to hair-raising adventures and tingling with excitement, while still being safe. This was the feeling she wanted to communicate to her readers. To begin with, writing seemed easy: 'I wrote the first books with the uncritical joy of an amateur. It was only when writing began to feel as important as painting that it became more laborious. Then I often rewrote my books three or four times.' Tove often improved her books before they were published in new editions. She completely rewrote *Comet in Moominland (Kometjakten)* and *The Exploits of Moominpappa (Muminpappans bravader)* and made corrections to *Finn Family Moomintroll (Trollkarlens hatt)* when her Swedish publisher brought out new editions of them in 1967. Tove also frequently designed new covers for the various editions and foreign-language versions of her books. To Maya Vanni, she wrote that she was ashamed of her first two books, *The Moomins and the Great Flood (Småtrollen och den stora översvämningen)* and *Comet in Moominland*, but also acknowledged that revising old books was a symptom of not having anything new in the pipeline.

Much has been said and written about escapism as a motive for the writing of the Moomin books. During the politically charged 1970s, books were supposed to have a message and the lack of a pedagogical, political or didactic tendency was usually noticed. In Finland, the Moomins prompted disapproval as they were seen as portraying an excessively bourgeois view of the family. When

A Black Moomintroll Walks around Town, watercolour, 1934.
Painted during Tove's first trip to Germany

the books were first published, there was also much discussion about their suitability in an educational context, though for quite different reasons. The Moomins' language, their drinking of palm wine and smoking of tobacco gave offence. What's more, the Moomins often said rude things and even swore at times.

The author made no bones about disclaiming any pedagogical intent: 'I write in order to amuse – but not to educate.' She said she had no philosophy or political tendency. She simply wanted to describe things that had fascinated or frightened her, and had made everything 'take place around a family that is perhaps best characterized by a kind of benign confusion, an acceptance of the world around them, and by the fact that they all get along extraordinarily well with one another'.

The Moomin stories were influenced by books that Tove read during her youth. You can see traces of Selma Lagerlöf's *The Wonderful Adventures of Nils* (*Nils Holgerssons underbura resa*) and Lewis Carroll's *Alice in Wonderland*. Rudyard Kipling's *The Jungle Book* possibly meant the most to her, and the books of Elsa Beskow[5] were also among her favourites. It is easy to find Moomin stories that are based on the Bible, and its influence can often be seen in the fates of the Moomins. Per Olov has described how the Jansson children eagerly studied the family Bible, absorbing its colourful narratives, and also the great impression the paintings of Gustave Doré made on them.

Tove's mother often told her biblical stories, as was natural for a pastor's daughter, though she never mentioned their origin. They often featured Moses in the bulrushes, Eve and the serpent in the Garden of Eden, as well as Isaac, and great storms and disasters. These narratives recur in many of the stories as motifs which, though clearly borrowed, are not out of place in the lives of the Moomins.

The work of the Swedish painter and illustrator John Bauer[6] meant a great deal to Tove. In *The Sculptor's Daughter* she writes about the effect of his drawings on her:

> *I walk through a forest drawn by John Bauer. He knew how to make forests, and since his drowning no one else has dared to [. . .] To make a forest big enough you don't include the tops of the trees or any sky. Just very thick, upright trunks that rise straight in the air. The ground is gentle hillocks, rolling further and further, getting smaller and smaller, until the forest is endless. The stones are there, but you can't see them. They have been covered in moss for thousands of years and no one has ever disturbed it.*

Tove read the horror stories of Edgar Allan Poe at the early age of nine, and her favourite adult authors included Victor Hugo, Thomas Hardy, Robert Louis Stevenson and Joseph Conrad. She received free copies of the books her mother illustrated. There were always books in the home, and the whole family read a great deal. Her brothers also began to write stories at a very young age.

Authors are constantly asked who they write for. In 1964 Bo Carpelan put the question to Tove, and she replied that in the first instance she wrote more for herself than for children. 'But if my stories are addressed to any particular kind of reader, then it's probably a Miffle. I mean those who have trouble fitting

5. Elsa Beskow (1874–1953) was a Swedish author and illustrator of children's books.
6. John Bauer (1882–1918) was a Swedish painter and illustrator.

in anywhere, those who are on the outside, on the margins [. . .], the fish out of water. The good-for-nothing one has managed to escape from or conceal.' She said that nearly all the many readers' letters she got came from Miffles: children who were timid, anxious and lonely. The readers of the Moomin stories seek consolation in the Moomin world, and they find it. By admitting their joys and fears, Tove said, children could experience the things that grown-ups often forgot, like contact with simple things, a sense of safety, and its opposite, a corresponding pervasive fear. She did not want to shut out the mystery, tenderness and cruelty that were a part of the child's world: 'In every honest children's book I think there is an element of fear. Anxious and self-confident children alike are unconsciously drawn to it, and to destruction.'

The worst thing is fear of the dark, which is a nameless terror. Yet it, too, can join forces with safety, providing a counterbalance to it and giving it meaning. Danger always lurks somewhere. An ordinary lamp quietly burning in a window makes the darkness dramatically black.

THE TWO WORLDS OF MOOMINVALLEY

There are several maps of the Moomins' world, and the geography of the stories is very precise. Ham had drawn excellent maps of the Jansson family's summer islands and the maps of the Moomins' world resemble them. Tove pointed out that Moominvalley was definitely part of the Nordic and Finnish landscape. In the first books, and in their early versions, there were many exotic elements – in Tove's view too many: palm trees, flowers and creatures. Some of these she pruned away. She wanted the natural environment in the books to be as realistic as possible: the moon had always to rise the right way, though it could be any size. The world of the Moomins was made up of sea, storms, rugged mountains and caves, but also of flowers and dense forest. Moominvalley was a homely, local and safe environment, along with its opposite as a backdrop to the adventures: an unpredictable and dangerous sea and a mountainous land prone to disasters. The Moomins always found it good to return from the great wide world to the calm of the valley back home. Though, of course, in order to return they had first to leave.

It is possible to find many prototypes of the valley's landscapes, characters and community. Tove's own family, her father, mother and brothers, can be seen in the principal characters in Moominvalley, as can many of Tove's friends. The origin of the Moominvalley landscape is generally considered to be Ham's

Undated early Moomin picture, gouache

parents' house, situated on the island of Blidö in the Stockholm archipelago and built by Tove's grandfather. There Tove spent many childhood summers with her grandparents, cousins and uncles. It was a large house with many rooms, in nearly all of which there was a tiled stove. The surroundings were gentle and luxuriant, with large trees. In *The Sculptor's Daughter* Tove describes her grandfather and his choice of site for the family home:

> [*Grandpa*] *came to a long green meadow that was bordered by forest and hills, which made it look like the vale of Paradise. At one end it opened on to a bay, for his descendants to bathe in.*
>
> *Then Grandpa thought: here I will dwell and multiply [. . .]*

The inhabitants of Moominvalley often stray from their valley and are subject to storms and disasters on the raging sea. Tove loved the sea in its various manifestations. She described it in her life, in her painting, in the Moomin books and also in other things she wrote. It was not to Stockholm that the Jansson family went in summer, but to the Pellinki archipelago. It was also there that Tove had the last house she ever owned, on the very small and barren island of Klovharu. As a place of residence it was simple in the extreme – nothing but sea and rocks.

The Moomins live in these two contrasting worlds: on the one hand, a luxuriant, marine landscape reminiscent of Blidö, with brooks, flowers, houses with tiled stoves; and on the other, the unpredictable seas of Pellinki with its barren islands, archipelagos, caves, mussels, sea creatures and boats. In the tension between these worlds the Moomin family settles down.

THE FAMILY IS BORN – *THE MOOMINS AND THE GREAT FLOOD*

The idea for the world of the Moomins originated in the overwhelming days of the Winter War. *The Moomins and the Great Flood* (*Småtrollen och den stora översvämningen*, 1945) was delivered to the publisher during the Continuation War, and it appeared shortly after peace was declared. It was a time of considerable gloom and the future looked far from hopeful. The mood of this period was certainly reflected in the book's atmosphere of fear and menace, and also in the development of its plot. While there can be no doubt that this is the story of a disaster, it also tells the story of the birth of a family.

A great flood has submerged the dry land and everyone is in mortal danger. It is an enormous environmental disaster, and the unpredictability of nature's forces generates the sense of adventure and excitement. The story is set in a landscape familiar to Tove from her experience of living on an archipelago – a landscape composed of water, sea and wind, fallen trees and creatures drifting in the tide. The narrative, which is based partly on old fireside yarns, deals with seafaring and a struggle with the elements.

It is a typical picaresque tale. Moominpappa has disappeared with the Hattifatteners, and Moominmamma and Moomintroll set off to look for him. The family bond that unites the Moomin pair is a strong one, but it is also open-ended. Sniff joins the family. The Hemulens and Hattifatteners are also represented among the tribes of the Moomin world, and the core members of the Moomin family are assembled. Other guests include the Ant Lion, and

Moomins in a Vast Landscape, watercolour, undated

the blue-haired Tulippa puts in an appearance. The story also embraces an enormous candy dream-world inside a mountain, where children can indulge in as many sweet things as they like.

The illustrations are based on the seascape and natural surroundings of Tove's summers at Pellinki, but there are also lush jungles, perhaps deriving from her exotic dreams of Morocco and Tonga. In a happy ending, the Moomins regain the calm of their beautiful valley. The adventure is over, and life can begin again.

The bonds of family and concern for others form the central nucleus of the Moomin world – they are the alpha and omega of the stories. In their search for Moominpappa, love and longing take Moominmamma and Moomintroll through dangers and adventures. The house that Moominpappa built drifts about in the flood like Noah's Ark, and comes to rest in a valley surrounded by hills. The house, the brook, the landscape, the colours and plants – they are all there, just as we encounter them in the later books. The Moomin family of

The Moomins and the Great Flood, cover of the
English edition from 2005. The same cover was
used for the Swedish edition of 1945

father, mother and son move into the blue house that from a distance looks like a tiled stove.

The title of the book's first edition was *Småtrollen och den stora översvämningen* (literally, in English, 'The Little Trolls and the Great Flood'). In 1945 the Moomins were completely unfamiliar to the public. They were thin, with long noses and sometimes even mouths. Yet they were clearly the pale, lovable creatures that the Moomins were later to become. The book contains several whole or half-page washes where the artist skilfully works in black and white, depicting the sea in a raging storm with different shades of grey. On the one hand, Tove emphasizes the sodden greyness of the flood and the steady rain, and on the other, the mighty tree trunks and giant flowers of the jungle-like forest. Unfortunately the printing techniques of the time did not allow her to recreate the sensitive variations of colour that characterize the original paintings and drawings.

Even in this early work, it is plain that the narrative operates on several levels. It is a quality that lies at the basis of all the Moomin books and makes them quite unique in children's literature. It was also the case that some bewildered publishers were unable to conceive of books that might be suitable for both children and adults.

Tove did not see the book as anything particularly special or life-altering, however. In a letter to Eva she declared that she really felt more enthusiasm for the books written by her brothers. At around the same time Per Olov wrote his collection of short stories *Ung man vandrar allena* ('Young Man Wanders Alone') and Lasse his novel *Härskaren* ('The Ruler'). Almost in passing, Tove mentioned that she had written a book she intended to illustrate herself.

Sketch for *The Moomins and the Great Flood*, watercolour, 1940s

IN THE WORLD OF WAR AND ATOM BOMBS –
COMET IN MOOMINLAND

Comet in Moominland (*Kometjakten*, 1946) was also born in the shadow of the war, and is even more closely bound to its time. Although it is not really a war novel, it is a book about great disasters that in many ways resemble military conflict. Tove began it during the Continuation War, but did not illustrate and finish it until the war was over.

Cover for *Comet in Moominland*, 1946

In *Comet in Moominland*, the Moomins continue their encounters with natural forces and disasters, but these are now even more violent, and occur at an even more rapid pace. Like the earlier book, this is also the story of a great journey. The action progresses through familiar landscapes, from the peaceful Moominvalley with its blue Moominhouse, with the scenes of destruction and horror once again echoing the Bible: a comet is rushing towards the earth, threatening to destroy the Moomin world, and with it the world as a whole. As the comet comes closer, the earth heats up and the natural world is turned upside down: the seas recede and dry up, locusts arrive from Egypt and hurricanes rage. Fear is evoked by several narrative devices familiar from children's books, such as an angry octopus, a condor and a poisonous bush. A volcano spits out fire and lava. The book's descriptions of volcanoes originate in Tove's own powerful experiences on Mount Vesuvius a few years earlier. By the time the comet finally crashes to earth the family has moved to a cave that they have insulated from the overheated, red-hot world. Surrounded by thundering, banging and hissing, their life in the cave is unpleasant, and they have no idea of what is happening outside:

> *The whole mountain shook and trembled around them and the comet howled as if terrified, or as if the earth itself was screaming.*
> *They lay still and held on to one another for a long time. From outside came the rolling echo of shattering rocks and soil. Time became dreadfully elongated, and each of them felt they were quite alone.*

These moments of terror are described with a realism that only an author who had experienced something similar could have achieved. During the war Tove was sometimes reluctant to go down to the bomb shelter, and would

Cover sketch for *Comet in Moominland*, watercolour, 1946

TOVE JANSSON

turn!

...et in Moominland. Jacket [Letters in black →

often defy fate by remaining in her studio during air raids. This incautious behaviour may have been linked to her aversion to such shelters, with their darkness, cramped space, overcrowding, and the smell of fear. One of the most problematic aspects of the bomb shelters was their isolation. During heavy air raids it was nerve-racking not to know what was happening outside. If the raids went on for a long time, it was all too easy to believe that everything outside had been destroyed.

The atomic bombs that were dropped on Hiroshima and Nagasaki in 1945 made the prospect of global destruction real. They meant that there was something even worse than what Finland had experienced during its wars. The possibility of global nuclear conflict caused shock, and it affected people all over the world – it was also mirrored in the work of artists and writers.

Much of this had a direct effect on Moominvalley, for Tove was still writing *Comet in Moominland* at the time of the bombing of Hiroshima and Nagasaki. The knowledge that the world could be destroyed by just the push of a button certainly influenced the book. The threat of total annihilation is therefore a major theme and a highly original one in a book for children.

The description of the change in the natural environment reads as though it came from news reports of the nuclear explosions. In the story the air becomes intolerably hot and the sky a fiery red. It looks as though life will not be possible for much longer, and only a cave can save the travelling Moomins. They go deep inside the mountain and stay there, without knowing whether anything of the earth remains. Moominmamma comforts her son and his friends with a lullaby:

> Sleep and dream, wake and forget.
> The night is near and the sky so cold,
> a hundred young lambs go into the fold.

It is wonderful news when they learn that the world has not been destroyed. The evil is in the past and the sky is blue again – the hot, red world was a nightmare that is now over. There is a sense of 'all's well that ends well', of the happy ending that children deserved: 'The sky, the sun and the mountain are still there, she said solemnly. And the sea, Moomintroll whispered.' Snufkin's mouth organ has all its notes again, and he plays it happily. This alludes to how the Finns would feel when the war was over and they were able to continue their lives. While restoring the country to the condition it had enjoyed before the war was harder than the process described in the stories, it was none the less possible.

The Moomins' strong family ties do not prevent them from opening their doors to strangers, however. Because of the Moomins' new bridge, the Muskrat is made home-less and so they feel that perhaps they have a moral duty to take him in. Then they meet Snufkin playing his mouth organ. Snork and the Snork Maiden also come to stay, and in future will become central char-acters – especially, for Moomintroll, the Snork Maiden. The extended family in Moominvalley is now almost complete.

Tove was pleased with her book and proud of it, and she wrote to Atos to tell him how happy she was: building castles in the air was not so stupid, after all. She described herself as 'a proud Moomin screwball'.[7] Her joy received further impetus from the knowledge that her next book had been accepted for publication.

Sketch for *Comet in Moominland*, watercolour, undated

FINN FAMILY MOOMINTROLL

After Tove delivered the manuscript of *Finn Family Moomintroll* (*Trollkarlens hatt*, literally 'The Magician's Hat') to the publisher, Ham happened to be visiting the publisher's office on business of her own. While there, she heard that they liked Tove's book: the lives of the Moomins would continue. The previous publisher had not wanted to publish any more Moomin titles, as the sales of the first two were rather poor. And even the new firm wanted to reduce the number of illustrations in *Finn Family Moomintroll*, and to cut two chapters from it.

7. 'a proud Moomin screwball': the Swedish word *krumelur* (*krumelurska* is its feminine form) means an ornament or curlicue. It has a secondary meaning of 'eccentric' or 'crackpot'.

Tove was quite happy with the book and its illustrations, and thought it was better than the previous one. She sensed a change in herself and believed she had found a new path. Perhaps she was already anticipating that the Moomin world would bring about some tremendous change in her life. *Finn Family Moomintroll* was a watershed, and it secured the future of the Moomin books and the Moomin world.

Finn Family Moomintroll (*Trollkarlens hatt*, 1948) is very different from its two predecessors. Moominvalley is no longer threatened by any major external disaster, and the characters have no need to flee or to hide. The book was written in conditions of peacetime, and perhaps for that reason the author felt that natural disasters were no longer an essential ingredient. Instead, the book describes the tensions between the characters and discusses questions of justice and morality: what is allowed and what is unacceptable? Who is right, who is wrong, and why? Are the concepts of law and morality that prevail in the world really concepts of justice, and what is the true relationship between right and wrong? These are not simple questions for a children's book. But they were matters of which Tove had deep personal experience, and which just at that time had particular relevance for her.

As its original Swedish title says, the book is about a magician's hat. The sudden discovery of the hat leads to a transformation in the creatures and objects that are exposed to its influence: eggshells become small, charming clouds one can ride around on. The hat turns Moomintroll into an ugly little man whom only his mother is able to recognize. Seeds that end up in the hat by mistake begin to grow, and soon the whole house is covered in giant plants, both inside and out. The jungle makes a splendid setting for games of 'Tarzan' in which the roles of Tarzan, Jane and Cheetah the chimpanzee are played by Moomintroll, the Snork Maiden and Snufkin respectively. Snork plays an enemy, and Sniff is Tarzan's son. Meanwhile Moominpappa concentrates on writing his memoirs.

At the time Tove wrote the book she was experiencing an intense phase in her life that brought with it a kind of emotional intoxication. The spectrum of her relationships, sorrows and joys was at its most far-reaching, and her emotions ranged from the most sublime happiness to feelings of anger and frustration. She still loved Atos, though with a love that was now in the process of cooling. But she also had Vivica, and the passion of their relationship and the great disappointment that followed. Then there was Tove's battle with her own occasionally violent negative feelings, a struggle that sometimes wore her out.

Thingumy and Bob with the big ruby. Illustration from *The Magician's Hat*, 1948 (published in English as *Finn Family Moomintroll*, 1956)

Finn Family Moomintroll had three godparents. After Atos and Eva, the third was Vivica, to whom Tove wrote in excitement that the book was finished; she told her about Tofslan and Vifslan (Thingumy and Bob), for whom she and Vivica were the prototypes. Now they were going to embark on adventures in Moominvalley: they would always be together and never be parted.

With Tofslan and Vifslan, the Groke also comes to Moominvalley. Tofslan and Vifslan are small creatures who talk strangely. Some people mistake them for mice, as they are so small and shy. They have brought with them a suitcase that contains a large ruby, an enormous, fiery red jewel they have stolen from the Groke, who is following them and demanding that they return it to her. As her Swedish name *Mårran* (from the Finnish *mörkö* – a bugbear or bogeyman) suggests, the Groke is a ghost who looks spiteful and radiates cold – she does not like anyone and no one likes her. For this reason she is utterly lonely, the personification of fear, malice and depression, and is one of the most contradictory characters in Moominvalley:

> *She sat motionless on the gravel path at the entrance, staring at them with round, expressionless eyes.*
>
> *She was not particularly large and did not look very dangerous either. All one could tell was that she was horribly full of spite and prepared to wait as long as she had to.*
>
> *And that was scary.*
>
> *[...] She continued to sit for a while and then slid away into the darkness of the garden. But where she had sat the ground was frozen.*

The Groke is a threat to the joy of life that forms the most important message in *Finn Family Moomintroll*. She is also the embodiment of fear and rejection.

Moomintroll, Thingumy and Bob. Illustration from *The Magician's Hat*, 1948

What's more, she symbolizes the long arm of the law lying in wait for the ruby – the object of the little creatures' love.

In the book there are also many descriptions of everyday pleasures. In the midst of all the adventures and miracles, Moomintroll is full of *joie de vivre*, and so are his friends: 'Oh to be a Moomin who has just woken up, dancing in glass green waves as the sun is rising!'

For this third Moomin book, Tove hoped to obtain a slightly better financial recompense. She knew exactly how she would spend the money; her dream was to buy a large houseboat in Sipoo. Her plan was that she, Atos and Lasse would be able to spend their summers there. All they lacked was the money to buy the boat, named *Christopher Columbus. Finn Family Moomintroll* was supposed to provide the answer to that problem.

But the book did not solve Tove's financial problems and the houseboat was never purchased. *Finn Family Moomintroll* received glowing reviews and was particularly successful in Stockholm. In Finland, too, it attracted more attention than its predecessor – though it was a long time before the Finnish translation appeared.

THE FIRST MOOMIN PLAY

The international enthusiasm for the Moomins that was sparked by *Finn Family Moomintroll* resulted in quite a hullaballoo and kept the author busy: interviews had to be given, negotiations conducted, rights enquiries answered. People wanted to produce all kinds of 'spin-offs' from the Moomins – everything from ceramic Moomin figures to Moomin films. The Moomin industry had really taken off, though hardly anyone suspected the proportions it would eventually reach.

The Moomins' popularity naturally also drew critical voices. The creatures' improper language and bad behaviour in both the books and the plays caused disapproval. An uncertainty about the intended audience was the main source of confusion. Many thought that a children's book ought to be written for children, and it seemed impossible to conceive that a book could be suitable for both children and grown-ups. A kind of anti-Moomin 'opposition' came into being, aggressively arguing about the poor creatures. And then there was the endless caravanserai of children. As Tove said, it all seemed to be getting quite out of control. To judge from her letters to Eva at this time, Tove found her incipient fame rather hard to cope with, especially the debates about the purpose of the

Tove on the opening night of the Moomin play, 1949

Moomins and the behaviour that might be appropriate for the 'poor trolls'. She had to explain repeatedly that the Moomins had no particular message or moral, and that they were not intended as educational models. She wrote that some critics claimed she was quite simply undermining children's morality. Though this did not seem to trouble her.

After conquering the world of books and picture books, the Moomins began to make waves in the theatre. Vivica had written to Tove in Brittany suggesting that they should stage a Moomin play at Helsinki's Svenska Teater. Tove was enthusiastic about this 'bold Moomin idea' – why should it not be possible to present the Moomins in the same way as *Sleeping Beauty*? She immediately began to plan the scenery, which ranged from a sky turned red by the comet to a radiant, Van Gogh-inspired sun in the bright blue heavens. In 1949 the play was presented at Svenska Teater. It was based on *Comet in Moominland*, and the script and set design were by Tove.

At first the theatre management was reluctant to include the play in its repertoire, as it was thought to be unsuitable for children. A children's play was supposed to follow a simple, traditional plot. It should not function on different levels, at least not levels of a kind that only adults could follow. The play's subject was also not to the management's taste. A theatrical production about the end of the world was too reminiscent of the recent atomic bombs and the horrors they had wrought. This was the crucial issue, and it was thought that perhaps children did not need to know about such things. Yet, largely thanks to Vivica, the play was performed. Its premiere took place on Holy Innocents' Day, 28 December 1949.

The play divided the audience. Some were horrified at the way the Moomins lived: they smoked and drank wine, and their language was colourful and sometimes risqué. They did all sorts of things that young children were not supposed to see and about which they ought to have been warned. In the opinion columns of the Swedish-language daily *Hufvudstadsbladet*, a lively debate took place. Some readers thought they had heard stronger language than was actually the case, they got things mixed up and misheard the dialogue. Parents wanted their children to see traditional princes and princesses, not prophets who drank spiced mulled wine. And so the author was obliged to defend herself.

Although the play was controversial, in the end it was a great success and there were soon requests for it to be performed in Stockholm and elsewhere in the Nordic countries. Tove agreed to this on condition that Vivica Bandler was the director. Vivica has described how she decided that the Moomins should speak Swedish in the Finland-Swedish way, exactly as it was spoken in Helsinki. In Stockholm, Finland-Swedish became identified as the Moomins' 'mother tongue'.

Producing the play was a demanding task. The days were long and the rehearsals tiring. By her own admission, Tove was completely exhausted. The working days often stretched to twelve hours, yet the pressure never let up. There was not even time for proper meals. In spite of everything, Tove loved working in the theatre, where she encountered a varied assortment of people and experienced the true intensity of the theatre world. She found the work fascinating and stimulating, and wrote to Eva that Vivica was a perfectly wonderful director. At the back of her mind was the knowledge that it could all either work out splendidly or go completely haywire. Such uncertainty was exciting, and therein lay its charm. For Tove, the potential for disaster was electrifying, it was a state of mind that she thrived on, and in the theatre it had a concrete and permanent presence.

When – after the play was finished – she returned to her studio to paint her 'old *natures mortes*', she longed to be back in the hectic world of the theatre. But painting was what mattered most to her, and it was what she really considered to be her life's work. Everything else was either a pastime to overcome fear and depression, or bread-and-butter work, however welcome that might be. She was glad to be able to write about the Moomins and draw them, and not need to worry about having to design sickly-sweet Mother's Day cards and other trivial tasks.

Yet money continued to be chronically tight. At first, not even the Moomin books brought anything in, and the flow of royalties from abroad was a mere trickle. But she stressed how glad she was that publishers had agreed to produce the books and that people had liked them. In 1951 she wrote to Eva that the largest sum she had received for a Moomin book was 30,000 Finnish marks, and of that, 30 per cent had gone on tax. The rent on the studio alone was 6,500 marks a month. On such a basis, the income from a Moomin book would pay only a few months' rent. Tove received no grants or stipends, and explained this by saying that those who allocated them thought she was rich – which was probably true, as many people had unrealistic ideas about the supposedly large amounts of money to be made from children's books and illustrations.

The Exploits of Moominpappa was later retitled *Moominpappa's Memoirs* (*Mumin-pappans memoarer*). The book first appeared in 1950. Moominpappa had begun to write his memoirs in *Finn Family Moomintroll* and in the new book he reads them in their completed version. The point of this appears to be to demonstrate how talented he is and how little understanding he has received. He is developed into a hero on whose exploits the book directs its focus. He is treated lovingly and with tender irony, as a brave and manly figure who is also an all-round genius. Even as a child, the alignment of his stars marks him out as a supremely gifted – though difficult – Moomin. His childhood has been bleak: as an infant he was left at the door of a foundling hospital, wrapped in a newspaper, frozen and all alone. His life in the loveless orphanage described in the story is presented as the worst thing that can happen to a child – it is uninspiring, strict, soul-destroying. Moominpappa recalls it in all of its dreadfulness:

> *Dear reader, imagine a Moominhouse where all the rooms are arranged in neat rows – rectangular rooms all painted the same pilsner brown. [. . .] A Moominhouse is supposed to be full of the most surprising corners and secret chambers, staircases, balconies and turrets [. . .] And even worse, no one was allowed to get up at night to eat, talk or go for a walk.*

He therefore runs away and embarks on a life full of adventure, the final climax of which is his return to Moominvalley and the Moomin family. Only there does he become Moominpappa: 'It's my garden and my veranda, and my family who are sleeping in the house.'

While Moominpappa is still a runaway, he builds a house for the first time. It is very similar to the later Moominhouse – tall and tower-like, from a distance resembling a tiled stove. With the help of Fredrikson the shipwright he puts the house on a boat and launches it so they can sail the seas in a houseboat.

It was while she was in the process of writing *Finn Family Moomintroll* that Tove decided to buy a houseboat, the *Christopher Columbus*, but it remained no more than a dream. So Moominpappa gets the boat instead. Named *Haffsårkestern* (literally, 'the ocean orchestra'), it takes him on incredible adventures – he encounters an immense storm and finally descends to the bottom of the sea where he is surrounded by strange fish and other creatures. While Tove wrote *Moominpappa's Memoirs*, she was planning her move to Tonga with Lasse, though they never got there. Once again, Moominpappa does better. He founds his colony on 'a rather large island shaped like a heart'.

In *Moominpappa's Memoirs* the gallery of Moominvalley characters is completed, especially with the addition of Little My, who is born on Midsummer's Eve. Not only does the sea bring Moominpappa adventure, joy and fear – it also gives him the one who matters most to him. Moominmamma enters his life like Aphrodite from the waves. A gigantic, roaring storm hurls her towards the shore, where she is rescued by the heroic Moominpappa. Even her handbag is intact, despite being tossed about in the surf and swell, she has not let go of it for a moment. The handbag is an integral part of her, containing all the things she will later use to take charge of those nearest to her, and to help them. These items provide a great deal of the building material for the emerging Moomin world – and make a significant contribution.

WHO'S WHO

Over the passage of the years, the Moomins, like human beings, changed in personality and looks, though they never became unrecognizable. Elements of Tove are present in every creature she created for the Moomin world. She is there in Snufkin's longing for peace and quiet and a place of his own, as well as in his love of nature. There are traits of her personality in the Hemulens' conscientiousness and devotion to hard work, in the Fillyjonk's endless longing and in Misabel's infinite sorrow. Every reader can identify with the Groke's desperate attempts at intimacy, especially at times when life does not go as it should and one feels that one's friends are moving away. Or readers can see their own fears embodied in the figure of the Groke.

Tove often said that Moominmamma was modelled on Ham. As in Tove's own family, the mother is the source and essence of warmth and safety. Her descriptions of the two mothers carving bark boats with a penknife on the veranda in summer bear many similarities. Both of them have the same warm and tolerant philosophy of life. They look after the people around them, and their love and compassion are inexhaustible and superabundant. Both mothers are resourceful, whether in dealing with nature, curing colds or coping with great sorrow.

Both mothers also have difficult relationships with men. They have to show understanding to husbands who do not necessarily take account of their feelings. In Signe Hammarsten-Jansson's life there was something very akin to Moominmamma's happiness and longing in *Moominpappa at Sea* (*Muminpappa och havet*, 1965). The book tells the story of Moominpappa's plan to move to a lighthouse island without giving much consideration to the wishes of the rest of the family. Mainly because of his own frustration, he takes them to a barren island where Moominmamma misses her home and escapes from her homesickness by painting the landscapes and flowers of her beloved Moominvalley. She can hide in those landscapes at will, find peace there, alone and content, even though they are only representations. Homesickness was also a feeling with which Ham was well acquainted.

Tove often said that Moomintroll was her alter ego. His early name was Snork, and in the Moomin world he became Moomintroll. Tove often drew this small creature in her letters and as an addition to her signature on the cover illustrations she designed for *Garm*. He was also frequently included in

Illustration from Moominsummer Madness, 1954

her monumental paintings, such as the Helsinki City Hall frescos and the Hamina mural. She also drew Moomintroll on the flag on the island of Bredskär.

Although Moomintroll may not be the quaintest or most colourful of Moominvalley's inhabitants, he is its central figure: everyone is related to him. Together, the son, mother and father form the founding cell of the Moomin family, a unit that is continually joined by new members.

Tove also comprised a good deal of Little

My, a character who does not mince her words, and whose sharp tongue often speaks the truth. Many of Tove's 'Little My' qualities are displayed in the drawings and texts she produced for the *Garm* cover illustrations, many of which made fun of life's commonly accepted truths and portrayed serious subjects with satirical humour of a kind she thoroughly relished. It has been said that the impulsive personality and creative intellect of Tove's close friend Eva Wichman may have influenced the creation of Little My, though the character also shows traits of her friend and lover Putte Foch.

Little My always says everything that's on her mind, even things that no one really wants to hear, but that are true and often made better for having been said. She is very eccentric – cheerful, angry, slightly mischievous and sometimes malicious, for example when she bites others on the leg or tail and then has a good laugh about it. She plays tricks, cracks jokes, and in many ways resembles the dwarfs and court jesters of former times. Truly tiny, she measures only one thousandth of a millimetre – so small one needs a magnifying glass to see her.

Little My is the best loved of all the characters in Moominvalley – something that says a good deal about the books' readers, for she is a little scamp. Of Little My's essential role, Tove said: 'She is very practical and helpful, you see. I needed something to put against the Moomin family's helpless sensitivity. If you removed her there would just be endless whining.'

In the Moomin community Little My is an indispensable counterweight to the other creatures, most of whom are invariably polite, kind and understanding. Her aggressive nature is liberating in a way, and represents something that everyone, including *The Invisible Child*, needs in order to be visible. You need to dare to be angry in order to truly exist, to be yourself among other creatures who are at once good and bad.

Illustration from *Moominland Midwinter*, 1957

Tofslan and Vifslan (who play the roles of Tove and Vivica) talk a lovers' language others find quite hard to understand. They always want to be together; they speak with a single voice and retreat into each other's company. They sleep in Moominmamma's handbag or in a drawer of the bureau, and prove that love is superior to notions of right and wrong. Love's glowing ruby belongs to those who give it the highest value, not to those for whom it is merely an item of exchange.

In the later books, Moomintroll's status as the author's alter ego is much more elusive. In the last book in the series, the Whomper Toft is both listener and narrator. He 'began to tell himself a strange story. It was about the happy family.' Toft's name looks a bit like 'Tove', and Tove often signed her pictures with the series' other Tove-like name – 'Tofslan'.

Although Toft, like Moomintroll, is male, he could easily pass for a little girl. In Moominvalley the differences between the sexes do not seem to be important. Indeed, with his short, fair hair Toft resembles Tove. He lives underneath

Toft and the tent. Illustration from *Moominvalley in November*, 1970

a boat, enjoys its tarry smell, misses Moominmamma and sometimes loses hope when he is afraid: 'The family doesn't exist anymore [...]. They've tricked me.'

In *Who Will Comfort Toffle?* (*Vem ska trösta knyttet?*, 1960), Toffle is joined by Miffle (*Skruttet* – sometimes translated as 'the little creep'). She too is small, shy and timid – qualities that Tove identified as her own. Tove often said that Miffle was one of her self-portraits.

The Groke has sometimes been interpreted as the darker side of the eternally sweet-natured Moominmamma. Some have speculated that her prototype may have been the critic and author Hagar Olsson, perhaps because of Olsson's dark and uncompromising vision of the culture and epoch in which she lived.

The Fillyjonk and the storm. Illustration from 'The Invisible Child', 1962 (published in English as *Tales from Moominvalley*)

The Groke introduces tension and a much-needed negative energy to the stories' descriptions of hours in the sunshine. Tove said that whenever she let the Groke get warm she found it impossible to write about Moominvalley. Who, then, is the Groke? She is no one and everyone. She represents the unhappiness and loneliness of the reader and author, or perhaps the cruel and wicked part of their nature. She exists inside people, and cannot be avoided. She bides her time.

Everywhere around us the world is swarming with Hemulens. They are teachers, officials, park-keepers and representatives of law and order. They bustle and organize and give instructions. They worry about the rest of us, because 'wherever he looked there was something to put right and he toiled his guts out to make them understand how they ought to arrange things'. A Hemulen's lot is not always a very happy one. Sometimes they are large and awkward, and look ridiculous. They are not very loving or lovable creatures. Tove herself had many of the Hemulens' personality traits. She kept a strict record of all her commissions, sales and receipts. With her clients she was careful, exact and reliable to the point of emotional strain. She obsessively kept notes on the events in her life, stored the information in archives and used it whenever the time was ripe.

The Fillyjonk lives with constant anxiety, an inborn fear that tortures her. For her the most important thing is orderliness, and she loves cleaning and tidying more than anything else in the world: 'How would I be able to live without cleaning and cooking? Nothing else is worth doing.' In the end she faces the calamity. 'Now it's happening. Now everything is going wrong. At last. Now I don't need to wait any more.' She is afraid of fear, but facing up to what she fears is liberating: 'Now I shall never be afraid again, she said to herself. Now I'm completely free. Now I'll enjoy anything.'

Too-ticky came into being in the book *Moominland Midwinter* (*Trollvinter*), which appeared in Swedish in 1957. At that time Tove's relationship with Tuulikki Pietilä was just beginning – it would span nearly five decades. It is easy to recognize Tuulikki as the model for Too-ticky by her appearance. Her personality is not split between several different characters in Moominvalley, but is represented by a single figure, in the same way that Ham is represented by Moominmamma. Although Too-ticky looks very masculine, she is always referred to as 'she'. She is wise, intelligent and practical – she knows how to carve, cook and fish.

The Hattifatteners are also inhabitants of Moominvalley and have been seen as representing the valley's sexual energy. The Hattifatteners are captivating but strange and slightly intimidating creatures. During thunderstorms they are electrified and really come alive and start multiplying. They also burn if they are touched. This electrification has been seen as a reference to unrestrained sexual desire, an interpretation that is supported by their appearance – they resemble penises or condoms. Their phallic world fascinates and entices Moominpappa like a force of nature, and he leaves his family and joins them. With his love of the sea, gales and thunderstorms, Moominpappa bears many resemblances to Tove's father, Faffan. Although Faffan did not sail away with the Hattifatteners, he would often disappear into the Helsinki night.

The Mymble is a wonderful female archetype, and she is the feminine opposite of the Hattifatteners. The name derives from the Swedish slang word *mymla*, meaning 'to [make] love'. The Mymble of Moominvalley is gentle, round and womanly, and she is very polygamous. She has around twenty children by different husbands, and one of the children is Little My. By nature, the Mymble is narcissistic and good-humoured. Her priorities are to enjoy life and be content, to sleep when she feels like it and wake up when it is worth the trouble: 'There

Snufkin. Drawing for a production at the
Dramaten Theatre, Stockholm, early 1980s

Snusmumriken.
pipa
ryggsäck
knappkänga
munharmonika
Hans kläder är medfarna
och inte helt rena, trasiga
i kanten, av något luvigt,
billigt material. Intrycket
ska vara hemtrevligt och
nonchalant.
Fjädern av en vild fågel.

muskamuikkunen
Snufkin

Tove

mintroll i kulisserna'   Snusmumriken

Illustration for *Comet in Moominland*, 1946

is nothing more pleasant than enjoying oneself, and nothing more simple.' Like the Hattifatteners, the Mymble can become electric.

Snufkin was born when Tove and Atos had their affair. Snufkin is the Moomins' non-Moomin – a human character. In his way of life there is much that recalls Atos, as well as Tove herself. Her brother Lars was also a spiritual prototype of this figure. On the outside Snufkin is obviously Atos. Both have a large, broad smile, often with a pipe in the corner of their mouth, and they both wear a wide-brimmed hat with a feather. Snufkin often has a rucksack on his back – just like Atos, he is forever on the move.

One distant relation of Snufkin may be Charlie Chaplin in the role of 'The Tramp', with his hat, his shabby clothes, his trousers that are too short and shoes that are too large. Both characters are lonely, well-meaning individuals, but while Chaplin's Tramp is miserable, arousing our sympathy in his efforts to escape his loneliness, Snufkin is active and unafraid, drawing our admiration for his self-sufficiency. Tove considered Snufkin's loneliness to be a positive thing, with its negative counterpart in the Fillyjonk's loneliness, which was 'fatal'. Snufkin's isolation is not the unhappy plight of the marginalized – it is something he has chosen for himself. He is neither responsible for anyone nor dependent on them; he has no particular attachments and does not want anyone else to rely on him. He is free – or apparently so.

Through Snufkin, Tove examined freedom from different points of view, especially the way in which people are fettered by great emotions. Snufkin says that if one admires someone else one cannot be free. His longing for freedom causes Moomintroll a great deal of pain and melancholy. Admiration and love therefore become very contradictory emotions. Complete freedom negates life's most powerful feelings, such as love, longing, anger, and even admiration, when it is deep and unconditional. The relationship between Moomintroll and Snufkin is very similar to that between Atos and Tove. Snufkin comes and goes, and Moomintroll experiences the same feelings the author experienced at the time she was writing the book, as she waited for Atos and those longed-for words of love and commitment – precisely what Snufkin is unable to give Moomintroll. Although Atos was the centre of Tove's life, his own life had many 'centres'. For his partner this led to feelings of loneliness, regret and longing.

The summer plans of Snufkin and Moomintroll may bear quite a close resemblance to the type of arrangement that existed between Atos and Tove. In summer, Atos would go his own way, and usually by himself:

I have a plan. But it's one of those lonely ones, you know.

Moomintroll looked at him for a very long time. Then he said: You're going away.

Snufkin nodded [. . .].

When do you leave? asked Moomintroll.

Right now! said Snufkin, and he threw all the reed boats into the water at once. He jumped down from the bridge and sniffed the morning air. It was a nice day for walking.

[. . .]

Will you be gone long? Moomintroll asked.

No, said Snufkin. I'll be back on the first day of spring, and I'll whistle under the window. A year goes by so fast!

Moomintroll understands Snufkin and his longing for freedom very well, even though the waiting is not easy. Like many other people who lived through the war, Tove was used to waiting. Fiancés, boyfriends, husbands, brothers and friends were engaged in the fighting, and other people had moved away, all in different directions. Women waited for their menfolk to come home on leave or for news of their death; they waited for the war to end and for peace to be declared. A person who was waiting could never be free: their longing became a sort of mental prison. Although she was accustomed to it, Tove found the waiting deeply wearing:

> *Moomintroll, who waited and yearned so terribly. Who sat there at home, waiting and admiring, and who said: Of course you should be free. It's obvious that you need to go away. And I understand that you have to be alone sometimes.*
>
> *And at the same time Moomintroll's eyes were dark with disappointment and helpless longing.*

Tove sometimes grew tired of Atos's countless ventures and his deep involvement in the study of Nietzsche. She hoped he would soon finish the book about the philosopher, as she believed such excessive admiration was severely narrowing his horizons. Such an attachment could also begin to feel like a millstone, just as Moomintroll's love feels to Snufkin. Once the idealized freedom is achieved, the feelings no longer cause trouble:

> *One never becomes completely free if one admires someone too much, Snufkin said quickly. That's something I know.*

Illustration for *Moominvalley in November*, 1970

The Muskrat. Illustration from *The Magician's Hat*, 1948

[...] When Moomintroll woke up from his winter sleep, he immediately began to long for you ... Isn't it nice to have someone to long for you and spend all their time waiting for you?

I'll come when it suits me, Snufkin snapped. Perhaps I won't come at all. Perhaps I'll go somewhere else.

Oh, then he will be sad, said the creep.

Although Tove's love for Atos had lost its freshness, and the radiance that was so important to her had faded, their friendship survived to the end. The relationship between Moomintroll and Snufkin also resembles the kind of deep bond that can follow a love affair. Can there be any farewell to a friend more beautiful than this, as Snufkin sets off once again?

Then Moomintroll got up on a chair and said:

Now I raise a toast to Snufkin, who is tonight hiking south – alone, but certainly as happy as we are. Let us wish him a light heart and a good place for his tent!

When she was with friends, Tove sometimes called Atos 'The Musketeer', after the character in Alexandre Dumas' novel *The Three Musketeers*. More often, however, she referred to him affectionately as 'The Philosopher', 'The Cosmosopher',

'Polysoph', or just 'Soph'. She also called him 'The Muskrat'. In the Moomin world, the Muskrat is the other unmistakable portrait of Atos Wirtanen, not so much by external appearance as by nature. The Muskrat is a philosopher and thinker. He is a little clumsy and unpractical, as Atos was.

The world of the Hattifatteners has many of the features of the lifestyle to which Atos aspired. His desire to subdue his private emotions and live 'objectively' may have had an influence on the Hattifatteners' nature. Moominpappa broods about these creatures who sail the seas and from whom all the feelings that cause sorrow, longing and regret have been washed away. Tove examined the consequences of such a life choice in her short story 'The Hattifatteners' Secret':

Imagine never being able to be happy or disappointed [. . .] Never being able to like anyone or be angry with them or forgive them. Not be able to sleep or feel cold, never make a mistake or have a sore stomach and recover from it, never celebrate one's birthday, drink beer or have a bad conscience . . .

THE MOOMINS FIND THEIR READERS

The early Moomin books received positive reviews in the Finland-Swedish publications *Västra Nyland*, *Nya Pressen* and *Arbetarbladet*. *Finn Family Moomintroll* was the first Moomin book to gain wide popularity – it was a breakthrough. Generally, translations of the Moomin books into Finnish had to wait a long time. The language barrier was a real obstacle, and the Finnish publishers were unbelievably slow. There were willing translators, however. The author Jarno Pennanen would have liked to translate the books for the Finnish publisher Otava, and he suggested this to Tove. He was certainly qualified and more than competent for the task. He had experience in the field of children's literature and under the direction of Professor Martti Haavio he had edited Finnish folk tales from the archives of the Finnish Literature Society and had even been granted permission to continue the work during his time in prison as a political detainee. The translation of the Moomin books into Finnish did not begin until they had already achieved success in Sweden and Britain. In Britain the first Moomin book was published in 1950 with the title *Finn Family Moomintroll*, and the following year it appeared in the United States as *The Happy Moomins*.

So long did it take for the books to become available in Finnish that *The Moomins and the Great Flood* (*Småtrollen och den stora översvämningen*, 1945) was not translated into Finnish until 1991. *Comet in Moominland* (*Kometjakten*,

1946) appeared *as Muumipeikko ja pyrstotähti* in 1955, nine years after its publication in Swedish. *Finn Family Moomintroll (Trollkarlens hatt,* 1948) was published in Finnish as *Taikurin hattu* in 1956, with a delay of eight years. *The Exploits of Moominpappa (Muminpappans bravader,* 1950) appeared in Finnish as *Muumipappan urotyöt* in 1963 – a whole thirteen years after the Swedish-language original.

The first Moomin picture book, *The Book about Moomin, Mymble and Little My (Hur gick det sen? Boken om Mymlan, Mumintrollet och lilla My,* 1952), was the first to appear in both Finnish and Swedish in the same year. It can be seen as the start of the Moomins' conquest of the Finnish-speaking public. *Moominsummer Madness (Farlig midsommar,* 1954) appeared in Finnish three years after the Swedish-language edition. *The Invisible Child (Det osynliga barnet)* was published in 1962 and *Moominpappa at Sea (Muuminpappa och havet)* in 1965, and they both appeared in Swedish and Finnish in those respective years. The Swedish-language books were published simultaneously in Finland and Sweden, except for *Comet in Moominland (Kometen kommer)* and *Finn Family Moomintroll (Trollkarlens hatt),* each of which appeared in Sweden one year later than in Finland. Not until the mid-1950s, when they made a tentative breakthrough to the Finnish-language book market, did the Moomins become familiar to Finnish-speaking readers from more than one book. By then the books had already been published in English and the comic strip series was syndicated in the world press in various languages. Readers of Finnish were very late in becoming acquainted with the work of an author who had practically conquered the rest of the world.

The reasons for this slow acceptance may possibly lie in the children's literature of the time. The most popular post-war Finnish-language children's book was *Pessi and Illusia (Pessi ja Illusia),* which Yrjö Kokko wrote at the front in 1944. It sold an enormous number of copies, more than 40,000, and in 1945 received the Finnish State Literature Prize. In the Finnish market, the Moomins were totally eclipsed by *Pessi and Illusia.* In 1952 the Finnish National Opera staged a theatrical adaptation of the book, and Tove was asked to design the costumes for it. She accepted the commission, but fell out badly with Kokko, who at the last minute demanded major changes of a 'national' kind. So deep were their disagreements that Tove wanted her name removed from the programme entirely. In the end, the show included some of Kokko's rather crudely nationalistic costumes and some of Tove's sensitive and cultivated ones. The final result was a curious one, and did not appeal to many in the audience.

V

Towards Fame

1950S MODERNISM

The war and the years of deprivation ended with the economic boom of the 1950s. In 1952 Finland paid the final instalment of its heavy war reparations to the Soviet Union. Then it became possible to start improving the well-being of the country's own citizens. The new, partial recovery was characterized by optimism and reconstruction. With the 1952 Summer Olympics being held in Helsinki, Finland acquired a more international, urban image. For the first time, the Finnish capital witnessed the arrival of people from many different ethnic backgrounds, and they were the source of much wonder and admiration. The buildings were repaired and new ones constructed to replace those that had been destroyed in the war. Architectural treasures were restored and the city's profile tidied up. For the Olympics, a new airport was built, with direct flights from various European cities. Finland was now to be seen as a prosperous Western country. Whereas in the past it was possible that the physical attributes of the Finns had not been sufficiently appreciated, leading to a certain sense of inferiority, Finnish identity received a considerable boost when Armi Kuusela was elected Miss Universe.

Although life was not entirely back to normal, it was at least improved. The supply of food was adequate and the shops were full of goods – people could even afford luxuries. The arrival of Coca-Cola was a sign of increased prosperity and internationalism and Finland's image was rapidly changing, especially to the outside world. On the inside, however, the damage inflicted by the war had left a deep wound in the national psyche, and there was a reluctance to air those issues in public debate. Silence was a solution to the pervasive sense of anguish, and people hurried to focus on the future. In the world at large the Cold War still persisted, and Europe was now divided by the Iron Curtain, its existence having a major influence on artistic life in Finland.

Tove working on a mural at the Aurora Children's Hospital, 1955–6

Once again Finland's artistic community opened its windows on Europe. The spiritual vacuum engendered by the war and the subsequent years of austerity was now filled as Finnish culture strove to align itself with modern Western thinking and artistic trends. At the same time, a conservative, nationalistic, aesthetic view of art also proved to be very robust. The period was characterized by division.

The 1950s have been called the golden decade of Finnish literature, and not without reason. The literary world was a swarming, seething microcosm, where the various political camps and literary standpoints, both modern and traditional, confronted one another. Many of the most important names in Finnish literature emerged at this time, and they sought new ways of expressing themselves; they included Marja-Liisa Vartio, Tuomas Anhava, Veijo Meri, Jouko Tyyri, Antti Hyry, Paavo Rintala, Paavo Haavikko, Lassi Nummi, Pentti Holappa and Eeva-Liisa Manner. Of the older generation of writers, Mika Waltari, Juha Mannerkorpi, Lauri Viita, Marko Tapio and Väinö Linna were still active. Modernism was extremely controversial, with the new poetry forming one particular focal point of discussion. Linna's novel *The Unknown Soldier* (*Tuntematon sotilas*) appeared in 1954. It gave rise to national soul-searching as well as a heated debate about the war, conditions at the front and the everyday lives of the soldiers.

This decade was also the golden age of Finnish design. Finnish glassware gained international fame, and the glass artists Timo Sarpaneva and Tapio Wirkkala were hailed as geniuses. The ceramic art of Rut Bryk and Kaj Franck, Armi Ratia's Marimekko with fabrics by Maija Isola, and the furniture of Alvar Aalto, distributed by Artek, won glory and renown beyond Finland's borders. Design was a guiding star for a country rising from austerity and it gave an important boost to the self-esteem that had been lost in the war. It also embraced graphic art, of which Tove Jansson's drawings were one example.

In the visual arts, the 1950s were characterized by enormous inspiration, but also by artistic disputes. Artists were increasingly able to travel to the centres of the art world, of which Paris was the most important. Visiting exhibitions reached Finland from abroad, each more important than the last. Previously not much abstract art had been produced in Finland, but now it was gaining a foothold. Tove's friends Sam Vanni and Birger Carlstedt were among the first Finnish artists to be interested in non-figurative painting. Carlstedt had already experimented with abstract work in the 1930s, but for a long time he continued to paint in a figurative style. Sam Vanni had been inspired by abstract art during his visits to Paris in the 1940s and 50s. Nearly all the works in his 1953 Artek exhibition were non-figurative, and the same was true of the show he put on two years later. The first exhibition raised some eyebrows. Although he was highly respected and had long been a favourite of the critics, he now received a very guarded welcome. E. J. Vehmas, the most influential art critic of the time, wrote a review of Vanni's abstract paintings in which he recalled his past talent in tones of condolence – Vanni himself likened it to an obituary. In spite of such resistance to change, or perhaps because of it, in the late 1950s an increasing number of exhibitions included works of abstract art, and the young students at the Athenaeum began to show an interest in the genre. In his role of teacher, Vanni was also one of the movement's most important standard-bearers, and it was from among his students that most of the prominent abstract artists of the next generation emerged.

In Finland's post-war art world, the most controversial and significant event was the Klar Form exhibition held at Kunsthalle Helsinki in early 1952. The exhibition came from Paris, and it opened an entirely new period of development in the Finnish art scene. Its importance is hard to over-estimate. It included works by Victor Vasarely and several other leading practitioners of Concretism. Non-figurative art now entered the public consciousness and inspired the younger generation of artists.

The question of whether art should be representational or non-representational was the central issue of the time and divided Finland's artistic community for decades. Many of the Finland-Swedish artists of Tove's generation belonged to the advance guard that led the revival of Finnish art in the 1950s. The first generation of abstract artists was composed almost entirely of Swedish-speakers and Finland's Swedish-language press generally showed more acceptance of the new art than its Finnish-language counterpart. In fact the Swedish-speaking critics were more at home with the terminology that the new art demanded, as they had been able to follow developments in the Nordic countries, particularly through the art criticism that was published in Sweden. For these journalists and critics the war years had not been the vacuum that they had for the Finnish-speaking critics, who suddenly found themselves called upon to judge abstract art without much warning, and as a result had problems commenting on what they saw and in following the new movements.

The Finnish public, meanwhile, formed its own opinion of abstract art, and expressed it with gusto. It was widely discussed in the newspapers, and critics considered whether it contained any love or emotion at all. The general consensus was that abstract art was empty and that 'all these ugly things are not rendered beautiful by the mere fact that they come from Paris'. Journalists wrote dismissive reviews of exhibitions, and satirical cartoons even appeared in the press. Tove herself drew some of them.

She did, however, show some enthusiasm for the abstract works in the 'Klar Form' exhibition. She thought it 'fantastic', though with some reservations. Eva had written to her about a Matisse exhibition she had visited in the United States, and Tove's response had been to sigh that she would rather have seen the Matisse. Although she understood 'Klar Form''s general significance, the works on display did not alter her artistic ideals. Matisse had been a crucial and much-loved role model for her, and also for Vanni. While Vanni now began to admire the abstract idiom of Vasarely, Tove did not.

RESTRAINED AMONG ENTHUSIASTS

Tove's attitude to the abstract art in Klar Form was typical of her attitude to art in general, and this was a harbinger of her future career as a visual artist. Tove wanted to hold on to traditional values, to what her father and art school training had taught her. Although the new art interested her, she did not take to it in her own work. By nature reserved and cautious, she preferred to keep her distance or circumvent the new art altogether, and to continue to follow the path that suited her.

Tove had also kept her distance from Surrealism and Existentialism, not to mention Socialist Realism. Over the years she had stated her desire to be a *'l'art pour l'art'* artist, and now she did so again – though it was ironic that this very label was being used in Finland to describe Abstractionism, which was regarded as being devoid of content, pointless: art for art's sake.

Tove called her art 'asocial', meaning that it was not tied to social reality. At the same time she repeatedly emphasized that she was an individualist. Popular fads did not appeal to her, and to some extent she found herself on the defensive. The assertion of her own individuality and freedom of choice may have been one of the factors that kept her from embracing the new ideas, which she seems to have rejected almost before being acquainted with them. Her respect for art and its long traditions meant that she found it hard to suddenly break with those traditions. Her father had taught her that one could make fun of anything except art – it was too serious a matter.

When in the early 1950s her close artist friends, particularly Sam Vanni, made the transition to an abstract style of painting, Tove was mystified: 'Just when I thought he was so good, he suddenly began to paint some kind of spiky stuff.'

The work of many or all of the Finnish artists who took up abstract art suffered a deterioration in quality right from the outset. They had more or less to throw away the techniques they had already learned and adopted. In the face of the new artistic trends, they were rather helpless, and their enthusiasm for it could not make up for missing skill. By comparison with their earlier productions, the first abstract works of artists like Ernst Mether-Borgström, Lars-Gunnar Nordström, and to some extent also Vanni, were rather thin. In order to develop, these artists needed time, strong willpower and trust in their own abilities.

Many of Tove's artist friends, like Vanni, Carlstedt, Rolf Sandqvist and Anitra Lucander, were interested in abstract art. It would have been easy for her, even expected, to be carried along by their enthusiasm. But there were clearly stronger forces that quelled any desire to take part in this crusade. Most of the artists at the Artek gallery directed by Maire Gullichsen were young and interested in the new experimental movement – and Tove could have joined them. It must have been distressing for her to realize that she had ended up outside the circle of artists who had been closest to her.

It is possible that she felt ambivalent about her own art, and that her emphasis on independence may have been a result of that uncertainty. One sign that this was so can be detected in her reliance on the approval of those around her, above all her father. Her admiration for him, her need for his acceptance and respect, was a part of this cautiousness and it could be restricting. By nature she was, after all, intelligent and witty, fond of satire, parody and humour. All of this can be seen in her books and illustrations, but in her paintings there is no trace of it.

NOT FOR ART BUT FOR LIFE

For Finnish artists, Paris was a crucial influence on their work. The busiest period of the Paris years was the late 1940s, when travel became possible again, though the enthusiasm for the art of the French capital lasted into the 1950s. Nordic artists sought one another out in Paris and Finland's Swedish-speaking artists in particular benefited from the experience and skill of their Scandinavian colleagues who had lived there longer. At the end of the decade the range of influences began to fragment and abstract art came to be dominated by Informalism, which was centred more in Italy.

Soggiorno, drawing, 1951. Vivica and Tove, who are always followed by
the Moomin characters, even to a hotel reception desk in Italy

Uca av Tove. "Soggiorno."

Unlike so many other Finnish artists, Tove did not undertake the artistic pilgrimage to Paris in the late 1940s and early 1950s. While money worries, a bank loan and work did much to keep her in her own country, those cannot have been the only reasons, as during the same period she did spend time in Italy and then Brittany, working hard at her painting there. The group spirit among artists and their enthusiasm for new ideas and exhibitions had not yet reached Italy, and it would not have been possible for her to come into contact with it on very brief excursions to Paris.

In 1951 Tove took a long trip to Italy, North Africa and Paris with Vivica. The trip was planned mainly for recreation and adventure, and she got both. The travellers lived life intensely and walked about the towns and cities to the point of exhaustion. That Tove had the Moomin world in her thoughts at the time can be seen from the many drawings she made during the trip. Her relationship with Vivica was going well, and with all its experiences she saw the journey as a 'horn of plenty'. Instead of visiting art galleries and museums, she sought out nightclub life until she was sick of it – or so she wrote to Atos. Tuulikki Pietilä was in Paris at the same time, and Vivica and Tove met her by chance at one of the city's countless nightclubs. But visual art did not take up much of the travellers' time: in its place their experiences provided many new themes for future books and also for the Moomin comic series.

It was plain that Tove had no interest in settling down in Paris like the other Nordic artists, even though she would have been well able to do so. She was now, of necessity, spending more time on writing and drawing than on paint-ing – especially on the Moomin books. In 1954 she travelled with her mother via London and Paris to the French Riviera. She wrote about her stay there in the comic series *Moomin on the Riviera* and in the short story 'Journey to the Riviera'. Both she and her mother had long dreamed of making the trip, which was made possible by scholarship grants and the fee for a mural commissioned by the Nordic Union Bank. Now retired, Ham was no longer bound by a regular work schedule. The trip was first and foremost a shared holiday for mother and daughter, a chance for them to relax and refresh old memories.

Despite the Moomins' popularity, Tove still saw painting as her most import-ant task, even though she had only had a limited amount of time for it recently. She honed and refined her art, continuing to paint landscapes, still lifes and human figures as she had done before. Remaining very faithful to all that she had learned during her training, she absorbed new impulses only with great caution. Immediately after the war she had often stressed that in her works she sought to go back to pre-war days, rediscovering the colours and shapes of that era, as though the war and what she called 'the lost years' had never been. But it was impossible to return to the past. Tove did not attain the 'radiance' of her 1930s work. However, in some of the monumental paintings there are traces of it, and above all it lives and pulsates in the Moomin picture books.

AN ARTIST STICKING TO TRADITION

Tove received her first Ducat Prize in 1938. It was a splendid welcome for a young Finnish artist who was just entering the field. An effort was made to distribute prizes, scholarships and grants equally among Finland's Swedish-speaking and Finnish-speaking artists, but there were sometimes violent debates about the rights and wrongs of this. Even back in Tove's days at the Athenaeum there had been 'language wars', something she detested.

The previous recipients of the Ducat Prize had been Essi Renvall and Sam Vanni, and after Tove it went to her fellow student Eva Cederström – Tove was thus in good company. Recipients of the award had to be under forty years old and to have taken part in the annual Young Artists' Exhibition (*Nuorten näyttely*). The year 1953 would be the last in which Tove could receive the prize again, as by the following year she would have exceeded the specified age limit. She was in competition with the sculptor Eila Hiltunen, who later created the much-loved Sibelius Monument; Lars-Gunnar Nordström, who became a famous Concretist; and Anitra Lucander, whose artistic career in many ways resembled Tove's own. When Tove was awarded the prize for the second time in 1953 – it was an important gesture of recognition – her work was judged superior to that of many other well-respected and talented artists.

During the 1950s, only two women won the Ducat Prize. Five years after Tove received it, the prize was awarded to Maija Isola. Like Tove, she became world-famous, but also like Tove, not as a painter. Isola designed fabrics for Marimekko, including the famous Unikko (Poppy) pattern.

One of Tove's most beautiful paintings of this period is *In the Warmth of the Stove* (*I kaminens värme*) of 1953. A dark-haired woman in a bathrobe is warming herself before a blazing fire. The flickering light has suffused the room and made the red and white of the bathrobe and the yellow of the background glow. The painting focuses on the central motif and much of the work remains abstract. It lives and breathes, and it represents a controlled and restrained modernism. The paintings of this period show that Tove was in the midst of a powerful process of development, but also that as an artist she was erratic.

In 1955 Tove gave a solo exhibition at the Taidesalonki (Konstsalongen) gallery. It had been nine years since her last solo show – far too long. During those nine years she had worked hard at her painting and so had plenty of work to display. Although she had taken part in several group exhibitions, including *Nuorten näyttely* and the triennial shows at Taideakatemia (Academy of Arts), the absence of a solo exhibition meant that she had been unable to demonstrate the principal themes in her own work – something that is essential for any artist. One reason for the long gap must surely have been the amount of time she had had to devote to numerous monumental works and illustration jobs, as well as to the Moomin books. But lack of time was probably not the only explanation, as Tove herself had constantly stressed that she was first and foremost a painter. A sign of the frustration that the circumstances of this period caused her may be gleaned from a notebook entry of 1955:

> *I can't reconstruct the time when I became an enemy of my own work, how it happened and what I must do to restore my natural pleasure in it. For a while I thought that these comic strips would help me. It was intended that the comic strips about Moomintroll, a half-forbidden, pleasure-tinged hobby, would turn into a new responsibility, and therefore that the pleasure would come back into my painting. The devil knows where it has gone, but it hasn't gone into that.*

The Taidesalonki show went well, some works were bought and the reviews were reasonably good. Yet people now saw Tove as a children's author, and above all as the creator of the Moomins. Her paintings did not arouse the same degree of enthusiasm. The critic on the main Swedish-language daily newspaper described them in pessimistic terms: 'Tove Jansson's solid, tasteful paintings are a pleasing phenomenon with us here at home. But if one imagines them in an international context, such as in Paris, they would scarcely attract attention [. . .]. The highly personal element that characterizes Tove Jansson's drawings and writing is decidedly less noticeable in her painting.' It was polite but crushing. Tove was seen as a skilled professional of the middle road, who did not surprise anyone with her art. For the young, ambitious artist it was a stern and cold judgement, and it undoubtedly affected her future life choices.

In the early 1950s the friendship between Atos and Tove was still strong, but now Atos was concerned about Tove's love for him, and not without reason. When Tove went off to Africa, Italy and France with Vivica Bandler, he feared he would lose her for ever. He wrote to her, asking her to come back 'instantly'. From Africa, Tove replied with reassuring words, though she made no promises, least of all any promises to return. As if to comfort him, she emphasized that he should always be part of her life and important to her. 'Of course it is true that we shall always be together, no matter how things change. Perhaps in different ways, but always in a good way. [...] I know you are worried that the trip is with [Vivica], but you should not be. It is quite unnecessary.' Her good relationship with Atos continued. In Tove's own words, she was his 'weakness' (*klockarkärlek*). The bond between them was increasingly based on friendship, though it seems they continued to have a physical relationship: 'We shall continue our relationship now and then, it is safe and domesticated [*hemvant*]. [He is] like my "ex", in a way,' she had written. But once Tove's sexuality had matured into lesbianism, she decided to end the relationship. She also rejected Atos's proposal of marriage, which had come too late.

Tove was sorry because it meant she hardly ever saw Atos. On the rare occasions when they did meet he was embarrassed and even intimidated by her new 'tendency'. She hoped that he would get used to the idea over time. Understanding his pride, she knew that he found it hard to digest the fact that his former girlfriend had moved to 'the wrong side of the tracks'. In 1954 Atos left Parliament in order to concentrate on his writing and in 1956 he contacted Tove and apparently asked to meet her. Tove replied by saying that he had been one of the best friends she ever had, and that almost no one else had given her as much as he had done. As if to warn him, however, she added: 'If you want to meet me, I am still here. I am now perhaps a little different than before.' The letters that followed were signed by both Tooti (Tuulikki) and Tove and were addressed not only to Atos, but also, after his marriage, to Irja. Tove was concerned about Atos's health and on one occasion sent him some of her own insomnia medication, urging him to consult her own trusted physician. Sometimes the subjects of their letters were very pedestrian – for example, she gave Atos advice on which flowers were worth planting in his garden.

Then Tapio Tapiovaara's wife died suddenly, and Tapsa was desperate and tried to revive his relationship with Tove. She said that she managed to reject him in a nice, polite way, something she stressed particularly to her friend Eva. From time to time she still met Sam Vanni, who was in the habit of visiting her once or twice a year in order to give her his opinion of her latest work. Vanni was successful: he sat on many panels and committees and taught at the Athenaeum. Tove had observed all this – and also that he had 'a much larger stomach'.

In Finland, the intellectual and lesbian circles were so small that the people in them 'stumbled over one another'. The Swedish-speakers among them formed an even smaller group, many of whom were interested in Vivica. In a letter to Eva, Tove said she suspected the world was full of women whose men did not fulfil their need for tenderness and eroticism, and that there was much that a 'ghost' could give them. She also wrote about Atos's new mistress, and of how the latter had become infatuated with Vivica. It looked as though he was about to lose another girlfriend to her.

There were all sorts of prejudices around at this time, and even Tove's closest friends found it hard to understand her new sexual orientation. Her best friend Eva Konikoff seemed unable to get used to the idea of her lesbianism. Tove was infinitely understanding and forgiving, and wrote that she had seen how hard it had been for Eva when she visited Finland. The only thing that upset Tove was that the people who mattered to her, Eva and Vivica, did not like each other.

When in 1953 Tove heard that her lesbianism had long been a subject of general gossip in the capital, she was shocked. Living a life of unguarded isolation in a world of her own, she had never suspected anything of the kind. Now the harsh truth was revealed in a threatening letter from an angry young man. Her privacy seemed to have vanished. There were anonymous letters, all manner of mudslinging and eavesdropping – she even suspected that her telephone was being bugged. Exposed to all kinds of things she had thought only happened to others, she was suddenly the object of slander and hatred.

Even enlightened colleagues could reveal their prejudices. One example of this is Marja-Liisa Vartio's story of how she met Tove at a literary evening. According to Vartio, Tove was by then already a celebrity and the object of envy in Helsinki literary circles. Other authors imagined that the Moomins, those 'strange fantasy figures', had made her rich. They also knew about her sexual orientation. Tove had offered Vartio a drink from her own glass, and Vartio had declined, as she 'knew that it meant the start of a flirtation'. Even among artists it seemed to be easy to lapse into homophobia and jealousy.

Lesbianism was such a sensitive topic that it could not normally be talked about, even with close relatives. Tove was aware that her parents knew. With her mother she had even discussed her friendship with Vivica. Faffan had heard the rumours, and had tried to enquire about them, but could not even bring himself to say the word 'homosexual' out loud. Tove concluded that her mother's silence stemmed from tact, and appreciated her diplomacy. To Eva, she wrote: 'I have a feeling that Ham understands but will never talk about it until she wants to.' For Tove, that decision meant loneliness. Not even decades of living with Tuulikki Pietilä eased the taboo, and mother and daughter never discussed the matter. Avoidance, concealment and silence about things that everyone knew about was very common in Finland. Vivica Bandler vented her feelings of disappointment caused by her own mother's silence about her homosexuality in a text that describes the pain in such a circle of silence:

> So now it was said. What you knew. What I knew that you knew. What must never be spoken aloud as long as you lived. And what I will finally be able to talk about when you are dead.
>
> How was it possible? That you kept so cleverly quiet about it, Mother? [. . .] Did you go around hoping like other poor mothers of your generation that I would be cured – or 'see sense', as I'm sure you called it.

Vivica remained not only an inspiring and helpful colleague, but also a close friend. She was 'the Big Ghost, the Original Friend'. Almost every year she spent a week on Tove and Tooti's island, and in return they visited her at her farm in the province of Saari. For Tove, Vivica was like a family member to whom she could always turn when she had problems. Together they created many remarkable plays for theatre, radio and television. Tove could also talk to her at length about her relationship with Tuulikki, and was herself in turn Vivica's confidante. Their correspondence was extensive and covered all areas of their lives. Tove wrote to Vivica about her work, trusted her judgement and was anxious for her to read and assess books she had only half-finished writing. If Vivica was busy, the books had to wait.

Vivica's close friendship with Ham continued, and she was concerned about her friend's ageing and increasingly ill mother. In the early 1950s Ham became seriously ill and had to go into hospital for abdominal examinations. When she came home, mother and daughter spent ten glorious days of vacation in Saari as Vivica's guests. Tove told Eva that Vivica was an infinitely loyal friend who would never betray her. Vivica would always be an important part of her life.

Tove and Vivica on the island in the 1950s

Tove considered that it was thanks to Vivica she had got rid of her naiveté and her desire to beautify things, qualities she had often thought were ingrained personality traits.

THE MONUMENTAL PAINTINGS

After the Second World War, Europe was rebuilt. There was a desire to create a new and better world in which art would play a prominent role, and the idea that artworks could dominate public spaces was born. Enthusiasm for monumental painting spread widely across Europe. The collaboration of art and architecture was one of the key themes of the 1950s: in Paris, the Groupe Espace association was founded in the late 1940s to promote a fusion of art and architecture and in the early 1950s a branch was established in Finland. Prominent advocates of the idea included the artists B. J. Carlstedt, Sam Vanni and Lars-Gunnar Nordström. Mural competitions were held and many of the mural designs implemented, although when monumental art was required for shops, schools, kindergartens and bars for everyone to enjoy, the works were usually commissioned directly from the artists. It was a social art, intended to encourage the sharing of good things and to make the new world more beautiful as it rose from the ruins of wartime. Many of the works were later forgotten. When sites were renovated, large murals had to be moved and some were even destroyed, as they were regarded as decorations rather than being valued as art. Hardly any other artist in Finland made as many monumental paintings as Tove did during those years. Her works were often called 'decorative paintings', perhaps because they were made for restaurants and cafeterias, or spaces intended for children. And they were indeed highly decorative.

Tove needed the monumental paintings, just as she needed her illustration work, as a source of income. She did not want to teach art, as she was nervous about public speaking and also perhaps of the students. This was also a reason why her own independent and lonely work appealed to her. At art school in Stockholm she had acquired a solid grounding in monumental painting, and with each new work she produced she developed and learned more. Many of her early murals, above all the two large-scale frescos she made for the Helsinki City Hall restaurant, testify to her abilities and talents.

In 1948 Tove was asked to paint a mural for a private kindergarten in the southern Finnish town of Kotka. Producing a work that eventually was seven metres long, she reflected how wonderful it was to make a painting for children, without the need to depict 'reconstruction work' or 'import and export'. She was probably remembering the murals she had created for Strömberg's factories, although the first painting she made there did not depict the factory work directly: she was striving to create something beautiful as a contrast to the employees' heavy working day. That painting, or its motifs, had apparently disappointed the factory bosses, and to make up for it she painted another mural depicting the distribution of electricity.

The Kotka Kindergarten mural was completed in 1949. It is an enormous fairytale panorama, including well-known figures from the Moomin books sitting around a campfire near a tent. There are also archetypal fairytale characters, for example a princess riding a white horse towards an open treasure chest, and there is much that is familiar about the landscape with its bays and arched bridges. Tove once said that her colleague and contemporary the painter Unto Koistinen came to look at the painting before it was finished, and snorted: 'Such shit.' The statement illustrates the low value that was placed on art for children – although, very possibly, it was the comment of an 'angry young man' directed against women's art in general.

Tove was eventually able to buy a studio, but had to take out a large mortgage. So she needed money, a great deal of it, as it was an interest-only loan. The ten-year bank loan, amounting to 1,200,000 Finnish marks, came to overshadow her life in a dramatic way. Vivica and Faffan were guarantors. The murals helped to ease the situation somewhat, and she was able to pay off the loan before the rise in interest rates would have made that impossible. The year 1953 was a particularly good one, with plenty of work. She wrote that during the year she had acquired more money and respect than ever before, and declared herself infinitely grateful for it. During this period she made one or sometimes two decorative paintings each year. The murals for the Kotka Vocational School and the Hamina Clubhouse were completed in 1952 – the latter, entitled *A Story from the Bottom of the Sea* (*En saga från havsbotten*) portrays the sea and the history of Hamina in terms of a fairy story. In the following year the murals in the Domus Academica Student Hostel were finished, while the painting in the staff cafeteria at the Helsinki branch of the Nordic Union Bank was completed

Sketch for a mural commissioned by the Nokia Rubber Factory, oil, 1942

in 1954. It depicts a square that looks like a piazza in Venice, and its background is a stormy sea with ships bobbing up and down on it. In the foreground there are people with umbrellas and parachutists. The work's pictorial narrative is not far removed from Tove's fairytale pictures.

The murals in Karja's Swedish Elementary School of 1954, and the paintings for the Aurora Children's Hospital and the Taikurin Hattu (Magician's Hat) Kindergarten in Pori of 1984, all contain fairytale motifs. For the Aurora Hospital commission, a contest between five invited artists was held. All the contestants were eminent artists, and besides Tove they included Gösta Diehl, Erik Granfelt, Erkki Koponen and Onni Oja. It must surely have been gratifying for Tove to prevail over four of the leading, recognized artists of the time.

Tove painted a composition that glowed with movement and colour, in which the characters of Moominvalley brighten the large wall surfaces. The Taikurin Hattu Kindergarten was a building that had been designed by Tuulikki Pietilä's brother Reima and his wife Raili. It was Tove's last monumental painting, and by that time she was seventy.

Tove painted the altarpiece *Ten Virgins* (*Tio jungfrur*) for the small church at Övermark in the west Finnish town of Teuva in 1954. It was her only church painting. Of the commission she wrote happily: 'It's a blessing that there are walls, as people are buying just as few paintings as before. Have been able to pay off a lot of the bank loan [. . .] But travel will have to wait.' Sam and Maya Vanni had gone to Paris. Tove wanted to go there as well and dreamed about it wistfully. She imagined her friends sitting in La Coupole, where she would have liked to be – though for the time being she had make do with the cafeteria, as the mortgage still had to be paid. It was cold in the church and the conditions were not conducive to painting. The work was very time-consuming and she felt under pressure. During the daytime she painted in the church, and in the evenings read the Psalms of David and drew sketches for the Nordic Union Bank mural. In addition to all this, she put the finishing touches to her Moomin book *Moominsummer Madness* (*Farlig midsommar*). Her sole recreation was the writing of letters to friends.

VI

The Moomins Conquer the World

WHAT HAPPENED NEXT?

Tove's first Moomin picture book, *The Book about Moomin, Mymble and Little My* (*Hur gick det sen?*; literal translation 'What Happened Next?'), appeared in 1952 in Swedish (the English edition was published in 2005), and was translated into Finnish in the same year. The book was visually bold and airy. The large pictures dominate the book and are drawn with strong but supple lines. The motifs are composed of large, mostly monochrome colour fields, while the accented lines and monochromatic surfaces are reminiscent of the cut-paper technique commonly found in the work of certain major artists of the time, and also in the drawings of young schoolchildren. It was unusual then to find such vivid colours in a children's book, though there was a good deal of black and white as well, with strongly marked areas of whitish blue, scarlet, lilac, ochre and bright yellow in between.

The cut-out holes in the pages are the book's most striking feature. Through the holes the reader can see part of the next page, and often, through more holes, part of the page after that. It is possible to gain a sense of what will follow next, though the hints are often misleading and surprise is guaranteed. The design of the book required a very precise skill and execution. There is a rumour that this idea of cutting holes in the pages originated in a frightening experience Tove had as a child. With her mother she had been looking at a picture of a troll peeking out from behind a stone in Elsa Beskow's book *Children of the Forest* (*Tomtebobarnen*, 1910). Tove found the troll so terrifying that her mother had to stick a piece of paper over it. Only the upper part of the paper was gummed, and so Tove could lift it up and look at the picture – and then she was really very scared.

The text of the book is in verse form. Playful end-rhymes invite the reader to recite them and sing them aloud. The areas of text also play a visual role – they

Tove and two Moomin figures at the Moomin promotion
in Stockmann's Department Store, Helsinki, 1956

Gaffsie fishing. Illustration from the picture book *What Happened Next?*(published in English as *The Book about Moomin, Mymble and Little My*)

In the Moomin forest. Illustration from *What Happened Next?* 1945

are an independent element in their own right, printed in decorative handwriting reminiscent of school.

In the story, Little My has vanished and concern for her interrupts Moomintroll's cheerful walk to fetch milk. After many adventures, Little My and Moomintroll return to wonderful Moominmamma. The plot has themes familiar to earlier Moomin books, such as disappearing, searching and finding, natural forces and Moominmamma's gentleness – but here they are handled more briefly, and the story moves along with the help of the pictures.

The book immediately attracted much attention and unreserved admiration. It may be regarded as the Moomin world's breakthrough to an international audience (and one that included Finnish-speaking Finland). For most Finnish-speakers it was their first contact with the Moomins. Tove was happy: 'People like the picture book best here, and it has been translated into Finnish.'

The following year, Tove was awarded Sweden's Nils Holgersson Prize. It was her first children's book award, but certainly not her last. A short time later she received the Rudolf Koivu Prize in Finland. The awards were well deserved: *The Book about Moomin, Mymble and Little My* was something entirely new in

Hattifatteners in a thunderstorm. Illustration from *What Happened Next?*, 1945

children's literature, both in Finland and abroad. Its illustrations represent a new, modern view of art and place it alongside some of the best artworks of the period. As graphic art and children's literature, the work was original and innovative, and there was nothing else like it at the time. In one of her short stories Tove describes a fictional comic strip artist, but the words could equally well apply to her own brilliant use of line: 'No one had such beautiful lines. So light and pure, they looked as though he had enjoyed himself when drawing them.'

MOOMINSUMMER MADNESS

Tove began writing her next Moomin book, *Moominsummer Madness* (*Farlig midsommar*, 1954), on the Pellinki island of Bredskär in 1953. The book is about the world of theatre and was dedicated to Vivica, Tove's mentor and inspiration in that milieu. Once again, the plot is built around a great natural disaster that sets events in motion and disturbs the familiar routine and security of the old way of life. A tidal wave caused by a volcanic eruption swallows up everything around it, including the Moominhouse, and the creatures end up in the water. Luckily they find a theatre that is drifting about in the flood and take refuge in it. They know nothing about the theatre or acting, and are not even aware that they are now living in a theatre.

When Tove wrote the book she already had some experience of writing plays and creating scenery, having staged *Moomintroll and the Comet* (*Mumintrollet och kometen*; the original title *Comet in Moominland* (*Kometjakten*) was changed for the stage version) in Vivica's production, which had toured abroad. Tove had become positively fascinated with the theatre, its radiance and intensity – and its ambiguity: nothing was exactly what it seemed at first sight. The book describes the moments before the volcano's great eruption, as heat and dry, burning ash-flakes herald the approaching disaster and destruction. Again, it is the landscape of the atomic bomb:

> *The night was full of unrest, there was a crashing and screeching outside the walls, and heavy waves thumped against the shutters. [...]*
>
> *Is it the end of the world? Little My asked curiously.*
>
> *At the very least, said the Mymble's daughter. Try to be good if you've time to, for we shall probably all be soon entering heaven.*
>
> *Heaven? Little My repeated. Must we enter heaven? And how does one get out of it again?*

Cover sketch for *Moominsummer Madness*, gouache, watercolour, 1954

In situations of life and death, Moominmamma focuses on small, everyday matters that are easy to deal with even when great disasters strike. She looks for bark boats she has carved; she is glad that the ugly hammock has gone. When the flood invades the basement of the Moominhouse, she is able to see the kitchen from a new angle, through a hole sawn in the floor. She is also glad that she did not manage to do the washing-up before the flood. It would have been unnecessary. Moomintroll and the Snork Maiden fall into the clutches of the police and are put in prison. Finally they all return to the family and everything continues as before. The danger is past:

> *A single puddle still reflected heaven, a swimming-pool just the right size for Little My.*
> *It was as though nothing had happened and no danger would ever be able to reach them again.*

Tove did not stick to any rules about what was suitable for her readers, not even for children. In the Moomin world, which is always full of love and concern

Illustration from *Moominsummer Madness*, 1954

for others, nothing is really forbidden except the act of forbidding. In *Moominsummer Madness*, Snufkin's enemies, the Park Keeper and the Park Wardress, live in a park where they have pruned all the trees into circles and squares. All the paths are 'as straight as pointers. As soon as a blade of grass dared to come up it was cut so that it had to begin to exert itself again'. In this park, which is surrounded by high railings, small, furry, subdued 'woodies' come to play. There are notices everywhere indicating all the things that are not allowed: No Smoking, No Sitting on the Grass, No Laughing or Whistling, No Jumping With Both Feet Together. When Snufkin sees this, he makes up his mind: 'And now we shall tear down all the notices, and all the blades of grass shall be allowed to grow as they like.'

TROLLS IN THE WINGS

Moominsummer Madness was a brilliant and inspiring basis for a dramatic adaptation, as the book concerns a theatre and the making of theatre. The play was given the title *Trolls in the Wings* (*Troll i kulisserna*), and Vivica directed it in 1958, this time for Lilla Teater. Tove wrote the script and created the scenery. She took part in the production work just as enthusiastically and loved to share in the frenetic activity and see her expectations of the first night transposed into reality, wondering if the evening would be a success or a failure, just as she had in the days before her first play was performed. The rehearsals electrified her, as they did everyone else in the show. Tove's close friend, Lilla Teater actress Birgitta Ulfsson, recalled Tove in the theatre: 'A little weightless wildcat bouncing back and forth between stage and auditorium with a paintpot in one hand and a notebook in her pocket. Fixing, correcting, she is very practical.'

Vivica had not been satisfied with the first play, *Moomintroll and the Comet*. Because of the large masks they had to wear, the actors were not able to express themselves by means of facial expression. Body language alone was not enough to project the message, however, and the baggy Moomin costumes concealed many of the actors' movements. With the wisdom of past experience, the masks were the first thing to be dropped from the new play. Tove wrote the script in consultation with Vivica, and when Vivica asked anxiously how the work was progressing, Tove replied that everything was going well and that she was not worried about how to create the 'Moomin spirit'. That would arise from the dialogue, which she planned to write separately, role by role. She thought it a much greater challenge to create a dramatic framework for the play, one that would hold it together.

The play was a great success, and it enchanted the audience. After being performed in Helsinki, the play was taken to Stockholm in 1959, and to Oslo in 1960, where the now legendary Lasse Pöysti and Birgitta Ulfsson, close friends of Tove, appeared in the leading roles. Once again Vivica was director. These successes led to numerous special performances, television series and radio plays. In Norway, Tove also appeared as the back half of the Lion under a yellow cloth, and managed the tricky choreography with flying colours. She was, after all, an enthusiastic and capable dancer.

THE COMIC STRIPS AND THE TWENTY MILLION READERS

Tove was just fifteen when her first comic strip, *Prickina and Fabian's Adventure* (*Prickinas och Fabians äventyr*), appeared in a children's magazine called *Lunkentus*. The strip was in a traditional style, but was still quite professionally done. In the following year she created *The Football that Flew to Heaven* (*Fotbollen som flog till himlen*), an action-packed strip drawn in clear black and white, with powerful depiction of movement. Three years later, after her training at Stockholm's School of Applied Arts, she produced another comic strip which showed a more professional level of technique. The drawings are full of detail, and this time done not only in black and white but also in shades of grey.

During the years that followed, Tove's interest in the genre seems to have waned. At the Athenaeum she was studying painting, and this may have led her away from the world of strip cartoons. Another factor may have been that cartoon drawing was not particularly attractive from a financial

Moominmamma painting her garden.
Illustration from *Moominpappa at Sea*, 1965

181

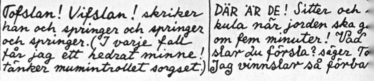

point of view: the fees were lower than those paid for other graphic work. But although Tove stopped drawing strips, she retained the skills she had acquired.

Atos found Tove's Moomin books inspiring, and he was the first person to suggest the idea for a Moomin strip cartoon series. As editor-in-chief of *Ny Tid* he was able to commission Tove's cartoons for the newspaper's children's section. The series she drew was based on *Comet in Moominland* and bore the pithy title *Moomintroll and the End of the World* (*Moomintroll och jordens undergång*). Its readers were apparently rather intolerant, as many of them were upset by Moominpappa reading *Monarkistbladet*, a monarchist newspaper, something that went against the ethos of a publication aimed at a working-class audience. Although the series was dropped after about six months, twenty-six episodes of the serial were published. Atos was convinced that it ought to be published abroad, and he began to explore the possibilities offered by the international press.

After *Ny Tid*, Tove offered the Moomin strips to a Finnish-language newspaper, either *Helsingin Sanomat* or *Uusi Suomi*, though she could not remember which. But the paper's editors did not even want to meet her, and they mislaid the samples she sent them. Not until the comic appeared in the London *Evening News* in 1954 was there any interest from the Finnish-language press.

In 1950 and 1951, English translations of Tove's books *Finn Family Moomintroll* (*Trollkarlens hatt*) and *Comet in Moominland* (*Kometjakten*) were published in Britain and the United States, taking the Moomins outside the Nordic countries for the first time. The reviews in Britain were very positive. In 1952 the British press group Associated Newspapers stated its interest in commissioning a suite

KOMETEN SLÅR NER!

ett ögonblick att förlora dår står mamma.... In ...fotogenlampan ramlar
vågen dånar på avstånd med er ungar, stäng dörrn, omkull, allt blir svart....
ken skälver.... nu – kommer det..... FORTS. Tove

Comic strip for the journal *Ny Tid*, undated

of Moomin comic strips. They were to have a continuous plot and be designed primarily for adults, and they would portray the so-called 'civilized world' in a satirical way. Tove was eventually offered a seven-year contract. It sounded good and she rejoiced: 'Only six strips a week, and never again will I need to draw idiotic little pictures, quarrel with troublesome authors, design Mother's Day cards, etc.'

The offer from the *Evening News* seemed like an excellent one. Tove accepted it in the belief that she would now be free of all her money worries and be able to concentrate on painting. In the latter respect she could not have been more wrong. The newspaper group invited her to London for a few days to negotiate terms. 'I left everything in a muddle, especially the mural for Nordic Union Bank I had promised to finish this spring, and flew away.' She spent two intensive weeks in London and each day was filled with all manner of excitement – meetings, conferences, dinners, theatres, new people, plus a new language to get to grips with – although she was very aware of the need to be careful and safeguard her own rights. However, the contract guaranteed her the first regular income she had ever had in her life. Money was important now, as Ham was about to retire. The financial security made her feel happy: '[. . .] what a wonderful, reassuring feeling it is to go to the bank at the start of the month and collect one's salary, which is always there and is always the same. You may think it sounds silly, but I have never experienced a situation where I can spend a certain amount every month.'

In London, the publishers later sent her on an induction course that lasted nearly a month: they explained what was expected of her and informed her of what she could and could not do. She was given a fairly free hand, but there were certain restrictions on subjects such as sex, death and the government. There must be nothing of an erotic nature, but Tove thought it would be difficult to portray that anyway, because of the Moomins' physical shape. She could refer to death if it had taken place back in the eighteenth century, which did not seem like an insuperable obstacle: her books had few dead people in them, and she told them that only one hedgehog had died in her books. She had to avoid matters relating to politics and the Royal Family, but Tove wanted to avoid them too. In fact, she stated her own demand to the *Evening News* unequivocally: 'And absolutely no politics! It would completely destroy the whole idea of something that is universally human, make the series too obvious and take away my joy in working on it.'

Not much was ruled out, then, but the requirements were considerable. There had to be suspense. In the three or four panels of each strip there was to be a rapid succession of events, including tricky situations that would be resolved in the next day's strip. Then Tove had to come up with a new story. Under the contract, the stories always had to have a happy ending and the characters were to survive even the most difficult situations. And no character was to eat another, even if it wanted to.

Sketch for comic strip in the *Evening News*, undated

Moomin comic strip for the *Evening News*, mid 1950s

In these comic strips Tove reused and reworked the narratives and principal themes of her books. She generally stuck to the subjects that were important to her. In *Club Life in Moominvalley* she poked fun at club life and people's reasons for belonging to clubs. For example, the members of one club have a moral right to fire catapults at unsuspecting passers-by. Moominpappa founds another club in which the most important thing is to socialize, enjoy oneself and follow the dress code, thus making the club's activities entirely self-serving. Moominmamma and Moomintroll are not members of any club themselves, but are recruited by the Brigand Club. After many adventures their punishment is decided – they have to be active members of all clubs for the rest of their lives. The cartoons Tove had drawn for *Garm* frequently acquired a new guise in the strips, where the themes are presented more directly through the Moomin characters: for example, in Tove's reflections on first and last loves, the first is often mistaken for the last, and vice versa.

Although the comic strip characters were already familiar from the Moomin books, new characters were also created by Tove. The strips were later released as books, editions of which continue to appear over fifty years after their first publication. They have lost none of their freshness and interest. Tove Jansson was the first strip cartoonist to make the separating lines between the panels into part of the story and this is considered to be her contribution to the history of the comic strip.

Ultimately the contract was for a period of seven years. It was signed in 1952, and in 1954 the strip began publication in the *Evening News*, then the world's most popular evening newspaper. The publisher sold the rights on, and soon the strip was appearing in many other newspapers around the world. At its peak, it was published in forty countries, reaching some twenty million readers. By this route it eventually found its way into the Finnish-language *Ilta-Sanomat*, and a short time later the Swedish-language *Vasabladet* and *Västra Nyland* began to publish it.

In 1954 the incomprehensibly tepid reception of Tove Jansson's international career by the Finnish-language press was illustrated in an article by *Helsingin Sanomat*'s London correspondent, headed 'Myy-sarjasta' ('The Little My Strip'). The article referred only to Little My, as the journalist apparently thought she was the only character in the story. It began with an account of how Little My, created by a Finnish artist's imagination, had 'made the British argue' about whether it was 'trash or a pleasant pastime created by an inventive brain'. The reporter said that Tove, referred to as 'Jansson', was probably one of the few, if not the only, Finnish strip cartoonist to have 'become popular in the foreign press', but hastened to add that Little My had received words of praise not only among the tens of thousands of people who read the strip, but also from other readers. In addition, the article went on, at least 'one necktie' portraying Little My embroidered in silver thread had been made. The necktie was the modest beginning of a Moomin spin-off and merchandise industry which eventually ballooned to the gigantic proportions it has reached today. Although this was something the journalist could not have envisaged at the time, it would have been hard to find terms more demeaning than these with which to belittle a Finnish artist, and the reason for the article remains a mystery. In general, positive publicity for Finnish art and applied arts was manna to the self-esteem of a nation that had just emerged from the war and the burden of war reparations. But still it seemed that the country was incapable of feeling pride or pleasure in the success of the Moomin comics – initially, at least.

In the spring of 1956, Stockmann's department store in Helsinki ran a big Moomin promotion. The newspaper *Ilta-Sanomat* printed a one-and-a-half page illustrated feature containing an interview with Tove in which she said that the Moomins were her true employers. As usual, Tove emphasized that she was really a painter. The journalist commented on the Moomins' fame, comparing it to an epidemic, a triumphal procession, and made a point of highlighting the Finns' lack of enthusiasm:

> *You see, in Finland we didn't want to know about the Moomins at all at first. [...]*
> *The Moomins were too clever for the Finns, all we wanted were pairs of princes and*
> *princesses, scary stories about witches and conventional tales about animals [...] Even*
> *now, when the whole of Europe is talking about the Moomins and people all over the*
> *world are reading Moomin books and comics, only two out of six Moomin books have*

Evening News delivery vans advertising the Moomins
during the campaign in London, 1954

been published in Finnish – in English it's six out of six, and the same in Swedish and German.

The journalist also wrote about the much-publicized 'Moomin Week' in London, when double-decker buses were decorated with Moomins and Tove Jansson made drawings of them in a television programme. These British Moomin celebrations were apparently the model for the Moomin campaigns at Stockmann's in Helsinki and NK in Stockholm.

Tove had become famous – 'the talk of all Europe' – and her twenty million readers could no longer be dismissed. She certainly enjoyed her popularity, even if it was not for her painting. To her contact in England, Charles Sutton, she confessed:

Furthermore, dear Charles, flattery and fawning are really something I have missed all my life, though I always dreamed they would be directed at my oil paintings. But it's all the same whether people like my still life works or the Moomins: the main thing is that they like something I have done.

For a long time fame had not been important to Tove – it had seemed more of a mixed blessing. Perhaps being a woman from a small country, she found it hard to be an international celebrity. Her attitude was probably not unlike that of the Joxter in the Moomin world: 'I don't think being famous is much fun, the Joxter explained. Perhaps to start with, but then it feels quite normal and in the end it just makes you feel ill. Like going round on a roundabout.' Tove now wondered if she had taken the right decision in promising to create the Moomin strips in such large volumes. It was a decision that had changed her life and career but had led to a result quite different from the one she had planned. She had thought she would be freed from the need to do illustration work of various kinds for so many different clients, which took up her time and energy. To produce six comic strips a week had at the outset looked much less demanding.

Although the first and second years of the comic strip work were exhilarating, after that the charm wore off and was gradually replaced by stress, and the work no longer seemed to have much meaning. Tove found it hard to comply with the rigid schedules and to keep churning out new ideas. For her it was far less easy than it was for her fictional comic strip artist who lacks ambition but is 'so fabulously skilled that the drawings flow out of him like diarrhoea'.[8] Being the conscientious, exacting and goal-oriented person she was, Tove suffered from anxiety and the fear of being unable to meet the deadlines. She found it impossible to balance work on the comic strips with the planning of Moomin products, her murals, her other painting, her exhibitions and writing. Not that she would have wanted to give any of it up, least of all her painting, as she still saw herself primarily as a visual artist. As a result she had to work at a furious pace, the worst effect of which was the lack of privacy, something she also complained about in a letter to Charles Sutton.

In 1979 Tove wrote for the Swedish daily *Svenska Dagbladet* a description of her career as a comic strip artist for the *Evening News*. It appears in almost identical form in her short story 'The Cartoonist' ('Serietecknaren'), which was published in the collection *The Dolls House and Other Stories* (*Dockskåpet och andra berättelser*, 1978; published in English as *Art in Nature* in 2012). It tells the story of a comic strip artist who has vanished. He is the creator of a character called Blubby, and all the characters are produced in marzipan, candle-wax and plastic and are used to decorate curtains and dressing gowns. There are also Blubby Weeks, presentations at charity events and almost all the other spin-offs associated

8. The quotation is from the short story 'The Cartoonist' in the collection *Art in Nature*.

with the Moomins. The fictional cartoonist is meticulous about his strip – there must be no mistakes – but he is unable to say no. Then he disappears. The new cartoonist is told:

> You've only got seven years – you'll manage that somehow. You're not going to go and hang yourself. [. . .] There was one fellow who did. Villa on the Riviera and pleasure yacht and all the rest of it and he went and hanged himself. Perhaps that's not so unusual, but he wrote a letter to other comic strip artists, warning them not to sign long contracts. They've got his letter at the newspaper in their secret museum.

Tove's short story is rather a gloomy description of the life of cartoonists in a large newspaper concern and undoubtedly the pressures she describes are similar to those she had experienced herself. Tove was also meticulous, and perhaps too conscientious. She kept a vigilant eye on her work, in which there could be no mistakes. Around the Moomins, too, events, promotions and peripheral spin-offs had begun to proliferate. She had much in common with the unhappy creator of Blubby.

Reality and fiction also coincided in other alarming ways. When Tove began her job at the newspaper she was given a little corner of her own to work in. Another cartoonist had worked there before her and had ended up in a psychiatric clinic. She only learned about this later. After six years Tove decided to cancel her contract, and her brilliant career as a strip cartoonist came to its logical conclusion. In the letter of resignation she wrote to the publishers in England in 1959 she described her attitude to the comic strips, the Moomins and her painting:

> During this time, my life with Moomintroll has begun to resemble a very worn-out marriage. You have probably long realized that I want to separate from him. You probably saw several years ago that I was tired of him. Well, now I am even more tired of him. I discussed this long ago with the conductor Dean Dixon, and he said politely but with frightening honesty: 'Take care, Tove, soon people will be describing you as another of those strip cartoonists who want to be artists.'
>
> I was an artist then. Even though I was playing with the Moomins I tried to paint a still life every Sunday. Now I draw Moomins with a feeling that is starting to resemble hatred, and sometimes on Sundays I stand before my own work as if it were a closed door.
>
> [. . .] I don't ever want to draw comics again. I'm sorry.

Tove felt that if she continued to draw comic strips, the artist in her would die, and she did not want that to happen. Because she was sick to death of the

Moomin strips, the work had to stop. Right from the outset her brother Lars had translated Tove's texts from Swedish to English and he knew the world of the strips inside out. During the first three years, Tove did the drawing and wrote the text herself. Eventually she felt that she had worn out her subject matter and was finding it very difficult to come up with new adventures. She began to devise the ideas for the strips together with Lars, but drew the pictures herself. When she announced her desire to stop, Lars wanted to continue the series alone. He had no previous experience of drawing, but now began to train hard under Ham's guidance, and according to Tove reached a startlingly high level of technical and artistic proficiency. The newspaper group accepted his sample drawings, though Tove warned him about the difficulty of the task. Lars began to draw and write the strips in 1960 and continued to do so for fifteen years. By 1975 he also wanted to give up, as he said he had started to have dreams about the Moomins. Lars was a skilled draughtsman and creator of dialogue and narrative, and was considered by some Tove's equal in the genre, and by others even better than her. She

Tove Jansson's comic strips seem to have an immortal soul. Their brilliance has not faded, and their charm has not worn off. On the contrary, they are reprinted over and over again, and they endure from one generation to the next. The British author Margery Allingham (1904–66) reflected on their secret in an introduction to a book about the series (published by Allan Wingate in 1957) that appeared in the London *Evening News*: 'I can only explain it by saying that it seems to be an elementary question of quality [. . .] But here there is perfect line and perfect economy and nothing else whatever to get in the way.'

In all her illustrations, Tove's line is wonderful. In the comic strips it emerges with a clear emphasis. With only a black line of Indian ink she creates movement and captures the moment, while showing the facial expressions of her characters with strokes that have no more than a hair's breadth. By means of tiny changes in the irises of the characters' eyes she creates moods that range from happiness to furious rage: the Moomins have no mouths. In 'The Cartoonist' she makes fun of her skill: 'Surprise, terror, delight and so on – all one has to do is move a pupil here and an eyebrow there, and people think one's so clever: fancy being able to produce so much with so little.' The movements demanded of the pen are small, but what they are able to communicate is quite another matter. Tove was well aware of that.

A seamless coexistence between picture and text is rare. Few people in the world have mastered both media with such assurance. According to writer Göran Schildt, the comic strips represent the most brilliant aspect of Tove Jansson's

Till Vivca.!

← Tove (avb.)

Tove threatening the Moomins with a meat mallet. Envelope drawn for Vivica

gift, because they consist of both pictorial and verbal art by the same creator. The success of a comic strip depends on the text and the pictures reinforcing each other, making the end result more than the sum of the parts. Where the text stops, the picture takes over, and vice versa.

Tove understood the importance of her comic strips and their subtle influence on her readers' sensibilities. Yet she found it impossible to continue creating them. Years later she remembered her cartoon years with near-bitter frustration. She felt the time she sacrificed had taken away from everything that was important to her. During those six years she had 'no time for painting, never mind books, friends or solitude'. She wanted to paint and be an artist, yet the strips meant an end to her financial problems, and now she could afford to renovate her studio. For fourteen years she had suffered from cold and draughts, and she decided she had had enough. She had the premises thoroughly refurbished: the windows were replaced, electric heaters installed and the exterior walls insulated. In addition, a large loft – really another floor half the size of the studio – was built.

VII

What Do You Do with a Seashell if There's No One to Show It to?

TOVE'S LIFE PARTNER, TUULIKKI PIETILÄ

On top of all the fatigue and stress the Moomin cartoon strip series caused her, the mid-1950s were also an intense time in Tove's personal life. During this period her letters were tinged with sadness – a melancholy brought about not only by weariness but also by loneliness. She had many good friends and relationships – and of course she had her own family – but she had not found a partner to whom she could truly anchor herself. In 1955, however, she met Tuulikki Pietilä, with whom she had been superficially acquainted at the Athenaeum, though they did not attend the same classes. Tuulikki was a few years younger than Tove, and the Swedish- and Finnish-speaking students generally kept to their own sets. They had met by chance in a Paris nightclub when Vivica and Tove were travelling together, but now, in 1955 in Helsinki, a love was born that was to endure for almost half a century, until the end of their lives.

At the Christmas party of the Finnish Artists' Guild Tove asked Tuulikki for a dance. Tuulikki did not agree, apparently for reasons of propriety. Later, however, she sent Tove a card with a picture of a striped cat, inviting her to visit her in her studio on Nordenskiöldinkatu Street. It was the winter of 1956. The very next summer Tuulikki visited Tove on the island of Bredskär. Their love had been kindled. Tove wrote: 'I am finally with the one I want to be with,' and on one of the walls of her studio was the card with the stripy cat – where it still remains.

It was almost as if their love was complete as soon as they met. After Tuulikki's first visit, Tove wrote from her island: 'I love you, I'm at once bewitched

In the warmth of the stove. Sketch for
Moominland Midwinter, gouache, 1957

193

and filled with a great calm, and I am not afraid of anything that may lie in store for us.' Tuulikki likewise confessed her great love. The pair were different, both in their appearance and in their approach to art, but their life experiences and their values were quite similar. By the time they began their life together they had both seen and experienced a great deal, and were mature adults – Tove was already over forty. A few years later she wrote to Eva that Tooti (the nickname she gave Tuulikki) was an easy-going, cheerful friend, the best one she had.

Their relationship was made easier by the fact that they were both artists, they had similar interests, and both wanted to work with their hands. Tuulikki was the daughter of a carpenter, and Tove the daughter of a sculptor. Tuulikki was skilled with knives and had inherited a talent for wood-carving, which ran in her family. Tove loved hard work: she liked nothing better than building houses and chopping firewood (it seems that she even chopped firewood for Atos's neighbours in Kauniainen). Later the couple's shared hobbies came to include travel, film-making, making Moominland installations and fishing. At long last, Tove's dream of a union between two independent people who supported each other and worked together had been realized.

Tove's life changed completely when she met Tuulikki. In spring 1956, she wrote to Vivica about how calm and happy she was, and that she was not suffering with her nerves as much as she used to. She felt in harmony with her world and was waiting quietly for Tuulikki to come to the island. Her whole existence felt untroubled.

When the popularity of the cartoon strip was at its peak, the island's tranquillity was frequently disturbed by the intrusion of admirers and journalists. In order to obtain peace and quiet, Tove and Tuulikki built their own cabin on the small island of Klovharun – really a skerry – far out in the Gulf of Finland, though uninvited guests sometimes found their way there too. In winter, both women lived and worked in their studios in Helsinki. Tuulikki managed to acquire a studio in the same building as Tove's, and for years they were able to visit each other by walking along an attic corridor.

The card with a picture of a striped cat that
Tuulikki Pietilä sent to Tove in 1956

In summer they lived in their

Tove and Tuulikki in their Wild West costumes, 1950s or 1960s

small house on the island, often with only each other and the seabirds for company. They usually moved to the island in early spring and stayed there late into the autumn. Now that she was living with Tuulikki, Tove lost her Moomin fatigue, which had been so severe that she even referred to having 'vomited Moomins'. Instead of being a soothing place of retreat, Moominvalley had become a kind of prison. With Tuulikki's help, her faith was restored. The stories about the Moomins and their world also became one of Tuulikki's principal hobbies.

Tove and Tuulikki were emotionally and intellectually bound to each other, and filled each other's lives more and more. Sometimes it was hard to make room for this symbiotic relationship in Tove's equally intense relationship with her mother, Ham. Mother and daughter were accustomed to spending large amounts of time together and to travelling as a pair. Now Tuulikki wanted to share these things with her partner. Both Ham and Tuulikki wanted the same thing, but without the other around. It was left to Tove to take control of the situation and deal with it 'fairly and equitably' since jealousy was an issue for both women. Tove wrote anxiously: 'Good Lord, how difficult women can be sometimes!', and travelled with them both in turn. It is clear that the

195

understanding sometimes broke down, as Tove reported to Vivica when all was going well, 'Tooti and Ham have been nice to each other.'

MOOMINLAND MIDWINTER

Tove's book *Moominland Midwinter* (*Trollvinter*, 1957) is a book about love and specifically about falling in love with Tuulikki Pietilä. It was published after their first year of living together. In March 2000 Tove ascribed the book's success to Tuulikki, when she wrote: 'That I was able to write *Moominland Midwinter* was completely thanks to Tooti.' Tuulikki taught her to understand the winter, just as in the book. Tove also said that she wanted to write a book on how 'hellish' life could be amid all the deadlines, royalties and fears of late delivery, referring to the worries she had experienced as a newspaper cartoonist. When she wrote *Moominland Midwinter*, she was still bound by her contract with the *Evening News*, was severely overworked and was also caught up on the carousel of celebrity. She lamented the fact that she was never able to be truly alone. She needed solitude. For her, as for all artists, it was only in solitude that new ideas could arise.

Moominland Midwinter is different from the earlier Moomin books. Its narrative is not driven by a disaster, and the Moomin family have not lost one another, but are sleeping peacefully – hibernating. The winter, with its cold, ice and snow, provides the dark yet wonderful backdrop to the story. The evil characters are the Groke and the Lady of the Cold, whose beautiful green eyes kill anything that crosses their path. Death has come to Moominvalley. It is possible to see this work as the first Moomin book to be written for adults rather than children, though at one level the tension of the plot appeals to children too, and they can enjoy it.

Too-ticky playing the accordion. Sketch for *Moominland Midwinter*, gouache, 1957

At the beginning of the book Moomintroll wakes up from his winter sleep. He is the only one awake and is trying in vain to wake his sleeping mother. Filled with curiosity and frustration, he goes out and finds an unexpected world of snow and ice. Even the sea is frozen. It is a side of Moomin life that has been kept secret from him until now. During his adventures, Moomintroll encounters the most frightening thing of all – death. It has been said that the realization that life is finite is a sign of adulthood. If that is true, then Moomintroll has now grown up. He looks for his own place in this strange world:

> The whole world has died while I slept. This world belongs to someone else whom I don't know. Perhaps the Groke. It isn't made for Moomins to live in.
>
> He hesitated for a moment. But then he thought it would be even worse to be the only one awake while everyone else was sleeping.
>
> And so Moomintroll made the first tracks in the snow across the bridge and on up the slope.

Part of being grown up is the ability to accept and even see the beauty in fear, loneliness and life's imperfections. Moomintroll does not return to Moominmamma and tries not to go back into hibernation. He merely says: 'The whole world has gone to sleep [. . .]. I'm the only one awake, and I can't get back to sleep again. I'm the only one, and I have to wander and wander, for days and days and weeks and weeks until I too become a snowdrift that no one even knows about.'

The primal sorrow – of missing a person close to you – has overwhelmed him. In the past, when Moomintroll was a child, Moominmamma's wisdom and warm lap chased sorrow away. But now there is no Moominmamma, no miraculous handbag with cures for sorrows great and small. Moomintroll is alone – and he must cope alone.

Although the book deals with loss, death and, above all, the terror of being left alone, it is also a story about finding great love. Moomintroll finds fresh footprints in the snow and goes crawling off to catch up with the hiker:

> Wait! he shouted. Don't leave me alone! He stumbled on, whimpering, through the snow, and suddenly all the fear of the dark and the loneliness descended on him.
>
> It must have been somewhere there all the time, ever since he woke up in the sleeping house, but only now did he dare to be really afraid.
>
> [. . .] And suddenly he caught sight of the light.
>
> Even though it was so small, it filled the whole forest with a gentle, red glow.

Next to the snow lantern Moomintroll has found Too-ticky, with whom he

Moomintroll, Too-ticky and the snow lantern. Illustration from
Moominland Midwinter, 1957

can live in the strange new world. Too-ticky has a knife in her belt and she is dressed in a red and white striped sweater, a tassel cap that covers the crown of her head and dark blue long trousers, a bit like a caricature of a French sailor. She has a strong and rather stocky physique, and her hair is fair and yellow. All these features were characteristic of Tuulikki Pietilä too.

Intelligent and pragmatic, Too-ticky knows to leave Moomintroll enough mental space, and does not seek to smother him with excessive nannying. In this way she supports Moomintroll's progress towards independence. The support can sometimes be tough, though. Moomintroll watches with horror as someone carries things out of his father's house: 'It's probably all for the best, Too-ticky said happily. You have far too many things around you. And things you remember, and things you dream about.' Too-ticky is a realist, and she demands a lot of Moomintroll. Moomintroll says: 'I said, apples grew here once. And you just replied: but now snow's growing here. Didn't you realize I was depressed? Too-ticky shrugged her shoulders – You have to discover everything for yourself, she said. And climb over it all by yourself.'

Too-ticky dwells on things we cannot comprehend: what are the Northern Lights – do they really exist or are they just an illusion? Neither character knows much about snow either: 'You think it's cold, but if you make an igloo with it, it gets warm. You think it's white, but sometimes it turns pink, and sometimes

Moomintroll and Too-ticky in the forest. Sketch
                                    for *Moominland Midwinter*, watercolour, 1957

Kap. 2. "magia d'inverno."

blue. It can be softer than anything and it can be harder than rock. Nothing is certain.'

These are the kinds of uncertainties with which they must live. Always sensible, Too-ticky tells Moomintroll about her own attitude to life: 'Everything is very uncertain, and that is what makes me calm.' This sentence is the key to the book. It tracks the normal progression towards adulthood and the realization that the world around one is constantly altering and changing form. Tove continually returned to this sentence in interviews, with such frequency that it was evidently one of the basic tenets of her philosophy of life – to accept perpetual change and uncertainty.

WHO WILL COMFORT TOFFLE?

Tove's second picture book in verse, *Who Will Comfort Toffle?* (*Vem ska trösta knyttet?*), appeared in 1960, only a few years after *Moominland Midwinter*. For a long time the book's working title had been 'The Romantic Tale of the Lonely Toffle' ('Den romantiska berättelsen om det ensamma knyttet'), but was changed to the less romantic one. Tove wrote the book over the period

Illustration from *Who Will Comfort Toffle?*, 1960

On tienoo äkkiä niin hiljainen ja musta
ja mörkö niin kuin vuori tuijottaa,
ja jäinen maa on täynnä kammotusta,
kuin kuustakin pois värit putoaa.
Ja nyytti sanoi: helppoa ei tule olemaan!
Tuo mörkö on niin kamala etten tuulluthkaan!
No ensin hurja sotatanssi rohkeutta toi
ja sitten hampaat mörön häntään jotta kipunoi!
Ja mörkö ällistyi ja juoksi, pakoon yksi kaksi —
siis tuttu kyynelien läpi näki nyytin voittajaksi.
Ei pienen tuutin peloittelu ole vaikeaa,
ja lohduttelu, arvaathan, on vielä helpompaa.

Page from *Who Will Comfort Toffle?*, 1960

when she was recovering from the stresses of the cartoon strip deadlines, and at times she felt completely drained. But she never let exhaustion get in the way of her work: in addition to her writing she held an exhibition of paintings and was also involved in theatre work. It was a happy time, because her new life as an artist had begun, and she had found a new love with whom to share her life. The new book was dedicated to Tuulikki and was immediately loved by everyone.

Tove wrote her story for small, timid children, and in the 'Miffles' (*skrutt*) Tove revealed a great deal of her own shyness and her tendency to withdraw. But there was also some of her own personality in Toffle. Tove said that she had received a letter from a little boy, in which he complained that he was always overlooked – no one really noticed him or looked him in the eye; he was afraid of everything. The boy signed his letter as 'Toffle' (*knyttet*). Tove thought that his self-confidence might increase if he found and rescued a 'Miffle' who was even more fearful than himself.

Who Will Comfort Toffle? is a picture book for children about being in love and accepting love: the plot consists of longing for someone and the desire to find a partner. Like his real-life prototype, Toffle is lonely and frightened. He wanders around deep in thought, and asks: 'What do you do with a seashell if there's no one to show it to?'

Toffle receives a message in a bottle from Miffle (the *skrutt*), and now has someone to defend. His courage increases, and he dares to challenge the Groke and bite her tail. The astonished Groke runs away in fright. Toffle's courage is rewarded, and love is ignited:

> *... and Miffle flew to Toffle's arms and whispered: now forget*
> *how horrible it was – remember all the fun that's left,*
> *I've never ever seen it, but I long to see the sea,*
> *and collecting pretty seashells is a wonderful idea!*

Because of the author's sexual orientation, the genders of the characters she created and their patterns of behaviour have been of more than a little interest to researchers and readers. It has been observed that in the story the brave Toffle is male, while the withdrawn and timid Miffle is a woman. The gender roles are therefore very traditional. The man is strong, and he rescues the woman. In the first draft of the manuscript Toffle was female, but for one reason or another Tove changed her to a boy.

There are no holes in the pages as there were in the previous picture book, and in that sense it is a technically simpler work. But it is presented in large, striking colour fields, which make the pictures very reminiscent of the abstract art of the time – in particular its Concretist school – and accords with its overall objective of 'staying on the surface'. Shapes had to be executed in two dimensions, and the artist was not allowed to create three-dimensional shapes by means of techniques like shading. As in Concretism, the book's colour surfaces are often monochromatic, with sharp edges. The pictures acquire movement through the contrast between the strong colours. The clean, bright, single-coloured surfaces and bold parallels function splendidly. The white contours create the impression that the pictures have been cut out, like loose pieces on a white background, and this cut-paper technique adds its own excitement to the book.

FATHER'S DEATH

Faffan died during the summer of 1958. The rapport between father and daughter had endured through many difficult periods. Over time it had become easier, and they rediscovered their love for one another. In 1948 Tove wrote to Eva with warmth and understanding in relation to Faffan. The letter describes her

Faffan, the monkey and the lump of sugar

by then elderly father sitting in Gambrini's restaurant with his beloved monkey, drinking a whisky and water. The monkey played an important part in their lives and was often the focal point for many strong emotions within the family. Faffan, the monkey and this visit to the restaurant formed the basis of 'The Monkey' ('Apan'), a short story about a man and his pet monkey, in which Tove describes the animal going on the rampage and the despair of the restaurant staff. Faffan and the monkey also played the main roles in the stories 'Pets and Females' ('Husdjur och fruar') and 'German Measles' ('Röda hund') in *The Sculptor's Daughter*.

Tove and her brothers had acquired the monkey, named Jackie, almost by mistake. After the war, people used to advertise goods they wanted to exchange for items like butter or potatoes. The Jansson children saw an advertisement by someone who wanted to barter a monkey. They thought it referred to a so-called 'monkey sail', which was something they were looking for, but it turned out to be a real monkey. When they first saw it, the monkey jumped up into Lars's arms and sat there happily: 'And we couldn't go home without it, because it wanted to come with us.' Instead of a sail they ended up with a new member of the family. Tove described how they all soon began to behave like monkeys – waving their hands, chattering and jumping up and down . . .

While the monkey had a cage in Tove's studio, Faffan became very attached to the creature: as Per Olov said, he found it easier to show love and affection to the monkey than to his children. Tove also referred to this in *The Sculptor's Daughter*: 'Papa loves all animals because they don't contradict him. He likes the hairy ones the most. And they love him because they know he'll let them do anything they want.' The siblings eventually gave the monkey to their father for one good reason – none of them wanted it. The little creature was difficult, not least because it smelled awful and stank out its environment; it was also disobedient, bit strangers and dominated everyone's life. Yet Faffan loved it. Per Olov took a photograph of the monkey trying to steal a lump of sugar from his father's mouth. Later he thought that Tove might have found the picture distressing, as it shows so clearly how Faffan spoiled the malicious, unpredictable little creature. Faffan gave the monkey the love and attention for which his daughter had longed so keenly. In another story Tove describes a little girl's jealousy of a monkey. The girl in the story is obviously Tove, but in real life the monkey did not become part of the family until she was grown up.

The Sculptor's Daughter was published in 1968 and is based in part on Tove Jansson's own childhood. When the book appeared, she was already much more than just her father's daughter. She had already built her own career and was considerably more famous than her father had ever been. The book's title was an expression of love for a man who, even after his death, remained a strong presence in the life of his grown-up daughter. He had been Tove's main and longest lasting authority on art; Tove never ceased to admire her father's art, and always had his large and small sculptures around her. She had received a great deal from him, though much that, for her own sake, she had to divest herself of – a process essential for many children of strong, dominant parents.

The relationship between Faffan and Tove also seemed to have improved, to the extent that they no longer became so furiously angry with each other. The distance between their homes, and above all the process of ageing, seemed to have had a calming effect on them both. Faffan looked after his family's welfare and, as Tove wrote, saw to it that there was enough to drink on the island. Faffan bought *jaloviina* (cut brandy) and made *kilju* (sugar wine) for them all during the long summer months. He was very proud of his daughter's success, too. In 1957 Tove attended a Moomin festival at a Stockholm department store with her father and mother. Ham, who was also proud of Tove, said jokingly that Faffan was 'as proud as a peacock'.

Although Tove had often had considerable problems in her relationship with her father, after his death she realized that she had loved him a tremendous amount, in spite of their quarrels and differences. Much later, in 1989, she wrote an imaginary dialogue in which she described Faffan. Mari, who bears a strong resemblance to Tove, and Jonna, who resembles Tuulikki, discuss Mari's father. Jonna asks: 'Did you admire him?' Mari replies: 'Of course. But he didn't find it easy to be a father.'

Faffan's death altered the whole dynamic of the family. Above all, Ham's life changed, but so did those of her children, especially Tove and Lars. Ham had to move out of the Lallukka Artists' Home as the studio had been expressly allocated to Faffan ('the sculptor Viktor Jansson'), and widows with family were not allowed to stay on after the death of the principal tenant. The household had to be packed up and new accommodation found. Ham moved into Lars's apartment on Neitsytpolku, very close to Tove's studio, and usually spent the weekends at Tove's place. After her father's death, Tove was surprised to realize how much he had meant to her mother. All her life Tove had wished she could rescue Ham from Faffan's yoke. She had planned to take her mother with her and move to a better place, or at least to a land where there was colour, warmth and no perpetually demanding husband. To Tuulikki she wrote: 'Ham is suffering dreadfully [. . .] and they must have loved each other much more than I was able to comprehend.'

VIII

Back to Painting

'WHO IS THIS BRAVE NATURALIST?'

Tove and Eva Konikoff had now been writing to each other for some twenty years. As time wore on, the letters became rarer, and in some cases they wrote partly in English. On Christmas Eve 1961, Tove wrote to Eva about all the things they had in common. In places, the tone of the letter was rather sad: many of their mutual friends were dead, and many others had left Tove's life in different ways. Melancholy seeped between the lines. Rafael Gordin, Tove's admired physician, adviser and friend, had died, and she no longer had any contact at all with Sam Vanni. Vanni had divorced his wife, remarried and had a son whom Tove thought was called Mikael or Daniel (his name was actually Mikko). 'Sam and I don't meet any more', she wrote sadly. Tapsa she had not seen for ages. Although Atos, too, had almost vanished from her life, every now and then they ran into each other on the street. '[H]e still seems to have the same brilliant charm. But now he's quite grey, and has learned to listen.' From time to time she met Vanni's ex-wife, Maya, who worked as a translator and lived on Topeliuksenkatu Street – Tove thought she seemed awfully lonely.

Tove described the family atmosphere for Eva. On Christmas Eve life was peaceful: Impi was making the Christmas dinner, Ham was asleep, Lasse and his wife, Nita, were there and Tove was playing with her black cat, Psipsina – Greek for 'pussy-cat'. She said she was spending the 'black-and-white' winter months illustrating her next book, *Tales from Moominvalley* (*Det osynliga barnet och andra berättelser*, 1962; literally translated as '*The Invisible Child* and Other Stories'), and early the following year the book was indeed ready for the publishers. After Faffan's death, Ham had stayed with Lasse at Neitsytpolku, but now that he was married and they were expecting a baby, the young couple had moved to

Tove in her studio, 1956. In the background is a full-sized sketch for *Country Celebration*, one of the City Hall frescos. Attached to it is a graphic print by Sam Vanni, beside it is a sculpture by Faffan, and in the foreground are artists' materials, Tove's own paintings and a radiator

207

Tove and her black cat Psipsina

Merikatu. Tove was very worried about her mother. Ham would soon be eighty and was increasingly unwell. She still lived at Neitsytpolku, where she shared the apartment with one of Tove's former girlfriends, for security.

In the same letter to Eva, Tove started reminiscing about her years as a cartoon strip artist, emphasizing how dreadful they had been and how happy she was to be free of the contract.

Now, thanks to the comic strips, she had financial resources and no longer had to worry constantly about debts and rent. Above all she had a strong support in Tuulikki Pietilä, who as an artist herself understood the anguish of artistic creation and the pressure from one's environment.

Making a fresh start was particularly hard considering Tove was leaving behind a celebrated career and twenty million readers – and doing so voluntarily. Her choice was certainly not dictated by a quest for honour and fame, and painting did not seem to hold out the prospect of anything like the glitz and prestige her previous career had offered. She had been like a juggler trying to keep all the balls in the air at once, and it had become impossible. Now she deliberately dropped the most coveted, glamorous ball – the cartoon strips – and focused the energy thus gained on the part of her career that had earned her the least amount of recognition: painting.

After the long break, Tove felt she had returned to square one and was now like a helpless beginner in the world of painting. The worst aspect of it was other artists' condemnation of her cartoon strip work:

> At that time the general view was that while it was fine to paint pictures, if one drew cartoon strips one had sold one's soul on the altar of commercialism. I could not believe that people actually called me on the phone and told me I had sold my soul. In the end I had to have my number removed from the telephone directory. By the way, my father was so proud of my cartoons that he took them with him to Gambrini's restaurant and showed them to his friends.

It is possible that the abuse Tove suffered from other artists made her embrace her dreams of being a painter all the more determinedly, awakening a desire to prove herself. Perhaps she even shared their view of the hierarchy of art and graphic art. Her return to painting was nevertheless brisk and dedicated. As she wrote in her notebook in April 1960, during the first four months she managed to produce as many paintings as she had in the last ten years.

As if to underline that this was a new phase of her life, she began to sign her works 'Jansson' – not 'Tove', as earlier. Known by both of her names as an author, as a painter she may have believed that the use of her surname on its own was more grown-up, that it gave her work stature and dignity – or perhaps she wanted to send the message that she was now a different artist, an older one, more goal-oriented and experienced.

In 1959, on the threshold of her new life, she painted a self-portrait and called it *Beginner* (*Nybörjare*). She portrayed herself in everyday sporting clothes, a woollen sweater and long trousers, leaning against the beloved bentwood chair she had painted so often. Her expression is calm and determined, and her gaze is directed at the easel. The focus of the work is on the essentials, while the details are trimmed away.

In the late 1950s and early 1960s, the Informalist school of abstract art began to dominate in Finland. Informalism was the *dernier cri* in Europe, and Finland's artists took to it 'like a hot knife to butter', as the saying went. The effect was that the composition and form of paintings dissolved, and the number of colours in them diminished. Even critics like E. J. Vehmas, who had been most hostile to abstract art, were enthusiastic. Peer pressure also made many artists who had been opposed to abstractionism jump on the bandwagon. Vanni also came under its influence, and for several years his paintings lost some of their controlled form and abundance of colours.

The ARS 1961 exhibition at the Athenaeum was a great celebration of Informalism and was one of the first major international exhibitions to be held in Finland. A large number of the works on display were in pure Informalist style. Olavi Hurmerinta's cartoon in *Uusi Suomi*, one of the country's two main daily newspapers, gives some idea of the pressure that Informalism created. The drawing shows the annual exhibition of the Finnish Artists' Guild, and all the works are large Informalist paintings. Among them there is only one naturalistic still life, which a 'bearded radical' of the day is studying in amazement. The caption is his question: 'Who is this brave naturalist?'

It was probably Tove. The work she entered for this Kunsthalle Helsinki exhibition was the grey-toned painting *Nature morte*. Representational in style, and thus rather different from the other works in the show, it was hung separately from them. All the other works were thoroughly abstract, mostly Informalist paintings, as in Hurmerinta's cartoon. Though it was too large for it, Tove's painting was displayed in the smaller exhibition hall for graphic art. She described her feelings on seeing the cartoon that made fun of her work: 'All the others were abstracts [. . .] but I had just painted my bloody jars and bottles on a table. I didn't know whether to feel flattered or embarrassed.'

The pressure to conform was considerable, and eventually Tove also succumbed to Abstractionism and the abstraction of pictorial motifs. In the short story 'An Eightieth Birthday', she wrote about the atmosphere of this period. Although the story is autobiographical, it reflects the sense of pressure she and many of her artist friends felt. I feel that the grandmother is largely based on Tove herself:

You know, back then Informalism was all the rage, everyone had to do the same thing. He looked at me, saw that I didn't know, and explained: 'Informalism, it means more of less painting incomprehensibly, just colour. It got to the point where old, very fine artists hid themselves away in their studios and tried to paint like the young ones. They were scared and didn't want to be left behind. Some of them managed to pull it off, just about, and others got lost and never found their way back. But your grandmother kept her own style, and it was still there when the whole thing had blown over. She was brave, or stubborn, perhaps.'

I said, very carefully: 'But perhaps it was just that she couldn't work in any way but her own?'

Was the grandmother brave and stubborn, or was she merely unable to paint in any other way? The same question may arise when one examines Tove's art. It is hard to give up what one has learnt, to change one's values and abandon one's principles even though others around one are doing so. At the same time it is also a source of infinite sadness to feel that one has been excluded from the cutting-edge movement of the day, been dropped from the new developments and the circle of one's closest artistic colleagues. Tove's picture books *The Book About Moomin, Mymble and Little My* (*Hur gick det sen?*, 1952; literally translated as 'What Happened Next?') and *Who Will Comfort Toffle?* (1960) prove that she did not lack a sense of colour and form, that she had plenty of skill and vision. She possessed all the talent and prerequisites that were needed for her to develop into one of the finest abstract artists in Finland.

THE HARD-WORKING ARTIST

Despite the external pressure and the lack of clarity about the future direction of her art, Tove worked hard throughout the 1960s, holding numerous solo exhibitions. In her decision to return to her career as a painter she was serious, perhaps more serious than she had ever been before. In 1960 she left the safe and familiar Bäcksbacka gallery and held a show at Helsinki's Galleria Pinx, which had been established only a few years earlier and was popular among young artists. The change of venue can be regarded as a deliberate gesture on Tove's part, aimed at joining the company of the modernists. Two years later she gave another solo exhibition in Helsinki, this time at Galleria Fenestra. Although the reviews were fairly good, they were not laudatory: among other things it was said that the works lacked certainty and that the artist was still looking for her own style. The shows that followed were marked by a similarly lukewarm reception – they included an exhibition at the Husa gallery in Tampere, and in the second half of the decade there were two more at Pinx, in 1966 and 1969 respectively. In 1969 Tove and Tuulikki also held a joint exhibition at the Alvar Aalto Museum in Jyväskylä. Five solo shows and a joint exhibition within the space of ten years demanded considerable effort and were a test of Tove's strength and energy.

For a long time Tove stuck to traditional representational art, but gradually she began to introduce abstract elements into her paintings. *Chairs* (*Stolar*, 1960) is figurative, but the background of the work is very simple. With soft

Chair, oil, 1968

lines it depicts two chairs like those she had in her studio, placed back to back. Little by little, the abstraction became more pronounced, and Tove's move towards it was similar to that of most Finnish artists – a slow progress achieved by cutting a few more figurative motifs from each new work. She created her first abstract paintings ten years later than those of Vanni, for example, but she was not the only artist to lag behind the new wave. Several of her paintings had brilliant colours, and grew in size. Against a background of wholly or partly non-representational colour fields, we often still find a recognizable object, like the bentwood chair – a subject she now frequently returned to – in *Chair* (*Stol*, 1968). The works of this period are stylish, executed with powerful brushstrokes, and are in harmony with the Informalist aesthetic of the time. Tove often chose concrete titles for these abstract works, such as *Ravine* (*Klyfta*, 1965), *Cockfight* (*Tuppfäktning*, 1966), *Suomenlinna* (*Sveaborg*, 1967), *Kites* (*Drakar*, 1968) and *Decision* (*Beslut*, 1969). The titles prompt the viewer to look for a narrative, though it is not always there.

Often Tove chose motifs that in themselves looked so abstract that even a perfectly naturalistic execution produced an abstract impression in the finished work. These were the works with which she usually had most success. They include *Storm* (*Storm*, 1963) and *Hurricane* (*Orkan*, 1968). Landscapes, especially the sea in all its manifestations, were her favourite subjects. The painting *Swell* (*Vågsvall*, 1962) is a powerful depiction of high seas and large waves, while *Force 8* (*8 beaufort*, 1966) is a study of the sea's surface lashed by the wind and full of shapes radiating energy. *Weathering* (*Förvittring*, 1965) is an elegant portrayal of a grey and white island against sea and dark sky.

Although Tove had decided to make painting her main endeavour, she did not obtain the peace and quiet she needed in order to concentrate on it. Instead she took on large illustration projects, continued to create new Moomins, and undertook other writing as well. Her illustrations were popular in Sweden, where her readers wanted much more than Moomins from her. At the very end of the 1950s she illustrated a Swedish edition of Lewis Carroll's *The Hunting of the Snark*, followed a few years later by J. R. R. Tolkien's *The Hobbit*. Soon after came Lewis Carroll's *Alice in Wonderland*, which was a demanding and important task. At the beginning of the next decade she also illustrated *The Hobbit* for a Finnish publisher. These were challenging and exacting undertakings and they took up time that she could have devoted to painting. She had no pressing need to do

Rocks, oil, 1960s

Weathering, oil, 1965

Force 8, oil, 1966

them, as by now her money worries were a thing of the past. Had she become so accustomed to stress that she burdened herself without reason, or was it simply that she could not refuse? It was uniquely fascinating work, and perhaps she really wanted to do it. The illustrations she produced are original and exquisite, but they met with an indifferent reception. People had their own ideas about the literary classics and found it hard to accept new ones. Some of the pictures were quite close to the Moomin world in appearance, though they did not reach the same multidimensional level.

A large part of Tove's time was now spent on numerous commissions for radio and television. In addition, she corrected the translations of her Moomin books and provided them with new covers. Her writing was becoming important again, and perhaps it was this that finally led her to put visual art aside. Her next exhibitions were retrospectives showing an author and artist with international renown, above all else as the much-loved creator of the Moomins. Yet in a Moomin-related interview she gave in Sweden in 1969 she still emphasized that she was first and foremost a visual artist.

By the early 1970s Tove's dreams of following that career seem to have faded, and her diligent exhibition work of the 1960s came to a halt. In deciding to make painting the centre of her activity, she had clearly been reluctant to give up anything except the cartoon strips. The internationally distributed television cartoon series had made her famous all over the world. Through those series grew the Moomin industry, which took up more and more of her time and energy. She had no time to focus on visual art, and this, coupled with the associated difficulty of concentrating, pulled the rug out from under her painting. Increasingly she was seen against the backdrop of the Moomin world, as in a headline that described the situation well: 'Moominmamma is above all more of a painter.'

Yet Tove ardently wanted to be a painter and saw the role of artist as the one she valued most. So why did she not devote more of her time and energy to it? For someone with so many talents, it was hard to choose. Her last short story may give some indication of her dilemma:

One could imagine a horrible story about the constant compulsion to choose: I find a 'someone', and one fine morning, quite suddenly, make him realize that he is subject to constant choice, unrelenting and inescapable, at every moment of his life. He can never be sure that he chose correctly.

Sketch for an illustration to *Alice in Wonderland*, mixed media, 1966

Tove was shy in the company of other artists, and often complained of feeling upset when she was with them. Clearly she was still lacking in confidence about her artistic works and the recognition they received. It was not easy for a female artist to maintain her self-esteem in these overwhelmingly male circles. Tove felt more at ease with writers and theatre folk than she did with visual artists and she avoided the events of the Finnish Artists' Guild. When she decided to go back to painting, she tried hard to rid herself of these feelings and wrote to Vivica about her attempt to get used to hanging out with artists:

I sometimes go to the Artists' Guild to get rid of my phobias and I've found that I'm no longer afraid of the artists, they can't upset me any more. If I continue to go there for a while perhaps I may even start to like them. And that's how it should be, that's how one meets one's colleagues.

Perhaps Tove found taking second place difficult to cope with. In one of her last essays, she wrote about this: 'And what I'm most afraid of – being a sore loser, being second-best . . .' Being in the rearguard of great changes and attracting reviews that were reasonable, but not glowing, put a dampener on her enthusiasm for painting – especially when, in her other career, she had achieved such brilliant success as an author and illustrator.

Cover sketch for *The Invisible Child*, gouache, 1962
Overleaf: Källskär painting, *Ahvenanmaa*, oil, 1960

TOVE JANSSON

IX

Books for Children and about Children

THE INVISIBLE CHILD – STORIES FOR CHILDREN

Seven years of intensive work on the comic strips and the spell of hard exertion as a painter could not but leave their mark on Tove's output. The British newspaper group had commissioned the cartoons specifically for adult readers, and it is noticeable that there is a striking difference between the Moomin books that were written before and after the comic strips. While the early books are characterized by excitement and big adventures, the later ones focus on the relationships between the characters and on personal dramas, sorrow and joy.

Starting again was hard. In a low state of mind, Tove reflected on her situation: it felt as if she had nothing to say. The cartoons were 'life-threatening to all forms of narrative', and she thought they had had the same effect on her painting. They were the reason for the decline in her vital energy: she felt that beauty, abundance and her *joie de vivre* – everything that had been at the core of her art – had deserted her. There was nothing left, and she could not write about a vacuum.

She undervalued herself by thinking that writing for children had been a 'dumping ground for [her] naiveté'. Now the child's world and the stories that had sprung from it seemed to have evaporated. She wanted to write for adults, but such a change in direction made her hesitant and she doubted her ability. Yet in spite of her anxieties, the idea also attracted her. She comforted herself by reflecting that even if she could not write for adults, she could at least produce pictures for them. Writing was more uncertain – but perhaps that was where the challenge lay.

Although Tove had now decided to write for adults, the gate to the Moomin world was not yet closed. In 1962, *Tales from Moominvalley* (*Det osynliga barnet*

Cover sketch for *The Invisible Child*, Indian ink, gouache

och andra berättelser; literally translated as *The Invisible Child and Other Stories*) appeared, followed in 1965 by *Moominpappa at Sea* (*Pappan och havet*) and in 1970 by *Moominvalley in November* (*Sent i November*), perhaps the very finest of the Moomin books. They are written as much for adults as for children.

Tales from Moominvalley contains Moomin stories of quite a different kind – they are not tales of adventure, and not really tales at all. Tove called the book a 'collection of short stories for children'. It was very important to her and she did not want to let it go until it was ready. The manuscript was 'to lie around for a year or two', she told Vivica when her friend asked if they could look at it together. At the same time she thanked Vivica for the enormous amount of help she had given her, both in working on the book and in the idea for it.

The Invisible Child is a wise book, in which the tension stems from the relationships between the characters, their different personality traits and the clashes that result. The narrative style is intensely psychological, and the title story has become a classic in its portrayal of childhood development. It is a description of how coldness and irony can destroy an ego that is still fragile. A child does not develop if she receives no love. She must feel secure enough to dare to be angry, or, in the words of Little My, 'learn to fight'.

Piece by piece, the book's invisible child becomes visible. Not until she dares to show her hostile feelings does she acquire her true face. Too-ticky and Moominmamma assist her in this process of becoming – the same figures who in Tove's life were the closest and most important to her. Thus in *The Invisible Child* there is much of the author herself. She wrote in her notebook that she wished that she too could one day find her own face: 'Like *The Invisible Child* I must learn to be angry, and show it. I will probably show it too much at first, and so for that reason too I need a margin of isolation. Hopefully my face will gradually grow on me.'

Tove needed to allow herself to be angry and to show her anger. She had always found it hard to show aggression, which did not mean that she was free of negative feelings, but that she was somehow secretly aggressive. She complained that she found it difficult to control her emotions and the aggressive feelings could break out suddenly and unexpectedly, in unsuitable contexts.

Depression was another emotional state that Tove frequently said she feared, and at times it left her unable to work. It was a condition from which other members of the Jansson family also suffered. In particular, her youngest brother's bouts of deep depression were of serious concern to her. In the short story 'The Fillyjonk Who Believed in Disasters', she captures the essence of depression in her perceptive description of the Fillyjonk, whose life is a vicious circle of fear of all kinds of natural disasters: cyclones, typhoons, tornadoes, sandstorms or tidal waves. The Fillyjonk is absolutely convinced that life will go badly for her, and she is completely overwhelmed by the ineluctable threat of disaster. Her depression is described as accurately as only someone who has deep personal experience of it would be capable of: 'What one can't ask, can't reason with, can't understand and can never question. What arrives behind a black pane of glass, far away on the road, far out at sea and grows and grows and is never visible until it's too late.'

Sketch for *The Invisible Child*, Indian ink

Tove Jansson

The book *Pappan och havet* (translated into English as *Moominpappa at Sea*) appeared in 1965 and is, as its title suggests, a story about the sea, an island and Moominpappa. But above all it is a book about Viktor Jansson, and is dedicated to 'a father' (*en pappa*) – meaning Faffan, of course, who had died in 1958. Tove wrote that she would have dedicated it directly to him, 'if it weren't a bit pathetic'. In the book, Moominpappa wants to be a real man and decides, without asking his family, that they are all going to move to an island with a lighthouse on it.

Tinged with personal memories, the story is a melancholy one. Tove wrote it after visits to Ibiza and Portugal that loosened a kind of mental knot within her and helped her to engage in a more prolonged and satisfying period of writing. Even so, the book did not have an easy birth. As usual she asked Vivica to read it, and told her there was no hurry, because 'I'm going to sit on it until I know it can hold its own'. Although the book tells of a father's longing, it is also about the longing for a father, a daughter's sorrow and the attempt to revive a past time.

When Tove had completed the manuscript, she asked her friend Lars Bäckström in Uppsala to read it. Bäckström was editor-in-chief of the Swedish cultural magazine *Ord & Bild*, and Tove had great respect for him. His opinion was important to her, because she was worried about the book: 'I would like to know if you think that I've kept the positive side of the community, though I've kicked them out of the happy valley and given them brand new complications – loneliness and melancholy and opposition in the midst of the perfect family.'

Tove was evidently reassured by her friend's reply, and she explained to him the great uncertainty she felt: 'It's possible that I've fussed so terribly about (and with) this story because it's a condensing of my own Grokes, and the bare bones of it are a kind of search for my sculptor father who died many years ago.'

However, a few years after the book was published, when *The Sculptor's Daughter* had already appeared, Lars Bäckström wrote about the Moomins from the point of view (then current) of the New Left and its re-evaluation of political attitudes. He said that the Moomin world was only possible in the marginal groups of the world's upper class. Other reviewers also wrote from a left-wing perspective, accusing the Moomins of escapism, introversion and bourgeois values. It is possible that the criticism had a far-reaching effect on Tove's future literary choices and particularly on the fate of the Moomin books.

One letter to Lars Bäckström reveals something fundamental about Tove's attitude and the surprising effect that the negative criticism had. Thanking him for his views, she even said that she thought he was right:

Tove Jansson

Cover sketch for *Moominpappa at Sea*, gouache, 1965

*For all their easy amiability these trolls are pretty ruthless members of the upper class,
and there is a veiled and cruel lack of warmth about the whole thing. They use people
and events in an unconscious, charming way and are really insufferably self-sufficient.
I think it's very good that you have seen through them – I have long had my suspicions
of them. Though I cannot change them, and neither do I want to.*

Moominpappa at Sea was the last Moomin book to have the Moomin family as
its focus. Whether this was the effect of the New Left criticism of the day and its
questioning of the Moomins' existence one can only guess – but it was certainly
not the only reason.

On a private level, the book is a story about Tove's father and his love of the
sea. Tove often said that her father loved disasters, storms and even fires, as they
cheered him up. Ordinary life was too monotonous, and he got bored. A passion for

natural disasters was something that father and daughter shared. Both found the turmoil of the elements electrifying – in this they were almost like Hattifatteners during a thunderstorm. Together they had always enjoyed the forces of nature. The lighthouse island itself is the book's other main character. It is like a little 'flyspeck' in the middle of the great ocean. While she was writing, Tove bought a new place in Pellinki and with Tuulikki Pietilä began to build a small house there. Moominpappa's lighthouse island is similar to their new island, Klovharun, or Harun. According to Tove, it too was as small as a 'flyspeck'. It lacked a lighthouse like the one on the island of Kummelskär that Tove had tried unsuccessfully to acquire, while in her fictional account Moominpappa does get a lighthouse.

Moominpappa at Sea is a hymn of praise to the sea in all its forms – its gentleness, its storms and its unpredictability. It is also a story about the difficulty of gaining independence and accommodating the demands of family life. Moomintroll moves away from the family to a cabin he has built, where he takes control of his own life and becomes independent. Moominmamma also discovers new aspects of herself. She paints her homesickness on the walls of the lighthouse, hides among the magnificent flowers she has created with her brush, and lives her own life the way she wants to, not just for others.

Tove let her mother read the manuscript. Ham thought that the book amounted more or less to a story about how hard it was to be married.

Moomintroll is frightened and fascinated by the Groke. He seeks her out and encounters her over and over again. To his mother, he wonders aloud why the Groke is the way she is. His mother says: 'She's like the rain or the darkness, or a rock that one needs to walk around in order to make any progress.' Tove's grief at her father's death may be the source of this darkness and great sorrow that must be overcome in order for life to continue. In the story Moomintroll dares to confront the Groke.

Although the book is really meant for adults, the presence of the Moomin family continues to make it accessible to children. And, like all the tales from Moominvalley, this one also has a happy ending. Moominmamma's homesickness subsides and the lighthouse begins to function properly. Even the Groke becomes a benign creature whose clumsy shape no longer covers the ground with ice.

THE SCULPTOR'S DAUGHTER

At the end of 1967 Tove sat at 'our table' in Helsinki's Lehtovaara restaurant, remembering the past and thinking about the future, as she wrote to Eva. More than a quarter of a century had passed since her friend had moved to America, and they had both been through a great deal. Although Eva had made a few visits to Finland, she never had enough time – too many people always wanted to see her – and Tove invariably found her visits disappointing.

Tove's life was once again at a crossroads. The Moomin period seemed to be over. After *Moominpappa at Sea* she had felt that the whole of Moominvalley had taken wings and flown away. Even the Groke was a warmer personality now, which meant an essential counterpoint was lost. Yet Tove was happy to announce that, even though she lacked the support of Moominvalley, she was now writing for adults. It was all very exciting, and she felt that she was working with great dedication now that she was writing short stories about children for grown-ups. From time to time she still suffered from a lack of self-confidence; she had doubts about everything, and often ended up rewriting the stories over and over again.

Tove found the writing of *The Sculptor's Daughter* (*Bildhuggarens dotter*, 1968) a painful experience in some ways. In moments of doubt, she sank into depression, though at other times she felt infinitely happy. 'At any rate I wrote – with desire.' And that was always the most important thing to Tove; it was a criterion

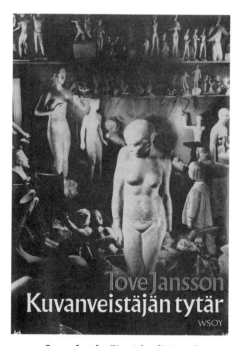

Cover for the Finnish edition of
The Sculptor's Daughter

Cover for the Swedish edition of
The Sculptor's Daughter

Cover sketch for *Moominvalley in November*, mixed media, 1970

of success. There were no illustrations in this book, as she wanted to emphasize that it was a book for adults, one that she wanted to distinguish from the Moomin books. As she was even reluctant to provide an illustration for the cover, Per Olov supplied a photograph instead. It shows a little girl with her hair in a pageboy style, standing in Tove's studio with her back to the viewer, looking at white plaster female figures. The Swedish publishers wanted her to design the cover because they wanted it to look like the covers of the Moomin books and this inevitably caused friction between publishers and author.

In the book, Tove defines herself through her father. It was the first book she had written for adults. She was no longer a creator of books for children, but a fully fledged adult author. This difference seems to have been quite crucial to her. Like so many of her works, the short stories in the book were based on real events – its provisional title was 'I, the Sculptor's Daughter'. The child in the stories was herself, though in fictional form. Sometimes she set the narratives in very different decades, occasionally adding elements of sheer fantasy – yet throughout there is a sense of and events of which she had personal experience. In the story 'Snow', in which she describes a mother and a little girl in a house surrounded by snow, everything, by her own account, is based on fact – with the only difference being that when the events took place she was no longer a little girl but already grown up. 'The Golden Calf' is also based on reality – except for the calf.

Throughout the book a playful irony is combined with the light touch of the Moomin books, as though the magic enchantment of the Moomin world had simply moved directly into the life of the Jansson family. But there are also many darker tones. The reader is offered the daughter's reflections on a world where only men are allowed to have parties, at which alcohol gets the upper hand and they become belligerent. Or a world in which a man's creative work comes before everything else, and if they feel they are being ignored their feelings may turn to jealousy.

HAM'S DEATH, AND THE THREE BOOKS OF MOURNING

When Ham died in June 1970, Tove lost the person she loved most of all. Ham was almost ninety when she died and she had been ill. During her final years she was often depressed, feeling that she was a burden to her children. Her sporadic disagreements with Tuulikki probably made the situation worse.

Tove was able to spend her mother's last two days with her in the hospital, and her brothers also visited every day. The death was peaceful and painless: 'She was able to go as she had wanted, without paralysis or lengthy waiting, and without losing one iota of her intellect. [. . .] So Ham sank into an infinite weariness.'

Although an old person's death is never a complete surprise, on a purely emotional level the death of a loved one always is. After her mother's death, Tove described her own life as calm but strange. It was the middle of summer, when nature was at its most beautiful, and Tove derived solace from that. In the middle of great sorrow, her work once again became everything to her. 'The summer continues, just as beautiful, and the work continues.'

Tove wrote letters to her friends to tell them about Ham's last days and the approaching funeral. To Eva Wichman she sent a poem Ham had written a year earlier in which she described her life in the style of Edgar Lee Masters's *Spoon River Anthology*:

> *I was pastor's daughter*
> *suffragette*
> *teacher*
> *girl scout leader*
> *interested in*
> *nursing*
> *books and riding*
> *a religious idealist*
>
> *loved an artist*
> *moved to his country*
> *saw 4 wars*
> *worked hard for*
> *life's meatballs*
> *had 3 wonderful*
> *amazing children*
> *so really it wasn't*
> *all so*
> *bad.*
> *– Ham*

Ham's death wrought a total change in Tove's life, and this showed most clearly in her books from this period. She had begun to write *Moominvalley in November* (*Sent i November*) some time before, though the book was published in the same year that Ham died. In it, death still remains in the background, just as it did in Tove's own life – something impending but not present. *The Listener* (*Lyssnerskan*) appeared in 1971, and some of the stories in it refer directly to this time of grief. *The Summer Book* (*Sommarboken*) of 1972 is the last of these books of mourning. It is a bright narrative of sun, sea and summer shared by a daughter, a father and a grandmother, and represented an attempt to revive the past and recreate those happy days.

MOOMINVALLEY IN NOVEMBER

Moominvalley in November is the last Moomin book, a farewell to Moominvalley and its inhabitants. Loss and the finiteness of life are the main themes. The members of the Moomin family are gone, yet they are somehow still vividly present. Creatures from the Moomin world that have made their way to the Moomins' residence are united by their longing and hope for the family's return. Will the family come home, is their return merely a fantasy or a reflection of the guests' shadow-play? It is all left open. Everything in the world is subject to change, and 'a leave-taking comes like a leap into the unknown', as it does in Snufkin's life.

The book's Whomper, Toft, is both part of the narrative and the narrator. He bears a strong likeness to Tove, especially in his appearance. Through Toft she grieves about her mother's approaching death. 'It's now she should come, she's the only one I care about! [...] I want someone who is never scared and who cares about me, I want a mamma!' Only Moominmamma can give Toft peace. Tove portrays him as a daydreamer, but, as she also wrote, 'the dream is more important than reality'.

Tove describes the process of ageing through the character of Grandpa-Grumble (*Onkelskruttet*). Grandpa-Grumble sleeps all the time and forgets things very easily. He cannot always remember whether his name is Crumby-Mumble,

Toft asleep in a coil of rope. Illustration
from *Moominvalley in November*, 1970

Grandpa-Grumble quarrels with his
reflection in the mirror. Illustration
from *Moominvalley in November*, 1970

Grindle-Fumble or Gramble-Fimble. He decides to be Grandpa-Grumble. With
the advancing years people have begun to treat him differently, and his life has
also changed in other ways. The author has observed the ageing of those close
to her and is able to describe the process as though she were able to penetrate
the skin of her characters. Grandpa-Grumble reflects on his life as an old man:

> *So many of them are introduced and immediately lose their names. They arrive on
> Sundays. They shout polite questions because they can never get it into their heads
> that one isn't deaf. They try to talk as simply as possible so that I'll understand what
> it's about.*

The old man wanders about the valley leaning on his walking stick, wearing a hat and talking to his reflection. Grandpa-Grumble's visual presence is almost identical to the picture of Ham in the German edition of *The Summer Book,* except that Grandpa-Grumble is shorter and plumper. Old age and ageing were subjects that interested Tove, and after Grandpa-Grumble she went on to create many other profound and very unconventional portraits of old people.

Moominvalley in November is set in late autumn, a dark, mysterious time. Winter has not yet come. The old is still dying, and the new has not yet been born. In Finnish mythology, November is the month of death, and its Finnish name – *marraskuu* – means 'month of death'.

The birth of *Moominvalley in November* was a challenging one. When Tove sent in the first version of the manuscript, she heard on the grapevine that the publishers did not like it and did not want to publish it. She reproached herself for this failure, and then put the blame on the fact that she had written the book over the summer, during which time she had been too restless. The island had had too many visitors. But in the end she confessed that these were just excuses: 'I suppose that one writes if one has something to say. At any rate, I believe in the idea of this book and in certain parts of it. The setting is a forest in Nov.–Dec. – Now I want to go – not to the island – but to Pellinki and spend a week digging myself into the sad decay of autumn, before the snow arrives.' In November she was indeed in Pellinki, in Gustafsson's small house – breathing in the darkening days. She wanted to gain an accurate sense of the time of year for her book, which is full of the brownish gloom of death and decomposition.

Waiting for the Moomin family

Tove was cautious about the completed manuscript of *Moominvalley in November,* and again she asked Lars Bäckström for his opinion: 'It seems to play in a minor key, I couldn't make it play any other way [. . .] what matters to me right now is not so much encouragement as choosing the right direction – perhaps I'm going the wrong way. But of course, one can't decide to be "childish" or "grown-up". It will be as it will be.' Lars Bäckström evidently managed to calm Tove, as she thanked him for his response and explained her uncertainty: 'My big worry was that the November book meant a step downwards, or backwards – and that I ought to wait until I was able to write about the family again. And I was afraid that it was too gloomy.'

It is true that *Moominvalley in November* is a book for adults rather than for children, and it is not a cheerful work. When she received a reader's letter from a girl who wrote that she was especially fond of *Moominvalley in November*, Tove replied that she was very pleased to hear it. She had thought the book was rather complicated and depressing, and would therefore be unlikely to appeal to children.

In *Moominvalley in November* Tove said farewell to her Moomin books. Above all, however, it was a farewell to her mother, the member of her family whom she loved most. Now that her mother was no longer alive, Moominvalley could not remain as it had been. A deep and quiet sorrow had been woven into the story – and that sorrow was hers.

THE LISTENER

The Listener collection of stories appeared in 1971. The book's blend of real-life and fictional material varies from one story to the next, but all of it undoubtedly has a strong connection with the author's own life – much in the same way as, in the book, she wrote: 'Desolation cannot be portrayed by anyone who has not experienced desolation and observed it very closely.'

In 'The Rain', Tove writes about the death of an old person. The story clearly has its roots in Ham's death a year earlier, and the author's own emotions come through very powerfully. Although the event itself is authentic and very personal, the story is also a universal narrative about what happens to a person who is dying and to the people who are being left behind. Death can be like 'one single cry, a rendering precise of the definitive, in the way that a graphic artist shapes his end vignette on the final page'. A life ends; the drawing is complete. Dying itself is something deeply private and sacred, even though it takes place in a hospital among all the machines and tubes:

> *The dying person is completely pure, completely silent, and then, out of the grey mouth, out of the altered face comes a long cry, it is usually called a rattle but it is a cry, the tired body that has had enough of everything, enough of life and waiting and enough of all these attempts to prolong what has ended, enough of all this encouragement and anxious fuss, all the clumsiness of tenderness, all the determination of pain not to show itself and not to frighten the people whom one loves.*

'The Squirrel' is a fairytale about the incongruous friendship between an animal and a woman. Tove said that she wrote it several times, polishing it over and over again, as is testified by a number of manuscripts that have been preserved. The story is set on an island, very obviously Klovharun, where an artist has gone for the autumn in order to write. A squirrel suddenly breaks the calm of her solitude, and its existence begins to affect her life on the island:

> She got up and took a step towards the squirrel, then another, the squirrel did not move, she stretched out her hand to the creature, closer, very slowly and the squirrel bit her, with lightning speed, like slashing scissors.

The story's ending is highly surrealistic: the woman sees the squirrel sailing away in a boat, his sole connection with the rest of the world. She is left alone on the island over the winter and can begin to write. Now she is calm. Tove said that the story was based on a real event: 'Yes, the squirrel actually existed. It came all the way to the outermost island on a piece of tree-bark. I put out food for it, and it spent the winter on the island. And when spring arrived it found a piece of plank and sailed away out to sea again.'

THE SUMMER BOOK

The Summer Book appeared just one year after *The Listener*. It is a bright book about sorrow, death and the happiness of living. The book's central characters are a young girl and her grandmother. Tove said that she got the theme of an old woman and a little girl from Ham, whom she often asked for ideas. Not until Ham died did she begin to work on the book. Its characters – Sophia, her father, Lars, and his mother, Ham, whose last summer is dealt with in the book – are easily recognizable. Although the events are at least partly fictional, the atmosphere is authentic and the thoughts expressed are sometimes so sincere that they can only be those of the author.

The old woman is saying farewell to the world, and her granddaughter is gradually approaching adulthood. Their dialogue opens up perspectives on existence: how the old woman can no longer remember her youth, how she finds it difficult to walk about on the island, how her life seems to be slipping away, how her memory betrays her and becomes fragile: '[B]ut now it's as if it were all slipping away from me and I can't remember and don't care.'

There is a great deal of death in the book. There are friends who are absent or no longer with us, as it's put euphemistically. The child is straightforward, and asks her grandmother a question:

> When are you going to die? the child asked.
> And she replied: Soon. But it's absolutely none of your business.

The child is interested in life after death, and she returns over and over again to the eternal questions: what is it like in heaven, does hell exist, how is God able to hear everyone's prayers, are angels men or women, and all sorts of other things. The child asks question after question:

> Are the angels allowed to fly down into hell?
> Certainly. A lot of their friends and acquaintances may be there.
> Now I've got you! cried Sophia. Yesterday you said there was no such thing as hell!

In the midst of these reflections on heaven and hell, the grandmother steps on a cowpat and starts singing:

> Too-ra-lay, too-ra-lee, you're not allowed to throw cowshit at me. Too-ra-lay, too-ra-lee, or else I'll throw it back at ye.

Everyday things and events that are slightly repugnant in their realism prevent the reader from becoming too deeply immersed in the charting of the borders between life and death. Nothing is allowed to grow too solemn or heavy – instead, everything is alive and pulsating, as long as life continues.

Tove had changed course and begun to write for adults. It confused the publishers, the critics and her public, as they were used to thinking of her as a children's author. To some extent *The Sculptor's Daughter* was seen as a less definitive shift, as it was, after all, about a child and could also be interpreted as autobiographical. But once *The Summer Book* and *The Listener* had appeared, it could not be denied that Tove really had begun to write for grown-ups. The books were liked – indeed, they were loved – and many people bought them. *The Summer Book* in particular was translated into several languages. Yet many people still found it hard to accept and to forgive her for abandoning the Moomin world. One critic expressed her disappointment by comparing Tove to a brilliant violinist who for some reason wanted to change her instrument and play the piano, while refusing to perform the pieces that were her tours de force because of her artistic conscience. According to this critic, the magic had left with the Moomins.

X

Finding Freedom and Colour

AT THE ARTISTS' RESIDENCE IN PARIS

In 1975, when Tove was sixty-four, Tove and Tuulikki had the opportunity of visiting Paris, where they stayed at the Cité Internationale des Arts. They had been there before and Paris was an important city for them both. Although Tove did not go there to paint (that was now a part of her former life), the visit did not lend itself to writing either, partly because she was so exhausted after completing a television drama in Sweden. The long spring in Paris that loomed ahead scared Tove. They were to stay in a small studio, which she anticipated could be difficult – she was used to her own work space and did not want to pretend to write under Tuulikki's watchful gaze. As it turned out, 'I pretended to write, but nothing came of it.'

When writing did not work out, she tried to paint. Initially it seems to have been no more than a kind of surrogate activity, as it was now a long time since she had either drawn or painted. But soon she was clinging desperately to the work as though her last hour were at hand, trying to rediscover the joy of creation and her desire to paint.

Tove said that even though she knew she could paint, it was hard to find the urge to do it. Fortunately, something began to move inside her and she rediscovered this desire. For her, it was the basis of all that was good and essential. And now that she had it she could paint and not be disturbed by anything – not by a request from someone who wanted to come and open a travelling exhibition of her illustration work, nor by anything else: '[I]f I don't get my teeth into my painting right now I will never try to paint again: this is the last chance. I don't even know if it's all that important, and I can't be bothered to think about it. The exciting thing is that now I don't care what people will think when they look at my paintings in future years. I am trying to see and to find my desire.'

Self-Portrait, oil, 1975

Tove took her time. First she made her familiar still-life paintings, then powerful works that are very different in style from much of the rest of her opus. She painted Tuulikki as a graphic artist leaning over her work, concentrating as she makes an engraving or paints a picture. The light streams into the studio through a window in front of the woman, who is surrounded by finished paintings on the walls and floor, and also by artists' materials, paintbrushes and bottles of Indian ink. Despite their ordinariness, the objects create an exciting atmosphere in the work, which is strong, intense, bold, and also painted with great skill. It conveys the artist's sense of freedom and her delight in painting and has something of the same fresh and irrational fairytale quality that characterizes many of Tove's works of the 1930s, or some of the colourful covers she designed for the Moomin books.

Tove also painted a picture of herself, which she later called *Ugly Self-Portrait* (*Fult självporträtt*). It reveals her as an artist with a powerful, direct technique, who painted her portrait with free gestures and an almost furious energy. The work lives and breathes and is the artist's spitting image. It possesses all the qualities she had sought for years: freedom, radiance, impulse and desire. Above all, it is painterly – perhaps the very thing for which she had striven all her life.

Tove has been recognized around the world as a master of the line. Her line was confident and powerful – and it sprang from her fingers ready-formed and full of life. With it she was able to express all the emotions of human existence. But her relationship to colour was more complex. Colour was enormously important to her and she directed most of her attention to it. When it seemed that the colours had fled from her paintings, or had become devoid of radiance or simply refused to obey her, she became depressed. The result looked dreary, grey on grey. When she felt that the colour had returned, her joy was immense.

The discovery of colour and painterliness in Paris was doubtless a source of delight to her. But since she had also found her own voice as an author and been preoccupied with the Moomins, she had become a different kind of artist altogether. There was so much else that she wanted to do – and so much that still tied her down. She had constantly to make corrections to the ever-growing number of translations and new editions of the Moomin books, provide new covers for them, supervise the burgeoning Moomin industry and write film and television series. At the same time so many books for adults were waiting to be written.

The Graphic Artist. Portrait of Tuulikki Pietilä, oil, 1975

THE DANGEROUS JOURNEY

In 1970, twenty-five years after the first Moomin book had appeared, Tove said farewell to Moominvalley in *Moominvalley in November*. Yet in 1977 she returned once again to that world in *The Dangerous Journey* (*Den farliga resan*). This story contains clear allusions to many of the literary and artistic works she loved and revered, such as *Alice in Wonderland*, the stories of Elsa Beskow and the art of John Bauer – especially his pictures of dense forests with mighty tree-trunks.

The visual origins of this third picture book can be found in Tove's early paintings, influenced by Surrealism, and in her monumental art, all of which have the same atmosphere of fairytale and mystery and an absence of mundanity. From a technical point of view, however, one can see much of the expressiveness, freedom and delight in colour that Tove discovered in Paris in 1975.

The book's overall appearance is very different from that of the two earlier

Sketch for *The Dangerous Journey*

picture books. Unlike those books, this is the work of a painter rather than a graphic artist and author. Here the colours dominate, the dramatic line has receded, and the accompanying text is no longer so important. Tove almost revels in painting, making the colours glide into one another, constantly producing fresh nuances. In some places, the watercolour edges are delicate and translucent, in others, strikingly powerful. The contours of the pictures and their colours are soft, and she employs very sensitive, light-toned pastel shades that give the impression of fading; elsewhere she creates three-dimensional shapes that are sometimes thick and at other times as light as a breath of air.

The landscapes are imposing, the volcanoes erupt, the forest is gloomy, the sea rages, and snow and wind threaten the wanderers. Only the description of Moominvalley is the same as before. Its inhabitants have found one another, and are happy in their sunny and flower-decked vale. With this image Tove took her leave of all the readers of her Moomin books.

XI

Life and Living

RADIO DRAMAS, THEATRE, AND TELEVISION SERIES

In the 1960s Tove's activity as a painter increasingly coexisted with the extension of her work into theatre, as well as into film, television and radio. She wrote new plays and adapted her short stories for Finnish and Swedish radio and TV. The Moomins continued their conquest of the theatre world, finding one new arena after another, and these dramas were immensely popular. In Finland, Ilkka Kuusisto's *Moomin Opera* received its premiere at the Finnish National Opera in 1974. In 1982 the Moomins' adventures featured in a production at Stockholm's Royal Dramatic Theatre, once again directed by Vivica. She still worked in close collaboration with Tove, who trusted her unreservedly – and the arrangement worked well.

As the director of several large theatres, Vivica was very busy, but she always seemed to have time for her friend. Tove sent her scripts and asked for suggestions for improvement, which she duly received. Vivica was an inspiring and capable professional partner. Her help was invaluable, especially in the early days.

Tove thought about the differences between scripts for radio, television and film, and came to the conclusion that each of them required very different methods of writing. She had to take into account their limitations and possibilities right from the start. It was the same as beginning a painting on the wet plaster layer of a fresco: one needed to know in advance what one wanted to achieve, what was possible with each individual technique, and what was not. The filming of the story *The Invisible Child* (*Det osynliga barnet*) was Tove's first experience of television work. She wondered how the producers planned to represent the child's invisibility, whether it could be shown by the little girl's dress being buttoned up over her head, or how, if the girl were invisible, they could film her eating a sandwich. These were fascinating problems, but she could always ask Vivica for advice.

Moomins from the Polish animation

Tove also wanted signature tunes for the productions. Their mutual friend Erna Tauro had worked with Vivica for a long time and seemed to be a suitable composer. In addition to writing the best-known Moomin music, in 1965 Tauro had also composed a setting of Tove's poem 'Autumn Song' ('Höstvisa'), a song that is universally loved and has been performed by many artists.

The first Moomin puppet animations were produced in West Germany in 1959 and 1960. Two series of six episodes each were based on *Finn Family Moomintroll* (*Trollkarlens hatt*) and *Moominsummer Madness* (*Farlig midsommar*). Swedish Television was enthusiastic about the Moomins and wanted to make a multi-part series about them – though in the end there were thirteen episodes altogether. The series, with the title *The Moomintroll* (*Moomintrollet*), was written by Tove together with her brother Lars: shown over several months in 1969 it received a huge amount of attention. Tove was surprised at the importance of television – people awaited the first episode of the Moomin series as if for some magical happening. *The Moomintroll* was directed by Vivica and the lead roles were played by a well-known group of

Moomin puppets from the German puppet animation

actors – Birgitta Ulfsson, Lasse Pöysti and Nils Brandt, who had performed the plays at Lilla Teater.

While Tove was planning the Swedish series, she received a letter from Japan. A Japanese television company wanted to make an animated Moomin series in colour, and to open negotiations for the copyright. Tove went to Vivica for advice. In her reply to the company, Tove said that although she greatly admired Japanese cinema, she regretted she had not seen any animations or films for children. She outlined the rights option that had been taken by Swedish Television, and said she would find out if her contract with them would be an obstacle to the project. Otherwise she professed to be very interested. A short time later she wrote to Vivica that Yasmo Yamamoto, the executive in charge of the project, had suddenly turned up in Finland with his secretary. Communication was difficult, as the only foreign language spoken by the pair was a little German.

The series was made in Japan and became popular there, though it was never screened in other countries as Tove refused to allow international distribution of the programmes. Almost everything about them seemed to run counter to the non-violent philosophy of the Moomins. In the Japanese series, Moomintroll is physically beaten by Moominpappa, and there is a war in Moominvalley. The rights to this first series have now expired in Japan and so the programmes can no longer be viewed.

During these years, theatre productions and films, as well as radio programmes and Moomin television shows, brought an awareness of the Moomins to a wider public. The business side of the venture, which had started around a decade earlier, grew into a veritable circus. In Finland, too, the Moomins rose to great 'commercial heights'. Tove told Vivica almost indignantly that someone had offered her a Peikko-juoma ('Moomintroll' soft drink for children). Tove received a perpetual stream of invitations from different parts of the world. Luckily her brother Lars was good at dealing with such matters, and as far as possible Tove left them in his hands. At this point the Moomins had still to reach the peak of their fame.

Although the experience with the Japanese Moomin animation had been a big disappointment to Tove, it failed to shake her faith in moving images, which now intrigued her more and more. From 1978 to 1982 a Moomin animation series was made in Poland, consisting of seventy-eight episodes of eight to nine minutes each. It was first shown in Poland and Germany, and later also in Britain, where it became extremely popular. The episodes were screened in Finland in the early 1980s, and the material was later stored and reworked for a variety of purposes.

Since the Moomin series saw success in Japan, the television producers there were keen to create more. This time Tove and Lars took a stricter line. They approved Dennis Livson (a Finnish producer of children's programmes with experience of working with the Japanese) as production coordinator. The series was put together under his watchful supervision, together with input from Tove and Lars, and involved an enormous amount of labour by the Japanese animators. It was created in two stages, and over a hundred episodes were made. They appeared on television in many countries in the early 1990s, with repeats that continued for years. With Dennis Livson's support, a film version of *Comet in Moominland* was also made. Most people are familiar with the Moomins through this Japanese animation series and its characters, and copies of the later programmes can still be obtained. It gave rise to an unprecedented Moomin boom that reached almost every corner of the world. The first Moomin books were read by thousands of people, and the Moomin picture books by many more.

In their turn, the comic strips reached tens of millions of readers. Through the Japanese animations the Moomins became loved in hundreds of millions of homes – in 1990 Tove visited Japan in connection with the series and was welcomed like a Hollywood star.

THE ISLANDS ARE THE BEST THING I HAVE EVER WANTED

Houses, buildings and the physical act of building a home meant a great deal to Tove. She spent nearly all her life looking for new places to live. For her, the act of moving house symbolized a beginning and an end, a new love affair and a new phase of life. New houses and places were like nests that she wanted to build for the people she cared for the most. She had wanted to buy a houseboat, the *Christopher Columbus*, on which she had planned to spend the summer with Atos and Lars. For Atos she had wanted to found an artists' colony in Morocco, in a house with hanging gardens. When her love for Atos faded, her interest in the project faded too.

The islands of Pellinki were the place in the world that Tove loved most. Initially the Janssons had rented a house for the summer from the Gustafsson family. The Gustafssons' son Abbe was the same age as Tove, and they became close friends. Later, in some of her short stories, Tove described the summers they shared. In Pellinki there was a surfeit of islands to move to, build on or simply dream about. When Tove was madly in love with Vivica, she wrote to her that she was trying to rent the lighthouse island of Kummelskär for them both. Kummelskär had been the object of her dreams ever since she was a little girl and she had wanted to be the lighthouse keeper there. Although the project was never realized, the dream remained vivid.

Tove's love for Vivica had also plunged her into great misery, however. Broken by it, she built a house on Bredskär with her brother which she called 'Vindrosen' – the Wind Rose. Building it was akin to therapy for her, for in building a house she also constructed for herself 'an outer and inner [house] of calm and indifference'. The act of building seemed to express a primitive instinct – a search for shelter in a cold world – and in the years ahead she did indeed seek shelter in the Wind Rose. With the passage of time, though, Bredskär became overcrowded. There were now too many of them in the little house, and they could not help getting in one another's way. Lars and his young daughter had returned from Spain, and Tuulikki had also joined the family – but Tuulikki and Ham had their differences. A new house was needed, if only 'to make Tooti calmer'.

The house on Klovharun

As Tove's reputation grew, an increasing number of uninvited guests came to Bredskär: journalists, film crews, admirers and a varied assortment of other people. The peace and quiet were gone, and yet it was peace and quiet that Tove needed. Once again she tried to rent Kummelskär, writing hopefully that she was going to Porvoo to try to 'charm the Public Works Department', but to no avail. Her disappointment showed through clearly in her comments, when she said drily that once again the officials turned her down because they thought she would scare away the birds and the fish – now it was the salmon, now the cod or the whiting.[9] Although she never succeeded in obtaining the island of her dreams, in the end she was granted the right to rent Klovharun, which she came to love.

The house on Klovharun was built very quickly. According to the law of the time, the construction timbers had to reach all the way up to the roof ridge if the whole structure were not to be torn down in the event that planning permission was not received – or so they believed, anyway. A memento of this is recorded in tiny handwriting in Tove's almanacs, where she kept a precise tally of how much cement they received, who did what, and which storms disrupted the builders'

9. The officials raised objections on the grounds that certain types of fish might be scared away by construction work – each time the type of fish they specified was different: sometimes it was cod, sometimes whiting, sometimes salmon. Tove mentions this in her letters to Eva.

work in late autumn. These notes were used more or less verbatim in the book *Notes from an Island* (*Anteckningar från en ö*, 1993), three decades later.

Tuulikki's brother Reima Pietilä and his wife, Raili, designed the house, which consisted of only one room with windows facing in all four directions, and a cellar two metres in depth. At night Tuulikki and Tove usually slept in a tent and worked in the house during the day, though it also served as a place to accommodate guests. Tove managed to complete a large amount of work on the island, writing and drawing even when they had visitors. Tuulikki and Tove also created tableaux based on the Moomin stories and made puppets for the puppet theatre they were planning. They spent a great deal of time carving tiny objects – miniature figures and settings for them – painting them and searching for all the necessary fittings.

As a place for two people to spend the entire summer together, the island was rather small and there were few distractions, and there was not always enough to fill the days. Nature provided the impetus for conversation, but even that was limited. Tove described the 'colourful' discussions they had: whenever the weather looked foggy, they would tell each other there was going to be fog; then they would say that the fog had arrived. Tove began to reflect, 'I grew tired of us, I thought we had become boring.' On such days it helped them to clamber up on the rocks and watch the boats out at sea or try to talk to each other on the two-way radio, though that was not always successful.

TWO TRAVELLERS

Tove's life had changed. Contrary to her earlier dreams and plans, she no longer contemplated moving away from Finland. Instead, she had an increasing desire to make journeys abroad with Tuulikki and then return

Tuulikki Pietilä and a sheep, drawn on the title page of the Faroese edition of *Moominland Midwinter* that had recently been published to her studio on her beloved island. She had always loved travelling and as a young woman had dared to tour the countries of Europe alone. In her view, the life of a traveller was a wonderful one, and luckily Tuulikki happened to share this enthusiasm. Everything travel-related became a large and important part of their lives. They studied the map of the world, learned one or two foreign languages, including English, and gained a basic knowledge of others. During her final years Ham was no longer able to travel, and Tove was reluctant to go away for long. So during this period Tove and Tuulikki's journeys together had become rather short.

Publishers wanted Tove to take part in events to launch new foreign editions of her books. Since her books were constantly being translated into other languages this meant a great deal of travel, and she had happy memories of some of these overseas visits. She often drew pictures in the copies of the books she gave to Tuulikki, usually with an inscription that referred to some aspect of the foreign trip. The picture on the title page of an Icelandic edition shows them both on the seashore, sitting on an enormous high rock. The inscription reads: 'Tooti and Tove on a Night of Destiny in Iceland, 1972'. In a Faroese translation she drew a picture of Tooti with a sheep beside her and the words: *Till min Färöiska Förföriska förfåriska Tooticki*, which may be loosely translated as 'To my Faroese Bewitching Sheepy Too-ticky'.

After Ham's death Tove needed someone who could fill the empty space her mother had left behind. Now there was nothing to keep Tuulikki and her in Finland. They had long dreamed of making a long journey together – and Tove wrote enthusiastically to Atos about their planned trip:

> . . . *and in October, Atos, remarkable things will happen! Tooti and I are going to travel Round the World! It's an old dream that we've long been saving and preparing for, and we won't be back until next spring. The direction – via Japan – was decided by some work I'll be doing in Tokyo, and that stage of the journey will be paid for by the Japanese. Then on to Hawaii, and San Pedro, you know – where Taube loaded up gasoline – and where Tooti's aunt lives, and Mexico, and by various methods (including paddle steamer!) up through the States to New York.*

Their journey began in England, as Tove had commitments there – and in Japan – thanks to her Moomin success there; their stay in Japan was also linked with the television series. Tove was enthusiastic about photography and saw it as a particularly fascinating art form. She had judged contests, written about it and actively followed the photographic work of Per Olov and Eva Konikoff. Through her work in television, Tove had also become familiar with the potential of the moving image, and with the way in which a TV studio functions. In Japan she bought her first cine camera, a Konica, and became so firmly attached to it that it almost became a third companion on the journey. For decades, making films was one of the couple's favourite hobbies, and for Tove it opened up opportunities in the film world. She and Tuulikki edited the films themselves, chose the music for them and wrote background voice overs. These films have been preserved, and through them we remain in direct contact with the couple's life together, both at home and abroad.

Tove and Tuulikki also worked diligently during their travels: sketchpads, pens, Indian ink and writing paper were always included in the luggage. Tove usually took along some semi-complete or unedited manuscripts. Tuulikki recalled Tove working on *Moominpappa at Sea* (*Pappan och havet*) during a trip to Portugal and Spain in 1964. The return home soon turned into a nightmare, as the manuscript, a thick blue notebook, vanished and would, it seemed, have to remain in Granada. But at the last minute it was found, having slipped down behind a bed.

Tove took *The Summer Book* (*Sommarboken*, 1972) with her on the world trip, completing it in landscapes entirely different from those of Pellinki where she had begun. Tuulikki remembered how once in New Orleans Tove wrote the first drafts of several short stories with great fervour: 'She sat in the tiny kitchen writing at a furious pace, there was paper here and paper there, and she was wonderfully happy!' While travelling, Tove gained new experiences and with them subjects for her books, some of which contain accounts of those experiences, or are at least partly based on them.

The couple had intended to spend only a few days in Florida. Their lodgings turned out to be an old people's city, a kind of waiting room for death. It seemed that in cities where the sun shone, death received a guarantee of sunshine too. Life in a nursing home immediately began to interest Tove, and they decided to stay a little longer. She began to take notes and write about what she observed. This was the origin of the novel *Sun City* (*Solstaden*), which appeared in 1974. The New Left intellectuals of the time still regarded Tove with caution, and she could not help being affected by this. Lars Bäckström wrote a positive review of the book, and Tove thanked him, describing her relief: 'I know that here I'm still an outsider and that I don't take a position on social issues in an objective way. And now you say that this is not a defect but an original genre, a freedom, even! How glad I was.'

Although the last Moomin book had been written, the Moomins did not desert Tove and Tuulikki. In fact a new phase of their existence had begun with the building of the Moominhouse and the three-dimensional tableaux of the Moomin stories. As described earlier, building homes had always been important to Tove: as a very young woman in the 1930s, she had built a cabin on the island of Sandskär in Pellinki with her friend Albert, as she wanted some privacy. To the islanders' astonishment the cabin withstood gales and storms and remained in place until Tove pulled it down, as did the interior and elegant entrance she designed for a cave.

In 1958 the physician Pentti Eistola built a miniature Moominhouse for his own amusement. He came to introduce himself to Tove and Tuulikki and to show it off, thus initiating a close friendship and also a diversion that the three of them shared for many years. Tuulikki, Ham and Tove were enchanted by the doll's house, and they built a charming greenhouse in its garden, with all the proper details. This really fired their enthusiasm and they all joined forces and began to build an even bigger house from scratch. It was an astonishing and almost perfect miniature world with all the trappings, from electricity to a cellar pantry stocked with jars of jam. It took the trio three years to build the house, which was over two metres tall and contained many rooms. During the winter they would gather in Tove's studio and when summer came they would pack up the materials and half-finished work and take it with them to the island, where the construction resumed. All the surfaces in the tiny cabin on Klovharun were frequently covered in miniature objects. As Tove described it to Maya Vanni, they had 'mainly worked on the "tableaux", the shelves are full of little figures, monsters, buildings, accessories, furniture [. . .]' She told her how the big Moominhouse came into being:

> It began several years ago when Tuulikki made some figures from Moominvalley just for fun. [. . .] Tuulikki's figures became more and more numerous – she made one of them sit on a chair, and of course the chair had to have a table, and the furniture had to have walls around it. That was when Pentti came into it all and the building of the house got going. We built it in the evenings now and then, taller and taller. The actual construction was done by Tuulikki and Pentti, but there were also small jobs like wallpapering, upholstering the drawing room furniture in red velvet, doing masonry work [. . .]

When the big Moominhouse was displayed in 1980 as part of an exhibition at the Museum of Finnish Architecture, Pentti Eistola was listed in the exhibition catalogue as 'chief designer, electrician and expert in problematic passageways' and Tuulikki Pietilä as 'craftswoman, maker of wigs and attributes, and also designer of the friends and creeping creatures that surround the Moomin family'. Tove herself was 'general worker, painter, cleaner and make-up artist' and Per Olov 'photographer and lighting engineer'. In addition, the catalogue said that architecture professor Reima Pietilä had checked the structure of the house and that many friends had donated linen, jewellery, porcelain and all the other items that were needed for a 'Real House'.

Tove and the big Moominhouse

For a doll's house, the Moominhouse is enormous. It is over two metres tall, has countless rooms, staircases and passageways, and its roof is made from 6,800 tiny handmade slivers of wood. The house itself is built in different styles: *Jugendstil* (art nouveau), Finnish national romantic, Empire, Russian-influenced, and many others. It certainly looks quite different from the round, blue house of the Moomin books. Tove admitted that when she had drawn it all those years ago she had not even been able to imagine what it would look like in reality. The big Moominhouse featured in various exhibitions around the world – in Bratislava in 1979 and in Stockholm and Helsinki in 1980. In the speech she gave at the private view, Tove said that while she knew that all children liked to play, she also knew that adults did too. If they were unable to share their play with children, they must have an alternative, and the alternative was usually called a hobby – that was what the project meant to Pentti, Tuulikki and her. Tuulikki was particularly enthusiastic about the house, and also about the dozens of other Moomin 'tableaux' – she was good with her hands, and wood-carving was her hobby.

Building the Moominhouse gave rise to Tove's short story 'The Doll's House', and also to the last Moomin book, *An Unwanted Guest* (*Skurken i Muminhuset*), which appeared in 1980 and features the house. Tove's short texts and Per Olov's

Moomin tableau, 1984–5. Scene from *Moominpappa at Sea*
with the Ocean Orchestra and Moomin characters

photographs conjure up an eventful night in the life of the Moomin family. The
night is dark and a full moon lights the landscape rather eerily. The Moomins
are awake, for something strange is happening in the Moominhouse. They
find an uninvited visitor called Stinky, who despite his small size is actually
a foul-smelling, big-time villain. Per Olov's photographs of the house and all
the most important Moomin characters that live in its rooms create a suitably
mysterious atmosphere.

At first, building the Moominhouse was a pleasant game. But the builders'
enthusiasm kept on growing, and Tove and Tuulikki began to construct tableaux
of various kinds in rapid succession, soon filling up both their living space and
all their time. Tuulikki had once wanted to be a sculptor and the tableaux now
gave her the opportunity to create three-dimensional compositions. With her
experience of set design, Tove was familiar with spatial concepts, though now
the dimensions had to be reduced to the very minimum. They made forty-one
tableaux based on Moomin stories – miniatures that either depicted events in

the stories or showed scenes of the kind encountered on stage. Whenever the couple travelled abroad or visited a flea-market, they looked for objects and materials that might be suitable for making these structures.

The Moominhouse, in its various forms, has become famous. Its most familiar representation is the round, blue house in Moominvalley, which from a distance resembles a tiled stove. This was the house that was used in the Moomin films and as the model for the blue plastic Moomin doll's houses that 'thousands of Finnish children have played with, and onto whose residents they have projected their desires, ideas and fears'. But like any home, the Moominhouse is much more than just a dwelling-place.

NOVELS AND SHORT STORIES

The Moominhouse also provided the theme of the short story 'The Doll's House', which appeared in a collection with the same title in 1978 (in English, the title of the collection was *Art in Nature*), dedicated to Pentti Eistola. The story is a powerfully surrealistic description of three men building a Moominhouse. Two of the men, the retired wallpaperers Alexander and Erik, are the central characters and it is they who start to build the house. Alexander becomes interested in making miniature furniture and then a doll's house, which is very similar to the Moominhouse. Erik helps with the work, moulds little apples, makes jam jars for the cellar pantry and polishes window frames. But in order to obtain lighting they need Boy, who is good at such tasks, and he becomes the third partner in the project. He succeeds in the difficult task of installing electricity in the doll's house, which he calls 'our house' as if he considers himself a full member of the team. This is too much for Erik, whose suppressed jealousy is provoked into violent rage. The psychological ownership of the splendid, lit-up doll's house is no small matter, and the struggle for it leads to bloodshed, though fortunately on a reduced scale.

Other stories in the book include the one about Viktor and the monkey in a Helsinki restaurant, the 'Cartoonist' story, and many others that are also based on events in Tove's life during the last few decades of her life – with changes and twists in reality of a kind that only an independent artist could have achieved. 'The Great Journey' is a story about the friendship and love between two women and the attempt of one of them to break away from her mother – a rather obvious portrayal of Tove and Tuulikki's life together, and of the trio's mutual jealousy:

Mamma could sit on her hair when she was young. And it's still the most beautiful hair I've ever seen. And Elena replied: I know, everything she has is the most beautiful thing you've ever seen. And Rosa: You're jealous! You're not being fair. She'll do anything for me to feel free. Strange, said Elena in a long drawn-out voice, it's strange that you don't feel free. And rather tedious for us.

Tove wrote three novels in the 1980s: *The True Deceiver* (*Den ärliga bedragaren*) appeared in 1982 and was followed two years later by *The Field of Stones* (*Stenåkern*).The short-story collection *Travelling Light* (*Resa med lätt baggage*) came out in 1987, and was often published together with the rather short novel *The Field of Stones*. In 1989 the novel *Fair Play* (*Rent spel*) appeared: it consists of self-contained, short-story-like chapters that portray the same characters.

The writing of *The True Deceiver* was a difficult process, and the work on it took a long time. When the book was complete, Tove wrote to Lars Bäckström: 'This book has probably caused me more trouble than any of the others: I've been working on it off and on for three years (Tooti says: more), have rewritten it again and again, boiled it down, changed everything [. . .] How glad I am that you liked the book – and even compare it to *The Summer Book*, the only one I know is good.'

When Tove thought she had reached a blind alley, she carried on writing 'stubbornly and laboriously'. *The True Deceiver* is about two female friends and their rather strange and tense relationship. One of the women, Anna, is an artist who draws rabbits and flowers for children's stories, and the other, Katri, is a person who pays careful attention to detail and practical matters. Tove said that the women were a portrayal of the different aspects of herself, and that the two characters were based on the Old Testament figures of Cain and Abel. Initially Anna is Abel, but in the course of the book the roles change.

The similarities between Katri and Tove are obvious, especially if one is aware of the watchful efficiency with which Tove took care of business negotiations and money matters, and how competent and not at all helpless she was at these tasks. She did not even employ a secretary to look after the jungle of international contracts and financial deals that had swollen to enormous proportions, though Lars gave her knowledgeable support and assistance. The artist Anna, with her drawings for children, is perhaps even closer to Tove, a kind of self-deprecating caricature of her: just how people might imagine an illustrator of children's books would look. But Anna does not write the stories herself, she merely draws the rabbits, while Katri investigates the fees that firms should pay for the rights to the drawings – just as Tove did when negotiating the rights to her Moomins, a task she often found extremely frustrating.

Something else that the creators of the Moomin world and the rabbits had in common was an enormous number of letters from children, along with the obligation to reply to them all and the fatigue this caused. What should one say in replying to a child? Should one be honest with them, even though it might often involve upsetting them, or should one stick to safe responses that inevitably meant lying? And how old did children need to be before one was able to truthful with them? All these questions are the subject of disputes between the women in the book. Tove was confronted with exactly the same questions and had to take them into account in her writing for children.

The Field of Stones is a shorter and more concise book, and it certainly caused Tove less trouble than *The True Deceiver*. *The Field of Stones* concerns the story of Jonas, who has just retired from his job as a journalist, and his two daughters. He reflects on his relationship to the words he has used during his career: 'I've destroyed too many words in this job, all my words are worn out and overworked, they're tired, if you know what I mean, they're not usable any more. They need a good wash, and then one needs to start all over again. [. . .] Do you know what it means to write millions of words and never be sure if you've chosen the right ones?' Jonas's despair about the difficulty of writing and the threadbare nature of his own linguistic style is doubtless shared by all writers. It was also shared by Tove, who just then was burdened by the fact that the sales of *Sun City* and 'The Doll's House and other stories' (*Dockskåpet*, a book of short stories, 1978; the English translation, entitled *Art in Nature*, was not published until 2012) had been rather poor and the knowledge that many readers still missed the earlier Moomin books.

To some extent it is possible to see Atos Wirtanen and his manic devotion to work as the prototype of Jonas. Jonas's former boss mentions that Jonas's hallmark expression was 'etcetera, etcetera'. Atos was known for using the same phrase. Jonas is supposed to be writing the biography of Y, a man who speculates in tabloid newspapers and whom Jonas calls the 'newspaper king'. Jonas works on his book in a little sauna hut in the country. But the work does not go to plan – the deadline torments him and the texts he writes seem devoid of life. In desperation he tries to solve the problem by any means possible: 'Now he stretched a point here and there, embroidered the truth, made up fables, knowing all the time that it was no good.' Nothing comes of the biography of Y: it remains only partially complete and ends up half-burned, under a rock.

Travelling Light appeared in 1987, when Tove was seventy-four. The title story is about the joys of travel, even when nothing seems to go as planned. What is really intoxicating is the traveller's departure, with its liberation from the everyday – perhaps getting away is more important than getting there:

> *If only I could describe the immense relief that filled me when they finally pulled up the gangway! Only then did I feel safe, or really only when the boat had gone so far from the quay that no one could have shouted . . . asked for my address, screamed that something dreadful had happened . . . Believe me, you cannot imagine my giddy sense of liberation.*

The novel *Fair Play* appeared in 1989. It is a story about Tove and Tuulikki's life – or at least something very close to their real life and experiences. Tove's pseudonym is Mari and Tuulikki's is Jonna; Lars is called Tom, and Atos, Johannes. Both Tove and Tuulikki had fathers called Viktor, and their boat was named *Victoria* after them – in the novel Mari and Jonna have a boat with the same name. The events clearly take place in summer on Klovharun and in winter in Tove and Tuulikki's studios, which are connected by an attic corridor exactly like the one in the real-life apartment building at Ullanlinna.

The book is about a couple's relationship, about jealousy, and the need for time to oneself and the peace and quiet in which to enjoy it. It is a book about how hard it is to live together, and about how much more difficult it is if one is in love. It is also about how two creative people can live together in such a way that the creativity of neither is restricted.

The couple's hobbies are described in the chapter 'Travels with a Konica' ('Resa med Konica'), which is specifically based on Tuulikki's passion for making films. The couple in the story really do experience all the things that happen between people who have lived together for a long time and who love each other, as Tove and Tuulikki do. In the book's chapters, which resemble self-contained short stories, the features of both their personalities come to the fore, especially Jonna's boldness and ability to fire her pistol when there is a need for it (and also when there is not). Tuulikki also kept a gun on the island, partly for security, to ward off unwanted intruders, and partly to put down wounded animals – though she probably also used it for recreation, aiming at tin cans and suchlike. They too discuss their relationship. Jonna remembers how Mari's mother, then aged almost ninety, still used to openly cheat at cards and how she absconded with Jonna's tools, chisels and knives, ruining them one after the other. Both Tuulikki and Ham were practised at wood-carving, and there was often friction between them, with obvious competition as to which of them could create the most beautiful carved object.

The short-story collection *Letters from Klara* (*Brev från Klara*) appeared in 1991. It too has a basis in real-life experiences, many of which had taken place decades earlier. Yet the stories are fresh and read almost as if the events in them had only just happened. The authentic atmosphere can doubtless be explained by the fact that a large number of the stories are based on Tove's notebooks and letters, and the episodes and moods she recorded in them. Now she presented them in fictional form, altering reality, but often only slightly.

The most amusing story in the book is 'Letters from Klara', in which Klara writes entertainingly forthright and clear-headed letters, now as a godmother, now as a younger friend or neighbour. The story 'Journey to the Riviera' is about the visit of a mother and daughter to Barcelona and Juan les Pins, and it corresponds fairly closely in place and time to a similar journey that Tove made with Ham after the latter's retirement. The relationship between mother and daughter is captured in an appealing way Although Ham had died some twenty years earlier, this did not lessen the story's intensity. The same journey also gave rise to the story about the Moomins on the Riviera, which deals with their misadventures in a sequence of hotels.

OPEN AND CLOSED

Many researchers have looked for references to homosexuality in Tove's writings. Although she did not talk about it in public, she made no attempt to conceal it either, and her relationship with Tuulikki Pietilä was known to everyone. The two women took part in official state events such as the President's Independence Day ball, where they were clearly the first to attend the event officially as a lesbian couple. Their relationship was so open and obvious that it was not newsworthy. It was hard to build a scandal on something that everyone knew – even the press, which liked to chase stories of that kind.

Psychological explanations of various kinds often have a chapter of their own in the analyses of Tove's books, and sometimes unusual views have been expressed. The Swedish scholar Barbro K. Gustafsson earned her doctorate in 1992 from Uppsala University's Theological Faculty with a dissertation on Tove's books for adults. She made a special study of *The Doll's House*, *Sun City*, 'The Great Journey' and *Fair Play*, and although her thesis also covered the Moomin stories, they were dealt with more briefly.

Wolves in the Winter Night, watercolour and Indian ink, 1930s

Perhaps surprisingly, Tove agreed to be interviewed by Gustafsson during her research work, and even participated in it actively by attending Gustafsson's dissertation defence. The fact that Tove was prepared to do this may partly be explained by a family connection: Gustafsson was the partner of Tove's beloved cousin Kerstin. When Kerstin, from a religious family, had realized that she was lesbian, Tove had been extremely supportive. Tove and her friends also helped Kerstin with many issues related to her lesbian identity.

Tove refused to give any public interviews about the dissertation defence, and did not want to talk about her private life or relationships. She returned to Finland as soon as the defence and the celebrations for Gustafsson's Ph.D. were over, though she did issue a press release. In it she followed convention, thanking Gustafsson for the clarity of her book and her extensive knowledge of the subject – she had, Tove thought, succeeded in uncovering a rarely explored area of the unconscious. She also said that though much was written about authors, it was perhaps best done after their death, if at all. As if to soften the blow, she stressed the degree of trust between herself and Gustafsson. She said that following the progress of the research had been like an adventure, and that it had almost allowed her to see herself as a pioneer.

In her study, Gustafsson focuses on a dream that Tove had in the 1930s and found strangely threatening. In it she had seen large, black, wolf-like dogs on a seashore at sunset. A psychologist had explained to her that the dream was about repressed drives and forbidden sensuality.

In her thesis, Gustafsson is perhaps prone to detect elements of homosexuality too easily in very ordinary matters connected with the sea and archipelago life. She also discussed the wild animals that Tove often returned to both in the Moomin books and in her works for adults. In *Moominland Midwinter* the dog Sorry-oo wants to join the wolves and learn to howl like them. The story concerns the desire to leave the species into which one has been born, something that proves impossible. In *The True Deceiver*, the wolfhound plays a central role in the power relationship between the two women. Numerous readers have seen allusions to homosexuality in the comic strip about a little dog that falls in love with a cat. It realizes that the love is wrong and becomes depressed. In the end the cat turns out to be a dog in disguise. This time the problem has a simple solution.

In Tove's books there are repeated descriptions of people or Moominvalley creatures becoming 'electric', and this is clearly an important theme in her writing. The Hattifatteners resemble a wandering flock of penises or condoms – in thunderstorms they become electric, and then burn anyone who gets close to them. It is very easy to imagine that the electrification is an allegory for oestrus. The Mymble is also able to become electric – with her countless children she is the most sensual character in Moominvalley. The Whomper Toft in *Moominvalley in November* is the master of thunder and lightning. He lets the Creature out of a locked cupboard, and all that remains is a smell of electricity. The Creature runs away and grows even larger during thunderstorms,

The dog Ynk (Sorry-oo), who wanted to be with the wolves. Illustration from *Moominland Midwinter*, 1957

when lightning fills the sky, but is too big, angry and bewildered to be so big and angry. In 'The Doll's House', electrification brings about a drama of jealousy between three men that leads to violence. There is a similar outcome in 'The Great Journey', where the mother feels the electrifying presence of her daughter's female friend, whereupon the daughter becomes jealous.

Fair Play is a book about the relationship between two women in their seventies who are set in their ways, and their daily life together. Gustafsson uses the narrative to examine their mutual roles in the light of the old custom of categorizing lesbians either as 'femmes' or 'butches', the latter having more masculine traits – a way of seeing a relationship between two women as a copy of a heterosexual one. Jonna and her prototype Tuulikki correspond to the 'butch' profile. Tove also portrayed Tuulikki as Moominvalley's Too-ticky, a rather burly, masculine figure who keeps a knife in her belt.

Quoting Lord Alfred Douglas and the line of verse that was mentioned at the indecency trial of Oscar Wilde, Gustafsson writes that homosexual love is the love that does not dare speak its name. Although the time in which Tove lived was quite different from Wilde's, there were similar prejudices and tensions in society – and, of course, they influenced her writing. Over the centuries women were not expected to write blatant erotic descriptions, but had instead to express themselves in allegorical terms. It was supposed that they did experience such feelings –and even more so when they were the result of unlawful love.

Tove's books contain no openly erotic episodes or writing of a sexual nature and in this her writing is typical of women's literature of her time. Sometimes it feels as though the characters in her books have to some extent been freed from sexuality. Their relationships are based more on understanding and friendship than on ardent passion, though their jealousy can sometimes take violent forms. Many things are veiled in highly metaphorical language. In the books that Tove wrote for adults, male and female couples are portrayed interchangeably without particular emphasis. In many of her books, as in her life, homosexuality was so natural that there was no need to make a fuss about it. While it was not to be denied, it was not to be given a high profile either. It was almost as though she backed out of dealing with her sexuality too openly, and in fact she forbade her biographer to write about her love affairs. Since the biography was written for children, this kind of advance censorship was possible.

In the story 'The Great Journey' ('Den stora resan'), two women in their seventies, Rosa and Elena, together with Rosa's mother, live a life of humdrum joys and sorrows and work on their creative tasks. Among all three, physical love is a taboo subject. Elena asks Rosa: 'What does she know, in any case? Nothing. She doesn't know anything about such matters.' The two women are unable to show their feelings for each other if Rosa's mother is present. They plan a holiday together, but Rosa changes her mind and goes away with her mother instead. She remembers the promise she made in the nursery: 'I'll take you with me, I'll steal you from Papa, we'll go to a jungle or sail out on the Mediterranean . . . I'll build you a castle where you shall be queen.'

Organizations that promoted sexual equality in Finland and the Nordic countries gave Tove awards for her pioneering work on behalf of sexual minorities, and she has certainly been an extremely important role model and author in the gay community. She had the ability to be completely open, yet at the same time quite private – as in the case of the dissertation, when she gave Gustafsson interviews and took part in the defence, but would not agree to answer questions from journalists who were interested in her private life. In relation to her lesbian identity, as shown by this very situation, she sometimes came out of the closet, and at other times she concealed the truth.

Tove's homosexuality inspired a great many researchers and readers to look for the most varied interpretations. Perhaps her slightly sardonic attitude to this excessive interest can be seen in her song 'Psychomania' ('Psykofnattvisan'), written in 1963 for the revue *Krasch* and set to music by Erna Tauro. The song is like an obscure parody, in which psychoanalytic terms form a wild, cacophonous reality all of their own. It is as though she is drifting among people who are intently looking for something and who begin to see signs of it everywhere. In fact, they can no longer see anything else because their heads are filled with 'psychomania'. The song is a lengthy one, and operates on many levels. It also demonstrates that its author was familiar with the psychological terminology of the day – Tove had always been fascinated by interpretations of the human mind and she knew the terminology back to front, so well in fact that she could play with it:

> *I pore and pore*
> *and where I pore*
> *the symbols gather more and more*
> *I sink right through the floor*
> *into depression*
> *and tendentious apperception . . .*

XII

Taking Leave

By the time Tove was in her fifties, everything was properly in place. She had the Ullanlinna studio and Klovharun, she had money and she was able to travel abroad and to make films. By this time Tove and Tuulikki were a well-established old couple with childhood, youth and middle age behind them. Yet still Tove had a great deal of work to do and no lack of drive to carry on. She was now an international celebrity and her career demanded time and constant attention. She had to approve or reject requests, especially those for permission to make use of the Moomin world. She had to give interviews, entertain guests and receive honours. She had to design covers for new editions and translations of her books, the text of which had to be read and corrected, and there were always decisions to be made about the Moomin merchandising industry, which had grown enormous. To a great extent, Tove was now in service to the work she had created and this did not leave much time for new projects.

Answering letters from children had long occupied a large portion of her time, and it was a task she considered important. Although she saw it as her duty, she also enjoyed communicating with her young readers. The greater the number of Moomin books that were translated and the more famous they became, the greater the flow of letters and the time needed to deal with them. Yet a failure to reply would have given her a bad conscience – something she dreaded. In her last book she had made use of (partly fictional) letters from children as the basis of the short story 'Messages' (published in English in the collection *A Winter Book: Selected Stories* in 2006). The story tells how omnipotent the children imagine the author to be, how many of their wishes are addressed to her and how impossible it would be not to answer their cries of distress. 'What am I to do about my parents? They're getting more and more hopeless. Write!' Or 'My cat has died! Write at once.' In old age, when Tove reflected on her life, she said she had received an enormous amount of love, and was partly referring to these letters from the children.

But answering them took precious time away from her other writing. In

1974 an interview with her appeared in the Swedish daily paper *Dagens Nyheter* under the headline 'Save Tove from the Children'. It was about how vast her fan-mail had become and how time-consuming the process of replying to each letter herself had proved to be. In the 1980s she estimated that every year she received some 2,000 letters, each of which she replied to individually, at some length. It was hard to find quiet time for her own work, so she proposed the introduction of a special authors' law. It would protect writers in the same way that the law protects birds during the nesting season. During the closed season, authors would be able to concentrate and write in

Paradise, oil, 1940

peace, as they needed both time and solitude. Becoming an artist took a very long time.

The islands of Pellinki were still for Tove a great source of creativity and the dearest place in the world. Ham, Faffan and Lasse's wife Nita had been a part of her summers there, but now they were no longer around. With Tuulikki, Tove had moved to Klovharun, where their life was mostly peaceful. Though once in a while they received visits from Tove's brothers, who brought their families and friends with them.

The search for Paradise had been a constant thread in Tove's life and art.

It is a recurrent theme, especially in her paintings of the 1930s, not only as a visual influence from the Bible, but also as a free-ranging fantasy, a land of Cockaigne, with blue waters, swimming and dancing – people mingling peacefully amid wonderful natural surroundings. In her large murals of the decade that followed it appeared as a theme again and again. Tove consciously wanted to give the people who used the premises a moment of Paradise (as she had done in the case of the Strömberg factory). Her most famous Paradise was, of course, Moominvalley.

In her personal life she sought her Paradise in different parts of the world and always had plans to move to a better place with the people who mattered to her most. This included the project of the artists' colony. In the end, though, she found it in Pellinki, and especially on Klovharun. Vivica Bandler wrote of the summers they spent together on the islands of Pellinki: '[E]verything was full of meaning, every dip of one's toe in the sea, every conversation. Being there was a glimpse of heaven.'

Life on the island was demanding, nevertheless, especially for people of advanced years: there was no well, so all the drinking water had to be brought in by boat. The island also lacked electricity and was a very long way from anything. The transporting of food supplies and the delivery and dispatch of mail were difficult – the two women needed help with all this and their friends began to worry about them. What if something were to happen, what if they were to injure themselves on slippery rocks, or fall ill? Telephone connections were bad, and in some kinds of weather it was even impossible for boats to dock at the island.

The archipelago's native residents provided many kinds of essential support to the Jansson family. Albert Gustafsson (Abbe) had played an important role in Tove's life ever since her childhood and they were both on familiar terms with nature. As a child, Tove played with Abbe and studied the sea and the islands with him, gaining much useful knowledge about archipelago life. In the story 'Albert' (*The Sculptor's Daughter*), while out fishing he frees a badly injured seagull from its torment by cutting its throat. Although it seemed cruel, it was an act of kindness to the suffering bird. The story evokes the narrator's infinite trust in the boy: 'Albert would always fix it. Whatever happened, and no matter what one had done, it was Albert who fixed it.' The real-life Albert Gustafsson was just as important as the Albert in the story.

As the children grew up, Abbe continued to be a close friend and psychological support, as well as a skilled handyman for everyday tasks. The family got kerosene from Abbe if it ran out unexpectedly, or pieces of hardwood for Ham and Tuulikki to carve. In 1962 he built the mahogany boat *Victoria,* four metres long, which became a favourite of Tuulikki in particular. Abbe's wife, Greta, was also a close friend of Tove. But Abbe's early death in 1981 left a great emptiness and the archipelago no longer felt the same after that.

During the winter that Abbe died, the house on Klovharun was burgled. Although the key hung on the wall beside the door, someone had smashed the windows, broken some things and stolen others. A few years later the same thing happened again. The vandalism felt like an insult to the house and made Tove and Tuulikki angry, as well as adding to their sense of insecurity.

The worst thing about their life on the island was the fact that they were growing old – they were not exempt from the creeping decrepitude that old age brings to everyone. The joints grow stiffer, one cannot keep one's sense of balance and one's strength begins to fail. Walking on slippery rocks, fishing and dealing with the boat when there were gales became more and more difficult, and in the end almost impossible. At some point old age can no longer be ignored and it forced them to accept restrictions on the way they lived, as Tove wrote:

> There came a summer when it was suddenly an effort to pull up the nets. The terrain became unmanageable and treacherous. This made us more surprised than alarmed, perhaps we weren't old enough yet, but to be on the safe side I built a couple of steps and Tooti fixed up some guide ropes and hand grips here and there, and we continued as usual but ate less fish. [...]
>
> And that last summer something unforgivable happened: I became afraid of the sea. Large waves were no longer associated with adventure, only anxiety and responsibility for the boat, and indeed all boats that ply the sea in bad weather. [...] That fear felt like a betrayal – my own.

They decided to leave the island with dignity – while they were still upright. And yet the departure felt like a little death. Perhaps they would have been able to go on visiting the island for a few more years, but in the end it felt better to leave when everything was still going quite well. So in 1992 they gave the island to the Pellinki local heritage association. The place where they had spent a large part of each year since 1965 was now in the hands of others. It was theirs only in memory.

But those memories were precious, and there were many of them. Out of them emerged the wonderful book *Notes from an Island (Anteckningar från en ö)* in 1996.

The pictures of the island's landscapes are by Tuulikki and the text is Tove's. Her notebooks and almanacs are filled with Klovharun's history. Every bag of cement and rock-blasting was carefully noted in tiny handwriting. The notebooks give an account of how the house was built, what it was like, and why it was so important: what it was like to live with nature, to watch the ice breaking up in early spring. Leaving the island became a prodigious farewell:

> So I would never fish again. Never again throw the slops into the sea and be careful with rainwater, never again suffer agonies over Victoria, and now no one, no one, had any need to be concerned about us! Good. Then I began to think: why can't a meadow be allowed to run wild in peace and quiet, and why can't the pretty stones be allowed to tumble about as they want to without being admired, and so on, and gradually I got angry and thought that the cruel bird war could look after itself and as far as I was concerned any damned gull that liked was welcome to suppose that it owned the whole house!

The most important thing in Tove's life had been creative work. She created, painted, drew and wrote enough to fill the careers of several people. Her creativity and artistic range had been immense – embracing painting, fairytale, short stories, novels, plays, poems, songs, stage sets, monumental paintings, illustrations and advertisements to political drawings and cartoons. There is no knowing where she found so much time and energy and just why the work was so important to her. She simply had a great need to create and do. It was a desire, an urge that she maintained for decades, something that became part of her personality. Indeed, she nurtured her creative ability for a very long time: her last collection of stories, 'Messages. Selected Short Stories 1971–1997' (*Meddelande. Noveller i urval 1971–1997*) was published in 1998 when she was eighty-four. In addition to older work, it also contained some new stories. Two years earlier she and Tuulikki had also put together the book about the island, and in 1998 the film *Haru – Island of the Lonely* (*Haru, de ensammas ö*) was completed.

Old age can gnaw away at a person, devouring their energy and creativity. In the novels and stories that focus on the subject, Ham and possibly Faffan were prototypes of the 'old person'. In *Moominvalley in November* Grandpa-Grumble only remembers what he wants to remember, and decides to give himself a new name. His old age is portrayed as thoroughly creative, even though it is accompanied by the troubles and pains of ageing. Life's fragility is also powerfully present in the old woman in *The Summer Book* (*Sommerboken*, 1972) who is experiencing her last summer, or at any rate one of the last. Yet the book is not depressing – far

On Klovharun. Tove and Tuulikki pushing the boat out into the water

from it. In *The Listener* there is an unflinching but poignant description of an old person's death. By way of contrast, there is also the story of Aunt Gerda's strange habit of making a chart of people and the relationships between them. The people and the relationships are constantly changing, and there can never be enough time – or even paper – to describe that complexity. In *Sun City* there are several elderly characters, and each of them is old in their own way. Tove describes the old ladies in the city of death with a surrealistic richness of colours.

In *Notes from an Island* Tove examines her own old age and her renunciation of her beloved island. 'Once in a Park' ('En gång i en park'), written in 1995 but not published until after her death, is a deeply personal story and describes the feelings of a creative person who finds she is unable to write or paint any more: the colours lose their meaning and the words will no longer come so easily. In 'Correspondence', Tove describes her exchange of letters with the apparently fictional Tamiko Atsumi. Through Tamiko, Tove writes:

> *Now I send a new haiku.*
> *It is about a very old woman who sees blue mountains far away.*
> *When she was young she did not see them.*
> *Now she cannot manage to reach them.*

275

When Tove was in her eighties she returned to the same idea, this time through a poem from Edgar Lee Masters' *Spoon River Anthology*. In that poem, too, a man does not get to see the mountains until he is old, but by then he is no longer able to fly to them. It seemed that Tove's ability to work was on the wane, even though her will to create was still strong. This conflict can be one of the most difficult experiences in the life of an artist.

When, as a young woman, Tove was depressed or overworked, creative activity did not always lift her mood. She would stand there helplessly, feeling that everyone had rejected her – but in time she always re-established contact with her creative impulse. In her old age she was not always certain that this would happen. Like a bad dream, there was the story of the artist 'who wakes up one fine morning and stares at his palette and has no idea which colour he should choose – there they all are with their beautiful names, like Cadmium Pourpre or Vert Veronese or Green Earth and Ebony Black right at the edge of the palette, and the painter no longer knows how to paint or what he has to do with the whole business – and what about a writer who one fine morning stands and stares at the alphabet?'

Tove wrote the story 'Once in a Park' during the last foreign trip Tuulikki and she took together. In it Tove describes moments during 1993 in Paris, the city that meant so much to her. The story's first-person narrator sits on a bench in a small park behind the Church of Saint-Sulpice, figuring out what he or she is going to write, and how to begin the book. Beginning seems to be the hard part: 'I try, but the more I try, the harder it becomes, more and more hopeless and insurmountable, to put anything together at all.'

In their letters, children had often asked her how to become an author, and what they ought to write about. Tove recalled telling them that they should write about things they were familiar with, things they knew about. That was what she had done, but now the situation was different: 'I made use of the subject of middle age until the cows came home, and when I got really old I also made from that what I could, but then I tried to write about very young people and it didn't work out so well.' She came to feel that she had written about all the things she knew about, and that now it was time to give up writing. 'I took my stick and walked over to the rubbish bin and threw the notebook away, a completely superfluous object that was not dignified at my age.'

Tove's last book was the collection *Messages. Selected Short Stories 1971– 1997* and by that time she had had an active career for almost seventy years.

To put together the collection, she went through her literary output and selected stories from different years. It was as if she were setting in order the life she had already lived and reviewing what she had written – a kind of tidying up before her death. Such collections chosen by writers themselves frequently resemble biographies. The stories in *Messages* are those that Tove felt most closely reflected her life of the past twenty-six years. Some of them concern, events and people that were important to her – families, her uncles and her cousin Karin, her travels with Tooti and Ham and the Konica camera.

The book also contains previously unpublished stories, based very closely on notebooks and letters from Tove's youth. Although, of course, she polished them stylistically and omitted passages of an intimately personal nature, the stories by and large reflect the contents of her notebooks and correspondence. Some of the narratives even preserve the letter format, giving them a feel of directness and authenticity. Their freshness has not faded.

Tove probably knew that this book would be her last, and that it was her final chance to produce something new. As she wrote in 'Once in a Park', it must have been difficult to accept. In the stories she looks back through her youth – the most important years of her life – one last time. A young woman dances the Viennee Waltz with Tapsa after the end of the semester at the Athenaeum, studies art with Sam Vanni while she lives her life in a country that is waiting for war, and sees off her best friend Eva Konikoff at the station as Eva takes the last train to Petsamo, fleeing Finland before the impending conflict.

Old people are often asked what they think of the life they have had, and how they would live it if they had their time over again. When Tove was eighty she was asked the same questions. She said that she had lived an exciting and colourful life, though it had also been a strenuous one. She was very happy with it. She said that the two most important things in it had been work and love. Then, somewhat unexpectedly, she said that if she were able to live it all over again she would do everything quite differently – though she would not specify how.

Then came cancer. Tove had been a smoker all her life, and eventually it took its toll. Outwardly, at least, she took her illness and the successive operations with calm. To a friend she remarked: 'You ask – yes, the cancer came back a few times, and always in new places – but they stitched me up very nicely.'

Tove thought it best to inform her closest friends of her serious illness.

Talking to those one loves most about one's anticipated death is surely one of the most difficult things in a person's life. One of her close friends described how Tove telephoned to say that she was soon going to die. Towards the end of the conversation she said: 'My dear, I thought this conversation would be so difficult, but it's not difficult at all . . . dying like this is so natural . . .'

Although stories from the Bible formed a partial basis for the plots in her books, and Gustave Doré's old Bible illustrations also had a special influence

Tove feeding a seagull

on the Moominvalley landscape, religion did not play a particularly important role in Tove's work. But when time is running out, people often start to take an interest in spiritual matters, and they want to discuss life after death with representatives of the Church. For some reason Tove met a pastor who, inspired by her serious illness, asked her: 'Have you given much thought to questions of eternity?' From Tove he received the answer: 'Yes, I'm eagerly waiting for that – and I hope it will be a happy surprise.'

A short chronology

Tove Marika Jansson, 9 August 1914–27 June 2001

FAMILY MEMBERS:
Signe Hammarsten-Jansson, 1882–1970
Viktor Jansson, 1886–1958
Per Olov Jansson 1920–
Lars Jansson 1926–2000

FINNISH NATIONAL EVENTS:
First World War, 1914–18
Finland's Independence, 1917
Finnish Civil War, 1917–18
Winter War, 1939–1940
Continuation War, 1941–4
Lapland War, 1944–5

TOVE JANSSON'S WORK AND ACTIVITIES:

1920s	Early illustrations, cartoon series and writings
1930–37	Study at Royal Institute of Technology in Stockholm and the Academy of Fine Arts in Helsinki. Further study in Paris in 1938
1943	First solo exhibitions (1943 and 1947), Taidesalonki, Helsinki, Finland
1944–7	Murals and wall paintings, including works for Apollonkatu girls' school, Strömberg's Electric Factory in Helsinki and large frescos for Helsinki City Hall
1944–8	*The Moomins and the Great Flood* (1945), *Comet in Moominland* (1946), *The Magician's Hat* (1948) (published in English as *Finn Family Moomintroll*)
1947–8	*Ny Tid* comic strip, *The Moomins and the End of the World*

1949   Children's play based on *Comet in Moominland* at Helsinki's Svenska
Teater

1950–51   Fourth Moomin book *The Exploits of Moominpappa*. *The Magician's
Hat* published in England as *Finn Family Moomintroll*, and as *The
Happy Moomins* in the United States

1952   First Moomin picture book *What Happened Next?* (published in
English as *The Book about Moomin, Mymble and Little My*)

1952–4   Murals and wall paintings, including for Hamina clubhouse and
Kotka vocational school, Domus Academica, Karja elementary
school and Union Bank, Helsinki. Altarpiece for Teuva Church

1954–7   Fifth Moomin book *Moominsummer Madness* (1954). Sixth Moomin
book *Moominland Midwinter* (1957)

1952   Contract for Moomin comic strip series in the London *Evening
News*

1955   Third solo exhibition, Taidesalonki, Helsinki

1959   Illustrations for the Finnish edition of Lewis Carroll's *The Hunting
of the Snark*

1960–62   Second Moomin picture book *Who Will Comfort Toffle?*(1960).
Seventh Moomin book *The Invisible Child and Other Stories* (1962)
(later published in English as *Tales from Moominvalley*)

1960–63   Solo exhibitions in Helsinki and Tampere

1965   Eighth Moomin book *Moominpappa at Sea*

1966   Solo exhibition in Helsinki. Illustrations for the Finnish edition of
Lewis Carroll's *Alice in Wonderland*

1968   First book written for adults, *The Sculptor's Daughter*. Revised editions of some of the Moomin books

1969   Solo exhibition in Helsinki and exhibition with Tuulikki Pietilä in
Jyväskylä

1970   Last Moomin book *Moominvalley in November*

1971–4   Short-story collection *The Listener* (1971), novel *The Summer Book*
(1972), novel *Sun City* (1974)

1973   Illustrations for the Finnish edition of J. R. R. Tolkien's *The Hobbit*

1974   Moomin opera staged at Finnish National Opera, Helsinki

1975   Residence in Paris at Cité des Arts, where she paints self-portrait
(*Ugly Self-portrait*) and *The Graphic Artist* (portrait of Tuulikki
Pietilä)

1977–80   Third Moomin picture book *The Dangerous Journey*. With her brother Per Olov, Jansson publishes photographic book, *An Unwanted Guest* (1980)

1978	Short-story collection *The Doll's House and Other Stories* (published in English as *Art in Nature*). Takes part in production in Poland of television series based on Moomin comic strips
1982–4	Novel *The True Deceiver* (1982), novel *The Field of Stones* (1984)
1984	Murals for Magician's Hat kindergarten, Pori
1986	Donation to Tampere Art Museum (original illustrations, paintings, both Moominhouses, and a number of Moomin tableaux). Tove Jansson exhibition at Tampere Art Museum
1987	Moominvalley exhibition opens in Tampere
1987–91	Short-story collection *Travelling Light*, novel *Fair Play* (1989) and short-story collection *Letters from Klara* (1991)
1992–4	Retrospective exhibitions in Helsinki, Turku and Tampere
1996–8	*Notes from an Island* (text by Tove Jansson, illustrations by Tuulikki Pietilä, 1996), short-story collection, 'Messages. Selected Short Stories 1971–1997' (1998)
1998	Film *Haru – Island of the Lonely*, with Tuulikki Pietilä

AWARDS INCLUDE:

Nils Holgersson Prize, 1953

Elsa Beskow and Rudolf Koivu Awards, 1957

Anni Swan Award, 1964

H. C. Andersen Medal, 1966

Swedish Academy Prize, 1972

Pro Finlandia Medal, 1976

Turku Academy, Honorary Doctorate, 1978

Selma Lagerlöf Prize, 1992

Finland Art Prize, 1993

Prize of the Swedish Academy, 1994

Honorary Professorship, Åbo Akademi University, Turku, Finland, 1995

Sources

ORAL SOURCES
Per Olov Jansson
Sophia Jansson
Tove Jansson
Birgitta Olfsson
Clara Palmgren
Helen Svensson
Anna Maria Tapiovaara

UNPUBLISHED SOURCES
Tove Jansson's notebooks

LETTERS
Eva Konikoff (E.K.)
Vivica Bandler
Atos Wirtanen
Ina Colliander
Eva Wichman
Letters from Vivica Bandler

NEWSPAPERS AND MAGAZINES
Helsingin Sanomat, *Uusi Suomi*, *Hufvudstadsbladet*, *Nya Pressen*, *Svenska Pressen*, *Nya Argus*, *Dagens Nyheter*, *Svenska Dagbladet*, *Stockholms Tidning*, *The Evening News*

TOVE JANSSON: MOOMIN BOOKS IN ENGLISH
Jansson, Tove. 2012. *The Moomins and the Great Flood* (London: Sort of Books)
Jansson, Tove. 1968. *Comet in Moominland* (Ernest Benn)
Jansson, Tove. 1953. *The Book about Moomin, Mymble and Little My* (Ernest Benn)
Jansson, Tove. 1955. *Moominsummer Madness* (Ernest Benn)
Jansson, Tove. 1950. *Finn Family Moomintroll* (Ernest Benn)
Jansson, Tove. 1958. *Moominland Winter* (Ernest Benn)

Jansson, Tove. 1960. *Who Will Comfort Toffle?* (Ernest Benn)
Jansson, Tove. 1962. *Tales from Moominvalley* (Ernest Benn)
Jansson, Tove. 1952. *The Exploits of Moominpappa* (Ernest Benn)
Jansson, Tove. 1966. *Moominpappa at Sea* (Ernest Benn)
Jansson, Tove. 1971. *Moominvalley in November* (Ernest Benn)
Jansson, Tove. 1977. *A Dangerous Journey* (Ernest Benn)
Jansson, Tove. 1980. *Skurken i Muminhuset*. (Referenced in English as *An Unwanted Guest*) (Helsingfors: Schildts)

TOVE JANSSON: OTHER WORKS
(where an English edition exists, it is listed in lieu of the Swedish)
Jansson, Tove. 2013 (1968). *The Sculptor's Daughter: A Childhood Memory* (*Bildhuggarens dotter*). (London: Sort of Books; Helsingfors: Schildts)
Jansson, Tove. 2014 (1971). *The Listener* (*Lyssnerskan*) (London: Sort of Books; Helsingfors: Schildts)
Jansson, Tove. 2003 (1976). *The Summer Book* (*Sommarboken*) (London: Sort of Books; Helsingfors: Schildts)
Jansson, Tove. 1977 (1974). *Sun City* (*Solstaden*). (London: Hutchinson; Helsingfors: Schildts)
Jansson, Tove. 2012 (1978). *Art in Nature: and Other Stories* (*Dockskåpet och andra berättelser*). (London: Sort of Books; Helsingfors: Schildts)
Jansson, Tove. 2009 (1982). *The True Deceiver* (*Den ärliga bedragaren*). (London: Sort of Books; Helsingfors: Schildts)
Jansson, Tove. 1984. *Stenåkern* (Referred to in English as *The Field of Stones*). (Helsingfors: Schildts)

Jansson, Tove. 2007 (1987) *Fair Play* (*Resa med lätt bagage*). (London: Sort of Books; Helsingfors: Schildts)

Jansson, Tove. 1989. *Rent spel*. (Referred to in English as *The Social Game*). (Helsingfors: Schildts)

Jansson, Tove. 1998. *Meddelande. Noveller i urval 1971–1997* (Referred to in English as *Messages: Selected Short Stories 1971–1997*) (Helsingfors: Schildts)

Jansson, Tove & Pietilä, Tuulikki. 1996. *Anteckningar från en ö*. (Referred to in English as *Notes from an Island*). (Helsingfors: Schildts)

Jansson, Tove. 1997. *Sam Vanni. Vuodet/Åren/The Years 1926–1959.* (Helsingfors: Helsingfors stads konstmuseum)

Jansson, Tove. 2002. 'En gång i en park' ('Once in a Park'). Svensson, Helen (ed.) *Resa med Tove. En minnesbok om Tove Jansson.* (Helsingfors: Schildts)

OTHER SOURCES
(where an english edition exists, it is listed in lieu of the Swedish)

Adachi, Mami. 2002. 'Att läsa klassikerna: Intertextualitet i Tove Janssons vuxenböcker'. In Svensson, Helen (ed.). *Resa med Tove. En minnesbok om Tove Jansson.* (Helsingfors: Schildts. 131–147)

Ahlfors, Bengt. 2011. *Människan Vivica Bandler. 82 skisser till ett porträtt* (Referred to in English as *Vivica Bandler, The Person: 82 Sketches for a Portrait*). (Helsingfors: Schildts)

Ahola, Suvi. 1996. 'Juuri tässä vai kaukana poissa? Paikallisuuden ja pelagisuuden suhde Tove Janssonin tuotannossa'. In Kurhela Virpi (ed.) *Muumien taikaa. Tutkimusretkiä Tove Janssonin maailmaan* (referred to as *The Magic of the Moomins: Exploring Tove Jansson's World*). (Helsingfors: Kirjastopalvelu. 82–94)

Bandler, Vivica & Backström, Carita. 1992. *Adressaten okänd*. (Stockholm: Norstedts)

Bandler Vivica. 2004 (2004). 'Tove'. In Svensson, Helen (ed.). *Resa med Tove. En minnesbok om Tove Jansson.* (Helsingfors: Schildts)

Björk, Christina. 2003. *Tove Jansson. Mycket mer än Mumin*. (Stockholm: Bilda förlag)

Björk, Christina. 2004 (2004). 'Än blommar svenska Mumindalen'. In Svensson, Helen (ed.). *Resa med Tove. En minnesbok om Tove Jansson*). (Helsingfors: Schildts. 21–45)

Bäckström, Lars. 2002. 'Rollfördelning'. In Svensson, Helen (ed.). *Resa med Tove. En minnesbok om Tove Jansson.* (Helsingfors: Schildts. 148–155)

Bäckström, Lars. 1996. 'Muumipappa tienhaarassa. Erään kirjevaihdon vaiheita'. In Kurhela Virpi (ed.). *Muumien taikaa. Tutkimusretkiä Tove Janssonin maailmaan.* (Helsingfors: Kirjastopalvelu. 179–194)

Carpelan, Bo. 2002. 'Den fruktbara osäkerheten'. In Svensson, Helen (ed.). *Resa med Tove. En minnesbok om Tove Jansson.* (Helsingfors: Schildts. 219–229)

Gustafsson, Barbro K. 1992. *Stenåker och ängsmark. Erotiska motiv och homosexuella skildringar i Tove Janssons senare litteratur.* (Uppsala: Uppsala Studies in Social Ethics, 13)

Gustafsson, Greta. 2002. 'Hon har alltid bara hört till.' I, Svensson, Helen (ed.). *Resa med Tove. En minnesbok om Tove Jansson.* (Helsingfors: Schildts. 193–202)

Happonen, Sirke. 2007. *Vilijonkka ikkunassa. Tove Janssonin muumiteosten kuva, sana ja liike.* (Helsingfors: WSOY)

Holländer, Tove. 1983. *Från idyll till avidyll. Tove Janssons illustrationer till muminböckerna.* (Tammerfors: Finlands barnboksinstitut)

Ilmonen, Anneli; Waaramaa, Teija; Bonelius, Elina (ed.). 2002. *Tove Jansson. Minnesutställning.* (Tammerfors konstmuseums publikationer 103)

Jansson, Per Olov. 2002. 'Om kärlekens vanmakt'. In Svensson, Helen (ed.). *Resa med Tove. En minnesbok om Tove Jansson.* (Helsingfors: Schildts. 9–20)

Kallio, Rakel (ed.). 2006. *Dukaatti, Suomen Taideyhdistys 1846–2006.* (Helsingfors: WSOY)

Karjalainen, Tuula. 1990. *Uuden kuvan rakentajat. Konkretismin tulo Suomeen.* (Helsingfors: WSOY)

Karjalainen, Tuula; Pusa, Erja; Oranen, Mikko (ed.). 1997. *Sam Vanni. Vuodet/åren/The Years 1926–1959.* (Helsingfors stads konstmuseums publikationer, no 53.)

Karjalainen, Tuula. 2006. 'Dukaattikilpailut ja 50-luvun modernismi'. In Kallio, Rakel (ed.) *Dukaatti, Suomen Taideyhdistys 1846–2006.* (Helsingfors: WSOY)

Kivi, Mirja (ed.). 1998. 'Muumilaakso. Tarinoista kokoelmaksi'. (Tampereen taidemuseon julkaisuja no 83. Tammerfors)

Konttinen, Riitta. 1991. *Konstnärspår.* (Helsingfors: Otava)

Kruskopf, Erik. 1992. *Bildkonstnären Tove Jansson.* (Helsingfors: Schildts)

Kruskopf, Erik. 1994. *Boken om HAM. Tecknaren Signe Hammarsten-Jansson.* (Helsingfors: Schildts)

Kruskopf, Erik. 1995. *Skämttecknaren Tove Jansson.* (Helsingfors: Schildts)

Kruskopf, Erik. 2002. 'Livets dans och det jordiska paradiset'. In Svensson, Helen (ed.). *Resa med Tove. En minnesbok om Tove Jansson.* (Helsingfors: Schildts. 66–79)

Kruskopf, Erik. 2010. *Ljusets byggare. Bildkonst I Finland på 1940–1950-talen.* (Helsingfors: SKS)

Kurhela Virpi (ed.). 1996. *Muumien taikaa. Tutkimusretkiä Tove Janssonin maailmaan.* (Helsingfors: Kirjastopalvelu)

Laajarinne, Jukka. 2011. *Mumin och tillvarons gåta.* (Helsingfors: Schildts)

Laukka, Maria. 2010. 'Tove Jansson'. I Kanerva, Arja; Lange, Kaisa; Laukka, Maria (ed.). *Mielikuvia. Suomalaisia lastenkirjakuvittajia.* (Porvoo: Lasten Keskus)

Muumitalo – Muminhuset. 1980. *Utställningspublikation.* (Helsingfors: Finlands arkitekturmuseum)

Palmgren, Raoul. 1984. *Kapinalliset kynät III. Itsenäisyysajan työväenliikkeen kaunokirjallisuus.* (Helsingfors: WSOY)

Pietilä, Tuulikki. 2002. 'Resa med Tove'. In Svensson, Helen (ed.). *Resa med Tove. En minnesbok om Tove Jansson.* (Helsingfors: Schildts. 229–254)

Rehal-Johansson, Agneta. 2006. *Den lömska barnboksförfattaren. Tove Jansson och mumin-verkets metamorfoser.* (Gothenburg: Makadam förlag)

Rinne, Matti. 2006. *Kiila 1936–2006. Taidetta ja taistelua.* (Helsingfors: Tammi)

Rinne Matti. 2008. *Yksitoista Tapiovaaraa: tuoleja, tauluja elokuvia.* (Helsingfors: Teos)

Ruuska, Helena. 2012. *Marja-Liisa Vartio. Kuin linnun kirkaisu.* (Helsingfors: WSOY)

Sandman Lilius, Irmelin. 2002. 'Visa om vänskap'. In Svensson, Helen (ed.). *Resa med Tove. En minnesbok om Tove Jansson.* (Helsingfors: Schildts. 29–45)

Tolvanen, Juhani. 2000. *Vid min svans! Tove och Lars Janssons tecknade muminserie.* (Helsingfors: Schildts)

Tolvanen, Juhani. 2002. 'Tove, jag och Henry Clay'. In Svensson, Helen (ed.). *Resa med Tove. Enminnesbok om Tove Jansson.* (Helsingfors: Schildts. 190–192)

Tomihara, Mayumi. 2002. 'Tove Jansson och japanska läsare: Mina möten med Tove Jansson'. In Svensson, Helen (ed.). *Resa med Tove. En minnesbok om Tove Jansson.* (Helsingfors: Schildts. 118–130)

Ulfsson, Birgitta. 2002. 'Vad gör man med en snäcka om man ej får visa den?'. In Svensson, Helen (ed.). *Resa med Tove. En minnesbok om Tove Jansson.* (Helsingfors: Schildts. 215–218)

Warburton, Thomas. 1984. *Åttio år finlandssvensk litteratur.* (Helsingfors: Schildts)

Westin, Boel. 2014 (2007). *Tove Jansson Life, Art, Words: The Authorised Biography (Tove Jansson. Ord, bild, liv)* (London: Sort of Books)

Witt-Brattström, Ebba. 1993. *Ur könets mörker. Litteraturanalyser.* (Stockholm: Norstedts)

Ørjasæter, Tordis. 1985. *Møte med Tove Jansson.* (Oslo: Gyldendal)

Ørjasæter, Tordis. 2002. 'I "Guldkalven" stämmer allt utom kalven'. In Svensson, Helen (ed.). *Resa med Tove. En minnesbok om Tove Jansson.* (Helsingfors: Schildts. 156–169).

Picture sources

Amos Andersonin taidemuseo / Kari Siltala 35

© Filmkompaniet / Filmoteka Narodowa / Jupiter Film / Moomin Characters™ 246

Helsingin taidemuseo / Katarina ja Leonard Bäcksbackan kokoelma / Yehia Eweis 60

Kansalliskirjasto 46, 51, 53, 110

Kansan arkisto 56

Keskinäinen Henkivakuutusyhtiö Suomi / Rauno Träskelin 64

Lilga Kovanko 161–2

Lehtikuva / Reino Loppinen / Press Association 156, 174, 206

Moomin Characters™ 7, 8, 10, 16, 18, 19, 21, 22, 29, 34, 37, 40, 42, 44, 51, 69, 77 , 85, 86, 103, 104, 130, 132, 140, 149, 150, 170, 185, 187, 194, 195, 196, 212, 213, 214, 228, 238, 242–3, 251, 255, 265, 277
– Per Olov Jansson 72, 79, 172, 203, 208, 216, 241, 244, 256, 256–7, 268, 277
– Eva Konikoff 38, 58
– Kjell Söderlund 218–9
– Len Waernberg 221

Orimattilan taidemuseo / Veli Granö 58

Puppenkiste 247

Suomen kuvapalvelu / Peter Lindholm 275

Svenska litteratursällskapet / Janne Rentola 83, 84, 95, 96, 99, 112, 113, 191

Tampereen taidemuseo 26–7, 68, 133, 179, 182–3, 222, 223, 229
– Jari Kuusenaho 428, 31, 45, 54, 70, 75, 100–101, 120, 124, 127,129, 131, 135, 184, 192, 199, 217, 224, 226, 258

Jukka Tapiovaara 61

Matias Uusikylä 264

Valtion taidemuseo / Kuvataiteen keskusarkisto
– Hannu Aaltonen 23
– Antti Kuivalainen 4
– Jenni Nurminen 47, 48, 50, 270–71

Marko Vuokola 25

WSOY 33, 137, 138, 144, 145, 146, 147, 152, 153, 176, 177,180, 181, 198, 200, 201, 228, 232, 233, 234

Cover image by: Reino Lappinen / STT-Lehtikuva / Press Association Images

Acknowledgements

Many people influenced the making of this book, and I thank them all. Tove Jansson's niece Sophia Jansson, creative director and chairman of Oy Moomin Characters Ltd, made it possible for me to read Tove's correspondence. This gave my interest a direction and opened up paths to me that I had not known about. My meetings with Tove's brother, the photographic artist Per Olov Jansson, were also important. The conversations we had over several years shed light on the life and atmosphere of bygone days. Per Olov also spent time looking at pictures from his archive for inclusion in my book.

Leena Saraste and Leena Mickwitz read and commented on my manuscript, and Erik Mickwitz helped me to clarify the interpretation of difficult phrases. Parallel with the writing of my book, I also worked on the compilation of a large art exhibition devoted to Tove Jansson in connection with the centenary of her birth. The synchronous nature of these undertakings has been of benefit to both, and so a big thank you is due to those who assisted in the exhibition project. I should also like to extend warm thanks to my publishers and to everyone who helped me in the completion of my book.

The long work of writing and research was made possible by a grant from the Alfred Kordelin Foundation, for which I also give sincere thanks.

My book is dedicated to Juho, Jaakko, Johannes, Alfons and Morris.

Helsinki 15.08.2013
Tuula Karjalainen

Index

TUULA KARJALAINEN is a Finnish art historian and art critic and historian who has previously worked as director of the Helsinki Art Museum and the Kiasma Museum of Contemporary Art. She is the author of the books *Uuden kuvan rakentajat: Konkretismin läpimurto Suomessa* (*Concretism in Finland*), *Ikuinen sunnuntai: Martta Wendelinin kuvien maailma* (a study of the work of the Finnish painter Martta Wendelin), and *Kantakuvat: Yheteinen muistimme* (a study of ten well-known Finnish works of art).